BIG
BOY
RULES

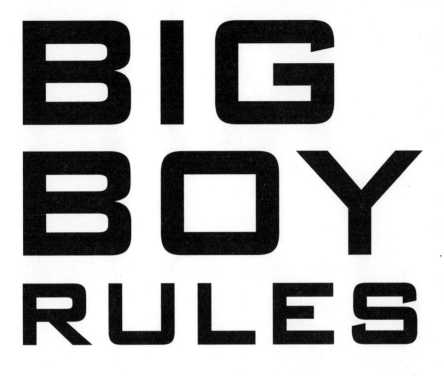

BIG BOY RULES

AMERICA'S MERCENARIES
FIGHTING IN IRAQ

STEVE FAINARU

WINNER OF THE 2008 PULITZER PRIZE
FOR INTERNATIONAL REPORTING

DA CAPO PRESS
A MEMBER OF THE PERSEUS BOOKS GROUP

"King Midas in Reverse"
Words and music by Allan Clarke, Tony Hicks and Graham Nash. Copyright ©
1967 Gralto Music Ltd. Copyright renewed. All rights in the U.S. and Canada
controlled and administered by Universal—Songs of Polygram International,
Inc. All rights reserved. Used by permission.

DESIGN BY JANE RAESE
Set in 12-point Adobe Caslon

Cataloging-in-Publication Data for this book is available from the Library
of Congress.

ISBN 978-0-306-81743-4

Published by Da Capo Press
A Member of the Perseus Books Group
www.dacapopress.com

Da Capo Press books are available at special discounts for bulk purchases
in the U.S. by corporations, institutions, and other organizations. For more
information, please contact the Special Markets Department at the Perseus
Books Group, 2300 Chestnut Street, Suite 200, Philadelphia, PA, 19103,
or call (800) 255-1514, or e-mail special.markets@perseusbooks.com.

10 9 8 7 6 5 4 3 2 1

FOR DAD AND WILL

CONTENTS

Prologue: On the Border   xi

1 Social Studies, Inc.   1

2 I Want to Kill Somebody Today   16

3 The Last Train   36

4 We Protect the Military   48

5 The Stories You Tell   68

6 Now You Are Going to Die   85

7 Your Blood   102

8 Scope of Authority: God   122

9 Hostage Affairs   143

10 BlackRwatey for Special Security   161

11 Faith that Looks Through Death   182

Epilogue: The Book of Wisdom   205

Source Notes   219

Selected Bibliography   235

Acknowledgments   237

Index   243

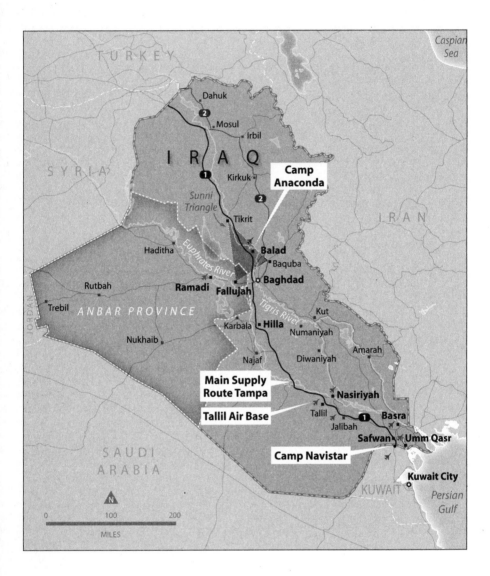

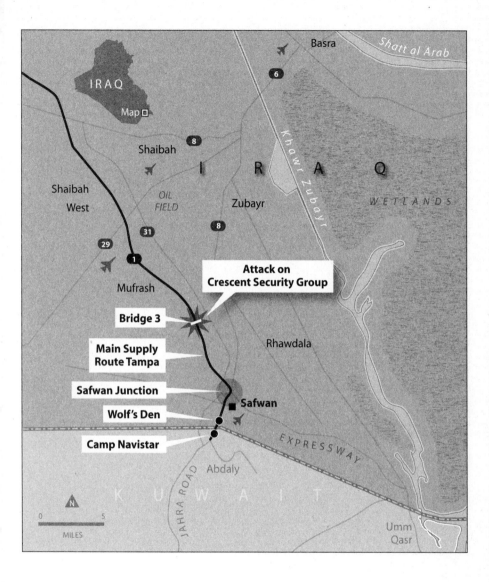

I'm not the guy to run with
'Cos I'll throw you off the line
I'll break you and destroy you
Given time
 —*The Hollies, "King Midas in Reverse"*

PROLOGUE
ON THE BORDER

THIS IS A BOOK ABOUT ORIGINAL SIN.

In the early days of the Iraq war, there weren't enough troops. As the situation deteriorated, a parallel army formed on the margins of the war: tens of thousands of armed men, invisible in plain sight, doing the jobs that couldn't be done because there weren't enough troops. The armed men traveled in convoys of multicolored pickups, modified with armor and stockpiled with belt-fed machine guns, frag grenades, flash-bangs, smoke, even shoulder-fired missiles. They wore bulletproof vests over their uniforms—usually khakis and polo shirts with the company logo—and covered their bodies in mosaics of tattoos. They protected everything from the U.S. ambassador and American generals to shipments of Frappuccino bound for Baghdad's Green Zone. They referred to each other by their radio call signs—Shrek, Craftsman, Tequila, Goat—never bothering to learn each other's names.

The armed men got to kill Iraqis, and the Iraqis got to kill them. It was U.S. government policy.

"I MEAN, THERE'S NO FUCKIN' WAY I'M GONNA LET them cut *my* head off on the Internet," said Josh.

He was twenty-three-years old and still looked like a marine, his dirty blond hair sheared down to his pink scalp. A tattoo swirled around his left forearm in meticulous cursive, almost like a Hallmark card: "The unwanted, doing the unforgivable, for the ungrateful." We were sitting on the border in the black Chevy Avalanche, me and the two mercs, blasting the air conditioning, waiting to cross into Iraq. The two of them were telling me about the death pact they had made. As death pacts go, there wasn't much to it. If they were about to be kidnapped, the other merc, whose name was Jon Coté, was to put a bullet in Josh's head with his Glock, then turn the gun on himself.

"Sounds reasonable," I told them, and it did.

Coté, an ex-army paratrooper, hadn't exactly dropped out of the University of Florida, where he had been an unlikely accounting major. It was more like a well-paid sabbatical. He said he was planning to go back to school in the spring, this time as an exercise physiology major. He was clean cut, well built, articulate, relentlessly cheerful; you could easily picture him up on a billboard wearing a milk mustache. "I'm the kind of kid who has to have fun no matter what I'm doing," he would say. One of the fun things that Coté liked to do was drive around Baghdad, where most Americans tried to melt into the floorboards, and blast Led Zeppelin and the Notorius B.I.G. through the open window while rocking back and forth in his seat, fingers splayed. Coté was also something of a health nut. On the front seat, he carried canned peaches and assorted nuts, along with his locked and loaded AK-47 and a dog-eared copy of *The Insider's Encyclopedia on How to Build Muscle and Might*. His name was pronounced "KOH-tay," and everyone called him that. As in, "Okaaay, Coté."

His friend Josh Munns was serious business; in 2004, he had fought his way into Fallujah with a marine sniper platoon. A year later, he found himself installing swimming pools in Redding, California, bored out of his mind. "I need something to shock my system to remind myself I'm still alive," he explained. That was one of the reasons he came back to Iraq. Another was the three-story fixer-upper he had just bought back in Redding with his fiancé. Her name was Jackie, just like his mom. Once a month, he took his paycheck—$7,000 in Kuwaiti dinars stuffed into a white envelope—to a Kuwait City exchange house, which then transferred the money into his California bank account.

It was about 9:30 A.M., early November 2006, and everything shimmered in the heat. The border was a moonscape of rocks and baked earth, the sun washed out by dust and diesel fumes spewing from the semis moving north. We were on our way to Basra, a once-peaceful city that now evoked the same dark imagery as other infamous Iraqi slaughterhouses, like Ramadi and the Triangle of Death. None of us wanted to go. The day before, insurgents had taken out three mercs from another company. The U.S. military, which catalogued troop fatalities by more than thirty potential causes, didn't count the mercs among the dead. The attack wasn't on the news—they almost never were, like they had never happened. But everyone was talking about it, calculating the new odds. "I hate that place," one of the mercs kept saying. "I hate that fucking place."

Our team leader, John Young, was a forty-four-year-old former carpenter and U.S. Army veteran from Lee's Summit, Missouri. He was small and wiry, maybe five foot seven. He shaved his head where he hadn't already gone bald, making it look like his sky blue eyes were sinking back into his head. Young had been in Iraq for nearly two years. One of his proudest possessions was a black flak jacket, frayed at the collar from where a bullet had come out of nowhere one afternoon, slamming him into the steering wheel and nearly ripping through his neck. The company displayed the tattered vest on a card table in the lobby back at headquarters, like a trophy won by the company softball team. Young knew that he wasn't normal, but he seemed to have come to terms with it. "I may be fucked up, but at least if I'm talking about it I know I'm fucked up, and that justifies my fuckedupedness," he told me, smiling. "And I'm okay with that today." He couldn't bring himself to leave Iraq. "This is me," he would say. "This is me."

Coté rolled down his window.

"Hey," Young said. "Do you guys know the way?"

There was a pause, as full and pregnant as the Mesopotamian sun. Coté and Josh shot glances at one another.

"Nooooo," Coté said, his voice rising. "Don't *you?*"

Young stammered something about "Harry's route," something about "we'll figure it out" and "MapQuest" and "I thought you guys knew the way."

I wondered if I'd heard that right. Did he say MapQuest?

"We'll talk about it later," Young said finally, turning to walk away.

Josh was fuming.

"Why the fuck am I riding point?" he snapped at Coté. "I don't know where we're going."

Coté chuckled.

"Yeah, it's not the getting hit part that bothers me," said Josh. "It's the getting lost and getting hung from a bridge part that bothers me."

ORIGINAL SIN.

A government launches a preemptive war predicated on a myth. Insurgents rise up to confront the occupiers. Lacking a sufficient fighting force, not to mention political will, the government rents itself a private army, piece by piece. Hundreds of companies form overnight, like mushrooms after a rainstorm, some with boards of directors and glass offices, others that are scarcely more than armed gangs. The companies hire from a vast pool of veterans and ex-cops, adrenaline junkies, escapees from the rat race, the patriotic, the bankrupt, the greedy, the terminally and perpetually bored. They hire Americans and Brits, South Africans and Aussies, Fijians and

Gurkhas. Peruvians who fought the Shining Path. Colombians fresh from the drug wars. They give them weapons (although many bring their own) and turn them loose on an arid battlefield the size of California, without rules, without laws, with little to guide them except their conscience.

Soon it's a $100 billion industry, an industry of arms, with unions and lobbyists and its own tortured nomenclature: in newsprint and polite conversation, they are all "private security contractors."

"I am so thankful for this war," one of them said to me one night.

He was a squat former marine who later became a mortgage broker, then traded it all in for The Sandbox. He'd spend three months in Iraq, take his R&Rs in Vegas, playing blackjack for $500 a hand, then return to wage war in a $5,000 Panerai watch.

It was so obscene I asked him to say it again.

"It's true," he told me. "I only came over here for the money, and I didn't even know I could do this job until two years ago. I didn't know it was *available* to me."

They were mercenaries—I mean, of course they were—fighting America's war for money. Over time, the word became as politically loaded as other Iraq staples, like "mission accomplished" and "WMD." Defenders of the practice, mostly the companies and their surrogates, parsed the meaning endlessly, like etymologists with guns. Critics dropped it like a cluster bomb. But, politics aside, it was fundamentally true: I never met a single one who didn't have his price. Monumental policy decisions that would decide the fate of the Iraqi people, the future of the American presidency—to them it was simply business: risk versus reward. One sweltering afternoon I sat at Burger King in the Green Zone, pondering the implications of an American pullout with a South African merc I knew. He quickly cut to the chase: "If it happened I wouldn't touch a plane ticket to Iraq for anything less than $35,000 a month. Because I'd most probably only have two months to earn it before I got whacked."

But the mercs had a saying, which I heard, in some variation, all over Iraq: "Come for the money, stay for the life." That was their way of summing up the million different reasons why they were there, why they kept coming back, including the reasons they couldn't articulate and probably wouldn't admit to if they could. There was the obvious: the camaraderie and the addictive thrill—Iraq as a reality, not as an abstraction. You were part of it, and it was part of history, and so you were part of history, too, even if you were dead. But it went much deeper, and it was mostly personal. Whatever your story was, that's why you were there; it didn't much matter whether the story was true, or whether you told it to anyone but yourself, or whether it changed over time, every day even.

I had my own story, of course. We all did—each and every one of us who didn't have to be there, which is to say basically everyone except the military and the poor Iraqis themselves. In many ways, this is a book about that, too: the stories we tell each other and the stories we tell ourselves, to explain our lives, and our deaths, and everything in between.

"DON'T WORRY, IT'S TOTALLY SAFE," SAID COTÉ.

He pitched his flak jacket and his helmet in the backseat of the Avalanche, cranked up the MP3 player, racked his Kalashnikov and headed down Route Tampa. It was after nightfall, the temperature plummeting, headlights devouring the asphalt as we drove. Out in the desert, you could see wood fires glowing, suspicious shadows, cinder-block houses lit by a single bulb. I tried to take notes in the dark but I couldn't see the words. Coté turned on the dome light to help me see.

"No, turn it off," I said.

In hindsight, it seems so incredibly stupid, driving through Iraq in a barely armored pickup, just me and the youngest fatalist I'd ever met. But that's not the way it felt at the time. Coté was twenty-one years younger than me—we shared the same birthday, February 11—but, all around him, he created the illusion of safety. It was a liberating illusion. I'd gone on countless missions in Iraq with the military, buttoned up in the back of a five-ton Humvee, driving in circles, waiting to get blown up. Often the purpose eluded me, as it did most everyone else. In Balad I once asked a lieutenant whose platoon had been decimated if he thought we were winning the war. He just looked at me and laughed: "Fuck, man, I don't even know what winning the war is." Coté had done his time—two tours, one in Afghanistan, one in Iraq—so you could easily understand the attraction: out here there were no orders and no rules, no shifting rationales about "fighting them over there so we don't have to fight them over here," no empty promises about "turning the corner in Iraq." It was just a sleek ride and an envelope full of cash. When he left the army, as a sergeant, Coté was earning $1,967.70 a month. He came back to Iraq two years later and was pulling down seven grand, same as a one-star general. And, by industry standards, he was underpaid.

We drove for hours in the dark. Coté set his MP3 player to shuffle and turned the volume down low. The only other sounds were the high-pitched whir of tires gliding over the highway, the squawking of the Motorola that kept us connected to the other mercs, and Coté's incessantly cheerful voice. He couldn't stop talking—about his parents' divorce, about his "ghetto" company, about his many girlfriends, and his shifting college major. Looking at his profile as he talked, moonlight pouring into the cabin, you figured no harm could possibly come to his pretty face, and so nothing could happen to you. I took off my own helmet and tossed it in the backseat, embracing the illusion of safety.

Coté was saying that he looked at his life like a book. "If the book is only twenty-three pages," he said, referring to his age, "I want them to be twenty-three really interesting pages."

When I heard a week later that Coté's death pact had failed, and that he had been sucked into the void, the most terrifying fate I could imagine in a country where any number of terrifying fates were imaginable, I couldn't believe that's all it was: a short, interesting, sort-of-happy life.

1

SOCIAL STUDIES, INC.

THE HUMVEES MOVED SLOWLY ON THE ROAD THAT CUT through the farms and the palm groves south of Baghdad International Airport. It was past dusk, cold, the sky a deep purple, and some of the soldiers wore night-vision goggles that cast the world in an eerie green glow. The mission was called ManPad Suppression. It required the soldiers to drive for hours in the dark, looking for the insurgents who sometimes launched shoulder-fired missiles at the planes.

The convoy rounded a curve and came upon a crossing. It was met by a van that stopped suddenly in the road. The van's door slid open, and several men emerged carrying AK-47 assault rifles and at least one belt-fed machine gun. The men opened fire on the Humvees.

For many of the Americans, it was their first taste of combat, and what stayed with them—more than the figures falling in the dark, the tracers that passed before them like red comets, and the jackhammer sounds of their weapons—was the floating intoxication, the seconds of pure juice that seemed to lift them from their bodies and the places they had come from until all they could feel or hear was their own breathing. It was especially true for Jon Coté, who had driven straight through the ambush.

When he got back to the base he banged out an email to his family and friends, writing in a fury about "this stream of red glaring rounds passing in front of us. All I could think was that there was no way around it and the only way to get out of it was to drive straight through it. So I held my breath, dropped the Humvee in first gear, floored it, and then pushed it into second. I drove right through the crossfire yelling *fuck yeaaaaah* with the guys in the back yelling *fuck youuuuu*.

"This is by far the coolest thing I have ever experienced in my life," he concluded, "and these are the kind of things that are going on in Iraq."

Jon looked like a recruiting poster in his desert camis, all handsome and confident. His email was armyboycote@hotmail.com. When he had enlisted in the 82nd Airborne, two months before 9/11, his aptitude scores were so high the army encouraged him to apply to West Point. He never responded. He preferred to stay on the line, where he could feed his addiction: rappelling sixty-foot walls, fighting with pugil sticks, jumping out of airplanes, and, finally, fighting America's wars in Afghanistan and Iraq.

"I am starting to find my way in life at what I was called to be, an INFANTRY MAN," he wrote to one of his friends back in Buffalo.

Iraq, it was the endless buzz. Night after night, the soldiers crisscrossed the redolent fields in their Humvees, looking for trouble. They passed through the whitewashed villages where people waved or glared, sometimes both, and they tried to use their spidey sense to sniff out the bombs that were buried in the road. Outside the wire, the buzz never left you, not from the moment you racked your weapon and put a bullet in the chamber and headed out the gate.

Late one afternoon the Humvees rounded a corner. There was a familiar *pop-pop-pop*, and, as they moved through the village—two dozen adobe houses set back from the road—the Americans poured gunfire in the direction of where they believed people were shooting at them. Jon again floored it as the convoy pushed through the kill zone, out of the village, everyone high on the juice and unharmed.

It wasn't until later that they learned that at least some of the shots had been celebratory—Iraqis firing into the air during a wedding—and that they had turned their weapons on civilians, several of whom had been killed. Numb, they drove back to the village with the platoon medic to treat the wounded. There were women who had been hit and a nine-year-old girl, her shoulder ripped apart by a 5.56 round. As the medic went inside to treat her, Jon and the other soldiers waited in the street, stricken. Many had joined the military after 9/11. This wasn't what they had signed up for: women and nine-year-old girls. They could hear her screaming from inside the house, over and over, until the screams became part of them.

Nothing much was right after that. In March, the company's twenty-year-old flag bearer, whom Jon had known since basic, came back from a mission and shot himself in the head with his M-4 while everyone else was asleep. He lay dying on the floor of the barracks, twitching as the company gathered around him.

When the unit rotated back to the States, in April 2004, the infantry was no longer Jon's calling. In many ways, he was still a model soldier, a decorated veteran of two wars. He had two Army commendation medals, the Army achievement medal, the expert infantryman badge, a good conduct medal, and the combat infantryman badge, the Army's award for engaging in and surviving intimate violence. "SPC Coté's professionalism, selfless service and dedication to duty are in keeping with the highest traditions of the American paratrooper, and bring great credit upon himself, the 2d Battalion, 505th Parachute Regiment, and the United States Army," read the citation for his second commendation. He had made sergeant in three years.

He couldn't wait to get out.

JON PICKED OUT HIS COLLEGE ON A WEB SITE: www.campusdirt.com.

The University of Florida (UF) in Gainesville looked like a male utopian vision of what college life should be, especially for the student who had spent much of his previous four years fighting America's wars in chaste Islamic nations. UF was the third-largest school in the country, with more than fifty thousand students. The average temperature during the school year was roughly eighty degrees. The campus teemed with oak trees draped in white Spanish moss and absurdly beautiful women draped in next to nothing. At night, the students crammed into the bars around University Avenue; women often drank for free.

Jon came armed with his GI money, his war-fighter cred, and his charisma. He tried to get as far away from his previous life as he could. He pledged Sigma Phi Epsilon, a party palace at the foot of frat row, moved into a beige apartment complex called Oxford Terrace, and enrolled as an accounting major. About two weeks after his arrival, he bumped into another Sig Ep pledge, Joey Dal Santo, on the stairs at Oxford Terrace. It turned out that Dal Santo, an eighteen-year-old business major, lived a floor above him. Jon invited him over for a drink, and the two set out for an introductory Sig Ep bash called the crush party.

Dal Santo was a wide-eyed freshman from Chicago experiencing the hormonal rush of his first few weeks in college. He watched, awestruck, as his new friend, also a freshman but one who was twenty-two years old and a veteran of two foreign wars, worked the crowd. Upperclassmen, sorority girls, UF football players fist-bumped him, yelled out his name and embraced him.

"Jon, how do you know all these people?" Dal Santo yelled above the din.

"Oh, I got to Gainesville a little early and I met a few people," Jon replied.

Two striking women sidled up to them. One was a twenty-one-year-old Bosnian blonde named Anja Magazin. Her friend Shiva Hafezi was an eighteen-year-old chemical engineering major who was born in Tehran. Anja began to flirt, and when Jon informed her that he was twenty-two she refused to believe him. In some ways he seemed younger, a smooth-faced kid unable to sit still, energy pulsating off of him in waves. "We're gonna have to see some identification," Anja told Jon, and so he fished out his New York driver's license and proved it to her.

Not long after, Anja and Shiva bumped into Jon at the campus gym. It was like running into a blizzard of words, Jon running on in his T-shirt and his gym shorts, talking about the fraternity, about the parties, imploring them: "You guys got to come over . . . we're gonna cook some food . . . we'll have some jambalaya. . . . I've got some friends I want you to meet . . . there's this girl, she lives next door to me, you guys will love her. . . . You *gotta* come over. . . ."

Soon they were all regulars at Oxford Terrace, Jon at the center of a multiethnic group of friends who were so close and varied and beautiful they looked like they had walked out of a sitcom. The group included Joey, Anja, and Shiva and Jon's neighbors, Fernanda Andrade, an aspiring Brazilian actress, and her blond roommate, Lauren Permuy. They went tubing at Cocoa Beach, spent New Year's Eve at Harbor Island, took a booze cruise to the Bahamas for spring break. They gathered most Sundays for dinner parties of jambalaya and chocolate martinis that Jon whipped up in his kitchen.

Jon's apartment was the embodiment of his new life; there were more bartenders' guides than textbooks. His small bedroom held a $2,000 king-size Princess Latex sleep set, an enormous television with speakers attached, a huge American flag, the 82nd Airborne flag, and a tiny desk on which rested his laptop, often idle. Jon's approach to scholarship was "to bring me Kit Kat bars while I was studying in the library," said Shiva. He passed his classes, but that wasn't the point. His undeclared major was liberation.

"My first impression of Coté was that he was the usual rum-soaked, lady-chasing, shallow frat boy," said Lauren. "He was an outgoing, good-looking guy that seemed overly confident with a smart mouth." After she hung out with Jon for a while, a more complicated picture emerged. To his fraternity brothers and his drinking buddies, Jon was a walking party. At mixers, sorority girls flitted around him in their sundresses, like moths slamming into a streetlight. "I'd be watching him thinking, 'I wish I was in that situation,'" said David Hankins, one of his fellow pledges. Jon inevitably blew them off. "Man, these little girls don't know anything about anything; all they are is loud," he told his friends. At packed clubs like Rue Bar and the Whiskey Room, dressed in jeans and tight pastel T-shirts bearing messages that read "Life of the Party" or "I'm Kind of a Big Deal," he'd draw his hand to his forehead like a shark fin and go after the hottest woman in the room. "He was that kid who would walk up to any girl in any bar and introduce himself with all the confidence in the world and people loved him for it," said Matt Sloan, the president of the Sig Ep pledge class that year. "He was *that* guy." When Jon finally settled on a girlfriend, she was literally a dazzler, one of the sparkly dance squad girls who performed at Florida basketball games.

Jon made everyone feel like they were living their lives in black and white. You wanted to be around him, to see what he might do next, to feel more alive. One night on the spur of the moment he dragged Dal Santo to Jacksonville to party around the annual Florida-Georgia football game. By 3:00 A.M., they were both half drunk, exhausted, with no place to stay. The only option was to sleep in Jon's maroon Ford F-150 or make the ninety-minute drive back to Gainesville. Jon said he'd drive.

"Don't fall asleep on me," Dal Santo told him.

"Don't worry, I'm fine," Jon promised.

Route 301 was pitch black, and Coté was doing about seventy when he turned to Dal Santo and said, "Hey, can you take the wheel for a second?" Reaching over, Dal Santo thought Coté wanted to adjust his seat belt, maybe grab a stick of gum or some water. Instead Coté put the truck on cruise control, climbed out the driver's-side window, and in one sweeping motion swung himself into the bed of the truck. He stood up, the wind buffeting his face, looking out over the cab like Leonardo DiCaprio on the bow of the *Titanic* as the truck hurtled into the darkness, controlled by Dal Santo, who was gripping the steering wheel in a panic.

"Jon, what the fuck are you doing to me?" Dal Santo screamed, quickly sliding over into the driver's seat. Coté just laughed. As Dal Santo took control, Jon walked across the bed of the truck, swung himself around through the passenger's-side window, and plopped himself down in the seat that Dal Santo had just vacated.

THAT WAS THE KID MOST EVERYONE KNEW. BUT SOME-times his friends witnessed a startling transformation. Jon would grow sober, introspective, dark. He posed profound questions about the world and about himself. The smart-mouthed drunk that Lauren Permuy thought she knew was, in fact, "one of the most fun-loving, sensitive, and caring people I have ever known." At times, Jon seemed contemptuous of the very life he had embraced. He called college "a charade" and said he felt like he had lived two life-times compared to the pampered children around him. Sometimes he disappeared for hours or even days, resurfacing without explanation. One night Dal Santo couldn't find him anywhere. His door was locked, his truck gone, and his cell phone rang unanswered. Dal Santo drove around Gainesville, hitting the bars, the frat, asking if anyone had seen him. Jon turned up the next day passed out on the floor of his apartment.

"Jon, I thought you were in jail; why didn't you pick up the phone?" Dal Santo asked him.

"Joey, if I'm in jail there's nothing you can do about it. Let it be," Jon replied.

At his core, he seemed to have a vague, untouchable sadness. Late at night, after attending parties that revolved around him, he would collapse on his kitchen floor, drinking, sobbing for reasons he couldn't articulate. Sometimes he called his brother, Chris, back in Buffalo and begged him to move to Florida. Chris worked as a parts manager at a Yamaha dealership. He was 361 days older than Jon, more cautious and responsible. He told Jon he couldn't just pick up and move his life.

"What the fuck is wrong with me?" Jon would ask him.

One night, Jon's friend Shiva Hafezi received a call from Jon's cell phone. When she answered she heard a woman's voice.

"I found your friend," she told Shiva. "He was on the side of the street. He wasn't feeling too well."

Jon had passed out in an alley near Rue Bar. When Shiva arrived at his apartment, she found him curled up in bed, crying. She lay down beside him and stroked his hair. "I kept asking him what was wrong. He said he couldn't say. I kept bringing up different scenarios. Was it about school? About his family? About a girl? He just kept saying, 'no, no, no.'"

Shiva told him to sleep, that he'd feel better in the morning. He told her he couldn't. He said he had nightmares.

"What do you dream about, Jon?" she said.

"Bad things," he told her.

"Is it about the war, about being in the army?"

He shook, the words coming out in spurts. "Shiva, I've seen things that no one should see. I've had my friends die and I feel alone. I don't know how to get these images out of my head. I don't know what to do."

"He cried until he fell asleep; he cried all night," said Shiva. "And I couldn't do anything."

The next morning she went home. Soon after the phone rang. It was Jon. She rushed back to his apartment and crawled into bed with him, holding him. "I tried talking to him about it. I thought maybe in his sober state I could talk to him and make him feel better. But there was a wall, a huge wall. After that, I knew he wasn't the happy guy everyone thought he was. I think that was the hardest part, because he found everything to be meaningless, and no one knew. Everybody just thought of him as the life of the party."

Shiva felt helpless. She was the daughter of Iranian immigrants who had sacrificed everything to give her an education. She was an intellectual who spoke fluent Farsi, a striver who would later be hired as a sales engineer with ExxonMobil, a job she planned to use as a springboard to launch her own business. But she felt she knew nothing about people or the world. Jon had given her confidence, had made her feel beautiful, had taught her about people and life. He was like a big brother. And what did she have to give back?

One night, Shiva was walking on campus in a downpour, wrecked by a failed relationship, "thinking my heart had split into about ninety pieces." She called Jon. He was with a girl, of course.

"Don't move," he told Shiva, "I'll be right over."

"I just knew he would make everything all right," she said. "When I saw him I collapsed in his arms. I just cried and cried. It's incredible to have someone just look into your soul and remind you that you are loved and you are cared about, that you are beautiful."

Jon drove her back to her apartment. When they got inside he lifted her up and placed her on the kitchen counter. He wiped off her face with his hand. "He looked at me and he said, 'Shiva, you're so beautiful. Don't ever let anyone get you down.'"

That night, Jon slept beside her, as she had with him, always just friends. The cheap mattress sloped off the bed, and when Shiva awoke the next morning she found Jon asleep, the top half of his body spilling onto the floor.

After that, whenever Shiva felt overwhelmed, Jon would leave notes for her around her apartment:

Shiva, don't forget you're beautiful.

Shiva, you're a strong girl. Remember to have confidence in yourself.

Shiva, don't forget what good things life has in store for you.

"He was beautiful," she said. "The world knew it more than he did. A perfect stranger knew it more than he did. His heart was made from pieces of this world. Why couldn't he take his own advice?"

Midway through the school year, Jon bought a motorcycle on eBay.

In many ways, the bike was an extension of its speed-addled driver. It was a Yamaha R1, with a top speed of 180 miles per hour. It went from zero to one hundred in five seconds. Customized versions of the R1 competed at Daytona. Jon's was blood-red, with black trim and dual silver exhaust pipes that fanned out like a ducktail behind the passenger seat. Chris, ever responsible, shipped him a $500 Arai helmet decorated with black, red, and white flames. Jon rarely wore it. Chris understood: "If some hot girl pulled up at a stoplight in a convertible, he didn't want her to have to guess whether the guy riding that hot bike was cute or not."

The motorcycle became fodder for a new round of did-you-hear-what-Coté-did-now? stories. He picked up a speeding ticket the first week he owned it. He popped wheelies on frat row. One afternoon, Sig Ep held an event outside Gainesville. Coté performed stunts for his fraternity brothers on the interstate. If they were going seventy, he'd drive past at ninety or one hundred, his feet up on the handlebars. Then he'd drop back to perform another stunt—a prolonged wheelie or a side-saddle pass, waving. At one point David Hankins, a premed student, looked up and saw Coté a foot from his window. Coté smiled, knocked, and sped away.

It was all good fun at first, part of the growing Coté lore. Over time, though, Jon's friends became concerned that he had acquired an instrument of his own destruction. As the year went on, they noticed, his mood swings were more frequent and severe. He was drinking heavily and in binges. He had all but given up on school, determining that his inexplicable major, accounting, was "pointless," which had been obvious to everyone but him. His tolerance for authority, never a strong suit, became nonexistent. One afternoon, a campus cop pulled him over for failing to use his turn signal. Coté had come to believe the Gainesville police were targeting him. He mouthed off and found himself in handcuffs in the backseat of a police car. Meanwhile, he was broke, having burned through most of his money on the R1, his truck, and continuous partying. He had no idea how he would pay for school in the fall.

That summer, Coté stayed in Gainesville at Oxford Terrace. He took a class and worked a couple nights as a greeter for Social Studies, Inc., a local business founded by Sig Eps. The job essentially required good-looking frat boys and sorority girls to stand outside the clubs, trying to persuade other good-looking people to come inside. It was a good deal, if low paying. Jon made forty dollars a night for one of his favorite pastimes, hitting on women.

Checkout Receipt

High Plains Library District

10/04/2019

Title: Big boy rules : America's

Due Date: 10-25-19

One of his coworkers was a Sig Ep named Matt Sloan, an eighteen-year-old psychology major from Sarasota. In many ways, Sloan was Coté's opposite, serious and focused. By the time he arrived at UF he knew exactly what he wanted out of life. After graduating, he planned to get his MBA, then a law degree, then become a sports agent. He was pledge class president (and, later, fraternity president), a leader in student government and the Gator Growl spirit group.

But Sloan felt indebted to Coté. Earlier that year, Sloan's myriad activities had all but sucked the joy out of college for him. Coté set him straight. "He told me, 'Listen, man, you gotta enjoy this; you only get to go to college once.' He related it to himself and his military experience. He said, 'I'm here to have a great time and figure out what it is in life that motivates me.' That pep talk has reverberated in my mind ever since."

Now, it was Coté who clearly needed help. Sloan could see that Jon was ratcheting up the risk, chasing bigger and bigger rushes. Every day seemed to bring some new story of a near-death experience, or that Coté had been spotted passed out somewhere. "Jon drank a lot—*a lot*," said Sloan. "I don't know if there was underlying depression, or whether he was just trying to find meaning in his life. He just didn't get a rush anymore. Mainstream America wasn't doing it for him. I feared that it was a by-product of post-traumatic stress. It all came down that summer. I think he asked himself, and a lot of people were asking him, 'Are you going to continue this risky lifestyle or are you gonna calm down?'"

"What are you doing, man?" Sloan asked him one night as they stood outside the Whiskey Room.

"I don't belong here," Coté told him.

He told Sloan he had been talking to one of his old army buddies who knew about a job that would make all his problems go away. The job would pay him more money than you could ever dream of. It would help him pay for college and give meaning to the "totally superficial" life he led in Gainesville. He tried to describe the job to Sloan, but even the name—Private Security Contractor—seemed vague. One thing was clear: It would mean going back to Iraq, but Jon downplayed the risk.

The more Coté described it, the more Sloan thought it made a bizarre kind of sense. "University of Florida, I mean, this place is utopia," he said. "We've got the weather, we've got the sports, we've got the academics, we've got the beautiful women. Jon realized that. He knew that this was *the* experience. And once he realized that it wasn't working here, it wasn't going to work in the States for him at all."

Sloan sensed that Coté was at a crossroads: it was Gainesville or Iraq. "It was like, 'Are you gonna keep doing this crazy shit, try to keep figuring out how to raise your blood pressure just to get that thrill, or are you gonna go back?' It was one of the two."

Jᴏɴ ᴜsᴇᴅ ᴛᴏ ᴘᴀʀᴋ ʜɪs ʙɪᴋᴇ ɪɴ ꜰʀᴏɴᴛ ᴏꜰ ᴛʜᴇ Whiskey Room, and when he closed the place at one A.M. that's exactly where it was.

He'd been drinking all night. He called his brother in Buffalo from the sidewalk and explained the situation. He had been pounding beers. He was waiting for a friend to take him to a party and had gotten tired of waiting. He wanted to ride his bike.

"Jon, that's a really bad idea," Chris told him. "I don't want you to do that."

They were back in their familiar roles, Chris urging responsibility and caution, Jon balking.

"I knew he was going to get on his bike," said Chris. "I told him to at least go the speed limit and not act like a fucking idiot."

Jon got on the bike. He wore baggy jeans, white Pumas, and a pink T-shirt. He was not wearing eye protection, in violation of Florida law, and certainly not the helmet that Chris had given him. He gunned the bike up University, stopped at a light near the football stadium, then blasted off. His front wheel rose from the ground as he performed the perfect wheelie on Gainesville's main drag, minutes after closing time at the bars.

Across the street, conducting a security check in the Murphree Hall parking lot, was Officer Eric L. Hutchinson of the University of Florida Police Department. Coté roared up University a few hundred yards, made a U-turn, then popped another wheelie, this one in front of Officer Ragen T. Howard, who was conducting a traffic stop. Howard radioed that a pink-shirted male not wearing eye protection was driving his motorcycle recklessly in the eastbound lane of University.

Hutchinson pulled him over. It was 1:53 A.M.

Coté wheeled his bike into a dormitory parking lot, his every move captured on a video camera mounted inside Hutchinson's patrol car. He dismounted his bike and lowered the kickstand as the stocky officer, who was wearing shorts, approached. The patrol car's flashers washed over both of them; they looked like two men having an animated conversation in a loud nightclub.

Coté raised his hands in exasperation, pleading. Hutchinson walked away. Coté leaned against his bike, pulled his cell phone from his pocket, talked for ten seconds, then shoved it back in his pants.

Hutchinson returned and marched Jon to the front of the patrol car. He pulled his arms behind him and slipped handcuffs over his wrists.

Jon was driven to the station house, where he was given a Breathalyzer test. His blood alcohol level was .10. The legal limit in Florida is .08. On his second attempt he apparently tried to beat the test.

"On the second sample Coté would not blow properly, and kept blowing air out of the side of his mouth," wrote Timothy L. Peck, the attending officer.

Coté sat down, resigned. He knew then that his driver's license would be suspended and that he was facing thousands of dollars in legal fees.

But he had already figured out a way out of it.

"He said he was going to be out of the country for a year, so he didn't care if his license was suspended," wrote Officer Peck in his report.

JON WALKED INTO THE PARTY AND SHOWED THE EMAIL to Shiva. It was from Mike Skora, an army buddy from the 82nd Airborne. He was writing from Kuwait:

i know it all came up fast. but you will be fine. i can get u
things here if u forget things. here are some things u might
need

    —gloves, nomax black or tan
    —good sunglasses
    —pants cargo tan, if none we can get us some here
    —shower things

you are coming on missions with me. i want you on my
team. we have good missions. im the baghdad team. we will
be going to a place near baghdad to drop off 10 trucks twice
a week. we work 6 days on, one off. but those 6 days we will
be resting like 3 days on an army base. this first week on the
mission you will be driving with me, then after that week
you get your own truck. your pay will be 7,000 a month. we
get paid once a month cash. you will get money at the end
of the month. the guys here are cool, some are complete
morons. im really surprised some guys are here. i know you
don't know much about the ak-47 cause we don't really use it
in the army. but you will be fine with it. our run up to
baghdad is a good one. the threat is medium. but I know you
will be fine.

He received the email from Skora four days after his DUI. That
same afternoon, he filed his application to withdraw from school
with the university registrar. Shiva scanned the email and the words
jumped off the page—Baghdad, AK-47, morons, medium risk—
what did it all mean? She marched him outside.

"Jon, what are you *doing*? Please, don't do this," she said.

He told her it was done. He recited his litany of complaints: his
lack of money, the emptiness of his life, his joke of a major, that he
was older than everyone else.

"Jon, you just got back. Why would you *voluntarily* go back?"
said Shiva.

"Shiva, it's *okay*, it's gonna be fun. It's what I need right now," he said.

He cleaned out his apartment and loaded the contents into a unit at Affordable Storage on South Main. He threw a black tarp over his bike and left the key in the ignition. He wrapped his leather motorcycle jacket in two layers of clear plastic and boxed up the Arai helmet that Chris had bought him.

The night before he left, he cooked up jambalaya for his friends at Oxford Terrace. On the wall of the apartment was a chalkboard that Shiva, Anja, Lauren, and Fernanda used for messages. Jon grabbed a piece of chalk and scrawled reminders for Shiva:

Remember how beautiful you are
Remember to be strong
Remember you got a big heart
Remember your booty is round and I'll always grab it

He took his green army cap, the one she loved to wear around the apartment, and placed it on her head. He grabbed his last bag and headed out the door. Shiva followed him down the stairs, crying.

"Don't follow me," he said.

But she did. He loaded the bag in his truck and hugged her goodbye in the parking lot. She was still standing there wearing his army cap as he drove away, away from utopia, to straighten out his life in Iraq.

I WANT TO KILL
SOMEBODY TODAY

JAKE WASHBOURNE STOOD IN THE MIDDLE OF ROUTE Tampa, his pale shaved head exposed to the blistering sun. A sleeve of tattoos ran the length of his left arm, as if it had been dipped in a vat of ink. His gloved left hand gripped the barrel of an M-4. Washbourne stood next to a gray Chevy Suburban that would no longer move. Moments earlier, the SUV had jumped the median at a hundred miles per hour, shattering both axles and flattening three tires. Now the two-ton vehicle sat in the middle of the highway like a felled beast.

As team leader, Washbourne was responsible for the $150,000 Suburban, once suitable for soccer moms, transformed into an urban combat vehicle with armor plating, bulletproof windows, and reversed seating to detect attacks from the rear. He was also responsible for the dozen armed men who were gathered near the disabled truck, conspicuous and exposed near the city of Hilla in south-central Iraq.

A blue truck suddenly appeared from around the curve. It was headed straight toward them, the driver either oblivious or filled with lethal intent. It was the classic Iraq dilemma: was it a car bomber or some bewildered Iraqi who had stumbled into a nest of armed men? Standing next to Washbourne, also holding an assault rifle, was a stocky Fijian army veteran named Isireli Naucukidi; everyone called him Isi. He saw the truck, too, now about a hundred yards away. Isi concluded that the truck wasn't a threat. He kept his weapon at his side. Washbourne concluded otherwise. He raised his M-4 and fired more than a dozen times, the rounds puncturing the blue truck until it stopped.

The mercs could see the wounded driver, his head rolling back, blood pooling on the seat and the floorboard. If the man had a bomb, no one could detect it. Iraqis had begun to gather on the side of the road, gesturing toward the truck. They wanted to help the wounded man but they didn't want to get shot themselves. Washbourne, his finger next to the trigger, waved them over. The driver, bleeding from his thigh, was then lifted from the blue truck and taken away.

Washbourne turned his attention back to the shattered Suburban.

"Okay," he told his team. "Let's burn this bitch."

EVEN THE HARD MEN WHO WORKED WITH JAKE Washbourne were wary of him. He was known as "J-Dub," his radio call sign. He was a former marine from Broken Arrow, Oklahoma, six foot three and chiseled. His company, Triple Canopy, based in Herndon, Virginia, was one of the largest private security firms in Iraq, with a reputation for hiring disciplined Special Operations veterans. But J-Dub didn't fit the mold. After hours, in the breezeway and the company bar, the Gem, he drank hard, and many of his colleagues believed his drinking affected his work. J-Dub was supposed to conduct security briefings before leading his men out onto Iraq's lawless roads. The briefings contained the latest threat assessments and locations of the most recent attacks. But J-Dub was sometimes absent from his own briefings. His subordinates would find him in his room, sleeping off the previous night's binge.

"Normally speaking, when that kind of shit goes on, guys don't last very long," said one of the men who had to roust him. "It was like, 'What the fuck?'"

J-Dub's job security was often attributed to his immediate supervisor, Ryan Thomason, who was also one of his best friends. A former Army Ranger, Thomason was known to colleagues as "Rhino." He weighed about 260 pounds, bench-pressed over 400, and looked like a college football player, which he apparently had been before the war. Rhino was loud, smart, undeniably entertaining; he fashioned himself part intellectual, part warrior. He liked to boast that he came to Iraq with a master's degree. Rhino had the words "Christian Crusader" tattooed into his bull neck in Arabic. As intimidating as he was, he also seemed to suffer from coulrophobia, a fear of clowns, and sometimes the mercs would paste clown photos to the back of his door, sending him into a rage. "He looked like this big Viking," said one former colleague. "He was this iconic figure with the big cigar stuffed into his mouth and the bullhorn voice. Guys loved him. He's really a great dude. But he's not the kind of guy you want in charge. He's one of those dudes you keep in a box with a sign that says 'Break Glass in Case of War.'"

In fact, Rhino was assistant project manager, the number-two man in charge.

They called it the "Milwaukee" project. It was basically a warzone taxi service, part of Triple Canopy's sprawling Iraq security operation. The company had been founded at the start of the war by former officers from Delta Force, the army's secretive Special Ops unit. The CEO, Lee Van Arsdale, was a former Delta Sabre Squadron commander who won the Silver Star during the Black Hawk Down affair in Mogadishu. By 2006, Triple Canopy had nearly $250 million in contracts, including the State Department's lucrative Worldwide Personal Protective Service contract, which it shared with Blackwater and DynCorp. On the Milwaukee project, Triple Canopy was under contract to KBR Inc., the Halliburton subsidiary, which was under contract to Laguna Construction, which was under contract to the Defense Department. A dozen or so Triple Canopy operators shuttled KBR and Laguna executives around Iraq in armored convoys; the client vehicle was known as the "Limo."

J-Dub, as team leader, earned $600 a day, or nearly twenty grand a month. The other "expats"—mostly Americans and Aussies— earned $500 a day. The remaining guards were Fijians like Isi, a cava farmer from the island of Ovalau, who earned $70 a day for the same dangerous work.

The mercs ran with M-4s and 9mm Glocks, the same caliber weapons used by U.S. troops. They occupied the same battle space as the military and ran the same bomb-seeded roads. But, unlike the troops, who operated under the Uniform Code of Military Justice, a legal framework dating back to the Second Continental Congress, the mercs were untouchable. None of the prevailing laws—Iraqi law, U.S. law, the UCMJ, Islamic law, the Geneva Conventions—applied to them. Shortly after he was hired by Triple Canopy, Chuck Sheppard, a former Ranger, began to wonder what would happen if he shot someone. What if there was a dispute? What if an Iraqi tried to press charges? Sheppard said Triple Canopy executives reassured him. "We were always told, from the very beginning, if for some reason something happened and they were trying to prosecute us under Iraqi law, they would put you in the back of a car and sneak you out of the country in the middle of the night. It was comforting. But we never saw nothin' on paper."

The mercs policed themselves under their own unwritten code. "Big Boy Rules," they called it. The military couldn't drink in Iraq; troops had to leave the country just to have a beer. Triple Canopy had its own bar, the Gem, which was located inside the company "man-camp" behind the blast walls of Baghdad's Green Zone. The Gem had an L-shaped bar, a big screen TV, speakers hooked up to an MP3 player and iced beer in a trough. On weekends the Gem filled up with tattooed contractors, U.S. embassy partiers, and women, vastly outnumbered, looking like prey. Sometimes, at the end of the work day, the mercs sat around and talked about killing. It made some of the experienced operators uneasy. "It was like romanticizing the idea of killing to the point where dudes want to do it," said a former Triple Canopy shooter. "You cannot put that out there and make it sound attractive and make it sound like a rite of passage. Killing is not a manhood determiner. Does that mean you're not a real man unless you've dropped a guy?"

"There was a certain group of guys who were always trying to measure their wieners based on how many times they fired," said another Gem regular.

J-Dub, his body a montage of piercings and ink, often served as bartender. He carried his head banger persona out with him into the streets. It was hard to figure. Triple Canopy was founded and run by some of the finest soldiers the U.S. military was able to produce. But the company, like many in Iraq, had expanded rapidly, maybe too rapidly, and in the process had promoted an employee who seemed almost a caricature of the modern mercenary and turned him loose in Iraq. "From the first time I saw him my spidey sense was tingling," said Mike Arrighi, a former homicide detective from Richmond, Virginia, who frequently traveled with the Milwaukee team as director of security for Laguna. "The motherfucker had the tattoos and the piercings below his lip; he didn't exactly engender a kind of friendly presence, if you know what I mean. Some of the best guys I met in-country worked for TC, but then you had this cartoon boy. We couldn't understand the divergence. There was simply no control."

The mercs of the Milwaukee team had a saying, a variation on the Las Vegas commercial: "What happens in Iraq, *stays* in Iraq."

STANDING IN THE MIDDLE OF ROUTE TAMPA, J-DUB ordered the team to empty the disabled Suburban of sensitive material. The mercs stripped the truck of communications equipment, loose ammunition, documents—anything of value. J-Dub then tossed a thermite grenade into the cab. The SUV began to smoke. He tossed in another incendiary grenade and the vehicle burst into flames. J-Dub picked up an AK-47—the insurgents' weapon of choice—and sprayed the burning truck with bullets.

"We stood there for half an hour so the vehicle could completely burn," said Isi.

According to Isi and others at the scene, J-Dub then instructed the mercs what to say if anyone asked what had happened. His story was that the convoy was attacked by small-arms fire and a roadside bomb. Another vehicle had simultaneously rammed the Suburban into the median, the story went, damaging the truck beyond repair. As the mercs sat exposed in hostile territory, the blue truck had suddenly careened toward them in a threatening manner and J-Dub neutralized the driver with well-aimed shots. He then destroyed the Suburban to prevent it from falling into enemy hands.

J-Dub recounted his story to skeptical U.S. Army personnel who came out to assist. He repeated it to State Department investigators who gathered the mercs in a conference room at a nearby base. He repeated it to me when I chased him down months later in Oklahoma.

"There was a small explosion in the median as we were going by, and that's when the car took us out," he told me. "We hit the curb and got totally airborne. It broke the axles, the drivetrain, dropped the transmission, and popped three of the tires. The vehicle was dead."

But many didn't believe it. Arrighi, who had been riding in the Limo, said he was later told, "It was all staged." Isi told me, "It was so stupid. It was just careless driving."

Still, Isi said he obeyed orders and wrote down the fake story when the State Department asked for statements. He laughed when I asked him why.

"Because I still want to work for the company," he explained.

In a day's work, J-Dub had lost a $150,000 company asset and wounded an Iraqi civilian. The weary mercs eventually made their way back to Baghdad. Rhino, who was serving as acting project manager because the project manager was away, was there to greet them. He instructed the mercs not to discuss the incident to anyone. That was for security reasons, his lawyer told me.

Rhino also had a message for the team, according to Isi.

"What happens in Iraq, *stays* in Iraq," he said. "Good job, boys."

NO ONE KNEW HOW MANY THERE WERE, NOT EVEN after they formed unions and trade associations like the International Peace Operations Association and the Private Security Company Association of Iraq, with officers and lobbyists who fumed whenever anyone suggested that they were, in fact, mercenaries, fighting the war for money. The estimates ranged from 25,000 to 75,000 or even higher. The Pentagon estimate was 25,000—an entire division of hired guns spread across the battlefield. The GAO estimate was almost twice that: 48,000. Once in Baghdad I met a South African merc who had formed another merc union, the International Contractors Association. His name was Jaco Botes, and his organization's purpose, he told me, was to bring regulation to an industry that was "changing the whole idea of warfare." Botes was lean, fair, and eerily composed, especially for someone who had been in-country three years and had been attacked nineteen times. He didn't talk about it much but at one point he said, "Someone you just spoke to . . . and then like that . . . there's nothing left of them." His voice trailed off. "It *angers* you." But he insisted he wasn't a mercenary. He said he was like a Brinks guard. He estimated there were 30,000 to 50,000 people like him in Iraq.

It had started small, a byproduct of all the mistakes at the beginning: not enough troops, ignoring the insurgency, starting the reconstruction prematurely. Soon they were everywhere: guarding the diplomats, the generals, military bases the size of small cities, and thousands of supply convoys filled with guns and ammunition and food. Suddenly no one and no thing could move around Iraq without them. Some human rights groups had mercs. The media had mercs. The International Republican Institute, chaired by John McCain, and the National Democratic Institute, chaired by Madeleine Albright, used mercs to spread democracy. The Iraqi politicians had them full time and the American politicians had them whenever the delegations came through to find out how the war was going. The market was so hot it became known as the "Iraq Bubble." The demand to be safe never stopped, so neither did the supply. The mercs came from the army, navy, air force, marines, from small-town police departments and the LAPD. And from other nations' armies: the British SAS, the Australian Defence Forces, the Nepalese Gurkhas. One Peruvian I met swore that there were ex-members of the Shining Path in Iraq, the terrorists who had massacred thousands of peasants during the eighties and early nineties. Terrorists fighting terrorists.

I didn't really blame most of them, even though a lot of people did, demonizing them and calling them all kinds of names, many much worse than "mercenary." The lessons of Vietnam were such that no one was about to criticize the troops for the disaster that the government had perpetrated in Iraq. But the mercs were fair game. I met an ex-cop from L.A. who did two years running the Baghdad airport road for perhaps the biggest merc company of them all, Blackwater USA (later Blackwater Worldwide). He was short and friendly, with salt-and-pepper hair, and went by the call sign "Miyagi" because of his resemblance to Pat Morita in *The Karate Kid*. He had one of the hardest jobs imaginable, driving up and down the most dangerous road in Iraq. Then one day a bomb went off next to him. The shrapnel tore through his thigh and nearly sliced off his dick; he needed three *stitches* to hold it together. (Afterward the doctor told him, "By the way, your boy is gonna be fine." To which he replied, predictably, "Since you're working down there, can I get an enhancement?") By the time I met him, Miyagi was broke, his marriage finished, and he was trying to find work near the beach in Santa Barbara. It wasn't easy. "People look at you weird," he told me, slightly bewildered. "They look at you sort of like you're a trained killer or something." But if ever there was a place that needed highly trained killers, it was Iraq. It was basic economics, really, a sudden windfall for the chronically and inexcusably underpaid, like veterans and cops and firefighters. If they had started handing out $20,000-a-month jobs for elementary school teachers in Iraq, they, too, would have turned out by the thousands. For most of them, this was all they knew. Here was an opportunity, fully sanctioned by the United States government, to sell those killing skills at a premium. And you could easily get your dick shot off in this job, or worse. It was the contractors' war, anyway. Not just the mercs but the janitors and the cooks, the truck drivers and the bomb disposal experts. By 2008, there were an estimated 190,000 contractors of all stripes in Iraq; they outnumbered American troops by 30,000. The total cost of these private contracts since the start of the war was $85 billion, or one-fifth of the U.S. government's overall spending on the war. It was, in all respects, the largest use of private forces in any major American conflict.

Contractors kept the Iraq war running, so it only figured that they fought it, too. But when it came to the mercs, the government didn't even have the decency to count them. Maybe because if it did, all the basic barometers that the Pentagon used to measure how the war was going—troop levels, number and frequency of attacks, and, especially, casualties—would have gone out the window. But there were never any statistics, as if mercs exist. They didn't die or get wounded or engage in combat. They were everywhere and nowhere. The U.S. Army Corps of Engineers employed at least a half dozen companies—thousands of armed men—to provide security on the $58 billion reconstruction of Iraq. It was some of the most dangerous, and frequently lethal, work in the country. But when the corps Logistics Directorate began to report casualty figures up the chain of command, the military deleted them, according to Victoria Wayne, who served as deputy director of Logistics until 2006. "It was like there was a major war being fought out there, but we were the only ones who knew about it," she told me. After a year of protests by Wayne and Logistics Director Jack Holly, a retired marine colonel, the casualty figures—hundreds of mercs and other contractors killed and wounded—were finally included in Army Corps of Engineers reports. But they represented only a fraction of the total—just those who worked for the Corps—and even then were not included in the official body count. Wayne called private security contractors (she and Holly never used the word "mercenary") "the unsung heroes of the war."

As the mercs expanded their presence, there was a kind of institutionalized ignorance that pervaded everything about them. It was as if the U.S. government desperately needed them to prosecute its failing war, but wanted to know as little as possible about who they were, what they did, and, especially, who was responsible for their actions.

In the spring of 2005, Bob Bateman, an American infantry major, was traveling through Baghdad in the backseat of an unmarked sedan. As the car approached a congested intersection, a Blackwater convoy came barreling through. The black armored Suburbans and Expeditions bullied cars up onto the sidewalk. At least one Blackwater merc started popping off rounds. Bateman later wrote: "I cannot say if the shots were aimed at us or fired into the sky as a warning. I do know one thing: It enraged me . . . and Blackwater is, at least nominally, on our side."

Blackwater was not nearly as notorious as it would later become. But the encounter was telling not only for its frivolous brutality but also for the official U.S. government ignorance that it ultimately revealed.

Bateman, a war-fighter/historian/blogger, had written books on the Korean war and conflict in the digital age. His wife, Kate, a liberal Democrat from Maine who spoke Hindi and Urdu, at the time was serving as vice president of her class at Johns Hopkins University's Paul H. Nitze School of Advanced International Studies. Kate began to ask pointed questions about the men who had blasted away at her husband. A few months after the incident, Secretary of Defense Donald H. Rumsfeld came to speak at Johns Hopkins. When the question-and-answer period came around, Kate was ready for him.

"I'm a first-year student here at SAIS," she began. "There are currently thousands of private military contractors in Iraq. . . . Since the private contractors are operating outside the Uniform Code of Military Justice, can you speak to what law or rules of engagement do govern their behavior?"

Rumsfeld stammered out a suggestion that the mercs fell under Iraqi law. "Iraq's a sovereign country," he said, dubiously.

Two months later, the commander-in-chief, George W. Bush, showed up at Hopkins. Kate pressed on: "My question is in regards to private military contractors," she told the president.

As she unspooled her question, Bush rested his left arm on the podium, his tilted face betraying utter bewilderment.

"I asked your secretary of Defense a couple months ago what law governs their actions," said Kate.

Bush interrupted her: "I was gonna ask *him.*"

The crowd laughed as the president then issued a mock plea: "Help!"

"I was hoping your answer might be a little more specific," Kate deadpanned, the crowd now laughing *at* the commander-in-chief.

She nervously plowed ahead: "Mr. Rumsfeld answered that Iraq has its own domestic laws, which he assumed applied to those private military contractors. However, Iraq is not currently capable of enforcing its laws, much less over our military contractors."

"Hmm," said Bush.

"Mr. President, how do you propose to bring private military contractors under a system of law?"

"Yeah, I appreciate that very much," he responded. "I mean, I wasn't kidding. I was gonna pick up the phone and say, 'Mr. Secretary, I've got an interesting question.' That's what delegation is. I don't mean to be dodging the question, although it's kind of convenient in this case [more laughter]. But I really will: I'm gonna call up the secretary and tell him you brought up a really valid question, and what are we doing about it? That's how I work."

But the answer, of course, was that there was no answer. The law, in reality, was Big Boy Rules.

As the security industry grew, a shadowy and motley workforce continued to pour into Iraq, thousands of operators of varying qualifications. "It was like the Mad Max Union Hall," said Arrighi, who started working in private security in Iraq in 2004.

The U.S. government rarely got involved.

"We could hire the Rockettes and give them guns, and they wouldn't know," Arrighi told me.

J-DUB WAS IN A GOOD MOOD. THE HILLA DEBACLE— the torched SUV, the wounded Iraqi—had been buried and forgotten. Five weeks later, J-Dub was due for a vacation; within hours he'd be on a plane back to Oklahoma. He geared up next to the Suburban, donning his flak jacket, his ballistic glasses, and his gloves. He racked a round into the chamber of his M-4.

"I want to kill somebody today," J-Dub announced.

The three mercs who were traveling with J-Dub later said they regarded it as an off-handed remark. Isi, the Fijian, told me that J-Dub often blurted out such comments before hitting the road. "From my point of view, he had a problem. Nearly every day he said he wanted to kill somebody," said Isi.

"Why?" Isi said he asked before they rolled out.

"Because I'm going on vacation tomorrow," J-Dub replied. "That's a long time, buddy."

Washbourne denied that he ever expressed an intention or desire to kill.

The Milwaukee team rolled out onto Route Irish, the infamous Baghdad airport road, en route to the airport itself. J-Dub took his place in the front passenger seat of the "Follow," the third Suburban in a three-truck convoy. Next to him was the driver, Chuck Sheppard, a tall former Ranger. He went by the call sign "Shrek" because of his vague resemblance to the cartoon monster. Sheppard had a reputation for competence and honesty; Triple Canopy was promoting him to team leader the following day. In the backseat, facing the rear, were Isi and a former marine sniper named Shane Schmidt. After getting out of the Marine Corps in 2003, where he did two tours in Afghanistan, Schmidt, then twenty-nine, had knocked around, working at the post office and at his godfather's steelyard in Wisconsin. He said he grew disillusioned by civilian life, in which "loyalty was a punch line to a very poor joke." He got the job through a former Delta he knew. On his bulletproof vest, Schmidt sometimes wore a small yellow duckie that his daughter had given him. His code sign was "Happy," an ironic reference to his surly demeanor, due in part to his dissolving marriage.

It was the second run of the day for J-Dub's crew. The morning run had ended with Schmidt pumping a round into the grille of a suspicious sedan that had been inching up on the convoy as it waited to enter the Green Zone. The car stopped without further incident, but J-Dub was jealous, Schmidt said, as if he feared he might leave Iraq without squeezing off another shot. "Son of a bitch, you got to shoot today and I didn't," J-Dub told him, according to Schmidt. But, then, in the early afternoon, the team was dispatched to the airport to pick up another client, a KBR executive.

The convoy drove west toward the airport at ninety miles per hour. Washbourne, as was common, was blaring "death metal music," according to Schmidt and Sheppard. Route Irish was known variously as "IED Alley"—for the improvised explosive devices, or roadside bombs, that frequently detonated in the median—and "Death Street." To avoid the bombs and the snipers, people drove the five-mile road as fast as they could. Within minutes, the Milwaukee team had arrived safely at checkpoint one, the first barrier to entry outside the airport.

The checkpoint—a maze of concrete barriers, bomb-sniffing dogs, and armed contractors—was always sketchy. Clusters of suspicious-looking men loitered near the charred carcasses of blown-up vehicles. A black statue of a winged man towered over the checkpoint, and it served as a kind of target for insurgents who occasionally lobbed mortars and rockets at the waiting cars. Sometimes vehicles detonated in line, incinerating everything around them.

Sheppard pulled the Suburban into a blocking position while the lead vehicle and the Limo awaited clearance to pass. As they waited, the mercs suddenly noticed a white "bongo" truck—half-van, half-pickup—inching toward them about 150 yards back. Exactly what happened next is a matter of dispute. Later, the four men would produce three distinct accounts. All three involved a Triple Canopy shooter putting bullets into the civilian truck.

According to Schmidt and Sheppard, J-Dub, fresh off his declaration that he wanted to kill, opened his door, stepped out of the truck, peered through the scope of his M-4, and shot several rounds into the bongo truck's windshield without provocation. "I seen the splash off the windshield; he fired into the grille and the windshield," Schmidt told me. "His intention was to kill him. If you're shooting into the windshield with a high-velocity rifle, you're not intending to scare somebody, you're intending to kill them."

In interviews and written reports, Schmidt and Sheppard said J-Dub then climbed back in the truck and warned them, "That didn't happen, understand?"

J-Dub later told me that he fired only warning shots into the grille of a truck that had advanced in a threatening manner. "They're a very pushy people," he said of the Iraqi populace. "After I went through the entire escalation of force I put two rounds into the grille of his truck. At no time did I fire six, seven, or eight rounds into the grill and the windshield. And there was no comments like, 'That didn't happen, you understand?' Or anything like that."

Isi said the bongo truck was never a threat. But he seemed confused as to whether it was J-Dub or Schmidt who indiscriminately opened fire. In an initial written statement and an interview with me, he identified the shooter as "Happy" (Schmidt). In his first statements to Triple Canopy, he identified the shooter first as J-Dub, then Schmidt.

Isi said he couldn't tell where the bullets hit. But everyone agreed the truck came to an immediate halt.

THE MILWAUKEE TEAM CONTINUED TO THE AIRPORT TO pick up the KBR executive. It then headed back down Route Irish toward the Green Zone.

The convoy was doing about eighty when it came upon an orange and white taxi, chugging along in the right-hand lane. The first two Suburbans—the Lead and the Limo—passed the taxi without incident. Then came the Follow.

What happened next is also a matter of dispute. What is not disputed is that three witnesses—Schmidt, Sheppard, and Isi—gave sworn statements that J-Dub turned his weapon on an innocent person for amusement.

"You know, I've never shot anyone with my pistol before," J-Dub remarked as the Follow approached the taxi, according to Schmidt and Sheppard.

As the Suburban passed on the left, they said, J-Dub pushed open his door, leaned out with his Glock, and fired "seven or eight rounds" into the taxi's windshield.

J-Dub was "laughing" as he fired, Sheppard told me. In an after-action report to Triple Canopy, Schmidt wrote: "From my position as we passed I could see the taxi had been hit in the windshield, due to the Spidering of the glass and the pace we were traveling, I could not tell if the driver had been hit. He did pull the car off the road in an erratic manner."

Isi would recall events a little differently. As the Suburban approached the taxi, he told me, J-Dub yelled out to Sheppard, "Cut him off! Cut him off!"

Sheppard obliged by swerving in front of the taxi, giving J-Dub a better shot, Isi said. He said J-Dub then opened his door and fired repeatedly into the taxi's windshield—with his M-4, not his Glock. Isi, who was facing backward, described the taxi driver as a sixty- to seventy-year-old man. He said he saw one hole in the windshield but could not tell if the driver had been hit. "From my point of view, this old man, he was so innocent, because he was ahead of us with a normal speed," Isi told me. "He couldn't have any danger for us."

Isi said the three Americans laughed as the Suburban sped away. Schmidt, he said, leaned over and patted J-Dub on the shoulder.

"Happy yelled out, 'Yee haw! Good shot, buddy. Great! Great!'" said Isi.

Both Schmidt and Sheppard denied that they felt anything but remorse. Schmidt told me, "No, I don't get a thrill out of killing innocent people. That was a moment of shame."

For his part, J-Dub called their accounts "an absolute, total fabrication."

"That shooting did not happen," he told me. "I would not do that. That is stupid. Granted, the Iraqi public may not be the nicest people in the world, but there is no cause for anybody to just hang a pistol out a door and just shoot people at random, for no reason whatsoever. It just infuriates the shit out of me.

"And as far as the statement goes where I said I've never shot anyone with my pistol, that is a lie. It was never one time said," said J-Dub.

"I am not a clever or witty man," he added. "I don't say things like that. I am not one for witty banter. And I'm not a morbid or sadistic fuck either."

When the team returned to the base, 9mm shell casings were found inside the truck.

Big Boy Rules.

That night, the mercs held a going-away party for J-Dub and other outbound operators at the Gem. J-Dub then left the country on vacation, even as word of a "bad shoot" spread through the Triple Canopy man-camp.

The Fijians usually kept to themselves, gathering in their trailers at the end of the day to sip cava, a bitter, slightly narcotic drink. They had their own supervisor, a Fijian army veteran named Jona Masirewa, who was chosen partly because he spoke the best English. The night of the shootings, Isi informed Masirewa, who asked him to write up a report. But both men were afraid to tell the company because of their lowly status as "TCNs"—third-country nationals. "It was a difficult thing for us because we are TCNs and they are expats," Isi told me. "They are team leaders, and they make commands and reports on us. And the team leaders were always saying, 'What happens today, stays today,' and if something like that happens, the team leaders, they start covering each other up."

Schmidt and Sheppard didn't know what to do. Schmidt later wrote that he briefly attended the going-away party at the Gem but "I didn't drink do [sic] to what had transpired that day." He said he feared "catching a bullet in the head" if he came forward. Sheppard said he was so shaken he spent the night at another location in the Green Zone. Both said they had feared for their lives and their jobs, believing that J-Dub would be protected by his close friend, Rhino. Some of the other mercs were offended; they believed that Schmidt and Sheppard were making excuses to cover up a possible atrocity; one told Schmidt to "man up" and tell the supervisors or he would.

By the time Schmidt and Sheppard came forward, two days after the incident, their accounts were nearly identical. As Triple Canopy began to investigate, one thing became immediately clear:

J-Dub's four-man crew had been involved in three shooting incidents in a single day, and none had been reported.

J-Dub was sitting at a Tulsa pizza joint, enjoying his vacation with his wife and a friend, when he got a call on his cell phone from the Triple Canopy's Iraq country manager, Kelvin Kai, from Baghdad. "He said that allegations were made that it was just a rampant day, is I believe what he called it, of shooting and mayhem," J-Dub told me.

The company's investigation took two days. Triple Canopy took statements from 30 potential witnesses and checked with the Iraqi police and the U.S. military, neither of which had a record of any shootings on the airport road. The Milwaukee project manager, Mark Alexander, filed a seven-page report in which he concluded "it is clear that there were up to three incidents where rounds were fired and no report was made after." Alexander wrote: "I believe that Schmidt and Sheppard initially did not report the incident because they believed Washbourne would try and make them look like they had more involvement than just witnessing the incident."

Alexander recommended firing J-Dub and placing him on Triple Canopy's "Do Not Return" list. He recommended removing Schmidt and Sheppard from the Milwaukee project and allowing them to return at another location if "they demonstrate they learned from the incident." He recommended issuing a written reprimand to Isi and Masirewa "for their failure to report the information."

Instead, Triple Canopy treated J-Dub, Schmidt, and Sheppard equally: all were fired. The company said they had failed to report the shootings immediately, according to company and U.S. military regulations. Isi escaped punishment after it was determined that he reported the incidents, even if Masirewa did not immediately come forward.

Schmidt and Sheppard responded by filing a lawsuit in Virginia's Fairfax County circuit court, arguing that Triple Canopy had fired them for reporting an attempted murder.

That's how it became public; if not for the lawsuit, I doubt it ever would have. Not long after the suit was filed, I went to interview Schmidt and Sheppard one afternoon with their lawyer, Patricia Smith, at a restaurant in suburban Virginia. What struck me, even more than the violence that the two men described, was the culture of lawlessness. It was the same war I had seen myself, and yet totally different. The military, for all its rigidity, was a culture of rules and accountability. That had been stripped away. In private security, Sheppard explained to me, "You got all the good things about the military—the camaraderie, the esprit de corps, you get to shoot things and blow things up—but with none of the other bullshit." Schmidt said there were never any rules of engagement, the bedrock for determining whether a shooting was justified. "I was never briefed on any rules of engagement," he said. "I was never briefed on company SOPs. The rules of engagement, the way they were briefed to me, was, 'If you feel threatened, take a shot.'"

A few weeks later I flew out to Oklahoma to see J-Dub. I didn't tell him I was coming because I figured that he wouldn't want to talk. I showed up at his apartment in Broken Arrow in the middle of a sunny afternoon. He came to the door in jeans and a T-shirt that revealed most of his tattooed left arm. I had never seen him, and I wasn't a hundred percent certain it was him. When I asked for Jake Washbourne, he told me he wasn't home. All I could do was hand Washbourne a business card and ask him to give Washbourne a message to call me.

I came back that night and his wife greeted me at the door. She was pleasant but said Jake had left town on business. As I drove away, I got a text message from J-Dub telling me he didn't want me to waste my trip and asking me to call. We agreed to meet at a Holiday Inn bar in nearby Tulsa. When I walked in, he apologized for lying and said he wasn't sure how to respond when a *Washington Post* reporter shows up on your doorstep. After a few beers, he agreed to meet me for an interview a couple nights later at a Tulsa bar called the Pour House. He brought along his brother and sister-in-law, who waited at the bar while we did the interview in a corner. Both of us taped the conversation.

Once again, I was surprised less by his account than the culture he described. He denied the allegations: "They're all unfounded, unbased, and they simply did not happen." By then, it had become apparent to me that whatever happened on the Baghdad airport road that day, the full story would never be known. But it was the context—a world so similar to and yet different from the American military experience in Iraq—that was striking to me. The main focus of J-Dub's anger was Schmidt, who, he said, had lost control in Iraq as his marriage unraveled.

J-Dub described several drunken episodes involving Schmidt, his subordinate, but none that seemed to keep Schmidt off the roads of Iraq. I later heard from other operators that Schmidt and Washbourne were both heavy drinkers, and yet both remained in the field.

Finally, I flew to Fiji to meet with Isi. I took a puddle jumper from Suva, the Fijian capital, to the island of Ovalau, descending over the water to a landing strip that had been hacked out of the jungle. Isi said he would be waiting for me at the airport, which turned out to be a tiny shelter with a few benches. When I arrived and he wasn't there, I hopped in a van, because the driver told me that no one would be back for another day.

We were slowly making our way along the half-paved road that rings Ovalau when a truck came up behind us, honking. It was Isi, accompanied by his wife. I swapped vehicles and we drove the rest of the way to the town of Levuka, which resembled the set of an old western, except that behind the dilapidated storefronts stood soaring green mountains, and in front of them the endless sea.

Isi was stocky and dark, about five foot ten, with thick weathered hands and an easy smile. He spoke passable English, his second language. Over dinner, Isi told me he had heard about the job with Triple Canopy from a former commander in the Fijian army. He flew to Suva and lined up inside a gymnasium with hundreds of other applicants, mostly former Fijian soldiers. He said he liked the job for a while, and the money was good, but after the Hilla incident and the shooting on Route Irish, he decided to come home and resume life as a cava farmer in Ovalau's interior, a job that paid him a fraction of what he earned in Iraq.

Isi made nearly ten times less than his American colleagues, but he was the only merc in the Suburban that day who reported the shootings immediately. He could have gone back to Triple Canopy, but he said he wasn't interested.

"I couldn't stand what was happening," he told me. "It seemed like every day they were covering something [up]."

THROUGH IT ALL, THERE WAS LITTLE DISCUSSION OF criminal action, even though J-Dub, as even he acknowledged, had been accused of "straight up murder on the airport road."

Triple Canopy said its only obligation was to report the incident to its contract holder, KBR, which was supposed to report to *its* contract holder, Laguna Construction, which was supposed to report to *its* contract holder, the U.S. military.

Triple Canopy sent a two-page report to KBR from the Iraq country manager, Kelvin Kai. It concluded that the three shooting incidents "did in fact occur," and that the incidents involving the bongo truck and the taxi "leave doubt that the Use of Force was required." KBR refused to say what it did with the report.

Triple Canopy officials also visited Lieutenant Colonel Michael J. Hartig, the army's director of security for the Green Zone. Hartig, when I interviewed him, said he got the impression that Triple Canopy was concerned mostly about the potential negative publicity. He said the officials vaguely described "some misconduct on the road." He said he was never told of specific allegations that a Triple Canopy employee had announced that he wanted to kill someone, then fired rounds into the windshield of a taxi.

"This is out of my venue," Hartig said he told the company. He said he referred Triple Canopy to the Joint Contracting Command for Iraq and Afghanistan. "I didn't want to get involved in this because I had enough going on in my life," Hartig told me. "It was like, 'Here's the point of contact. Have a nice day.'"

I called the U.S. Central Command, which oversees military operations in Iraq, to see if an investigation occurred. No one seemed to have any idea what I was talking about. After several calls, the Centcom spokesman, Major David W. Small, grew testy. He suggested that I was wasting his time.

"We're fighting a war here," Small told me.

THE LAST TRAIN

THE LOW DESERT—THE BAKED EARTH AND THE scrub—reminded me of Iraq, but then everything reminded me of Iraq.

Out on the horizon, a rust-colored mesa sent shadows across the Nevada plains. I half expected to see a pair of low-flying Black Hawks, their noses angled forward against the blue sky. Mark was having trouble finding his glasses. He rummaged through the cramped compartment, looking in the trash can, on the floor, and behind his seat. Finally he remembered that he left them downstairs, where Dad sat under a white Amtrak blanket that he had bought on one of his previous rail excursions, back when he was still healthy. Mark came back a few minutes later wearing his glasses. "Pay dirt," he said. He then sat down to write the statement he had to give before a federal judge that week to try to keep himself out of prison.

We sat facing each other, my little brother and me, the flipped-up backs of our laptops nearly touching. A freight train passed in the opposite direction, a few feet from our window, boxcars of yellow and green, some marked up with graffiti. Then it was gone.

The trip had been Dad's idea, a way for the three of us to get away while there was still time. It was bound to be an ordeal—we could have flown from San Francisco to Boise in a couple hours—but Dad hated the invasive security, how the romance of flight had been stripped away. He felt the same way about driving; more than twenty years earlier, while still in his early fifties, he gave away his Monte Carlo and never drove again. For him, the train was the last bastion of dignified travel. And so the previous night, after my nephew's eighth birthday party, I took Dad back to my house to spend the night before our trip. I gripped his bony arm and led him up the stairs to the front door. Dad collapsed on the couch, heaving, and I went back to the car to haul out his lung-cancer gear: the two scuffed oxygen tanks, his state-of-the-art walker, and the drugs—liquid morphine and Vicodin, the stool softeners and Ambien to help him sleep through the night. After a brief rest, Dad of course headed straight for the backyard to smoke a string of Kools. I sat down at the computer and finished my own letter to the judge. I was one of Mark's many character witnesses ("Please save my brother!"), like Carl Bernstein, the Watergate reporter, and Fay Vincent, the former baseball commissioner, both of whom submitted affidavits. Dad then announced that he wanted to take a bath. He shuffled to the bathroom and peeled off his smoke-infused clothes. Even now, the image of my 106-pound father is burned into memory: his skin stretched like rice paper across his ribs, a matrix of crude purple lines tattooed into his chest after four weeks of radiation. I lowered Dad into the tub, lit a scented candle, dimmed the lights, and handed him a joint. He took two big hits, then exploded into a coughing fit before sitting back, content.

"This is perfect, *perfect*," he said.

The taxi arrived at eight the next morning. Dad pushed his green walker into the train station at Emeryville, and then a cheerful yellow shuttle took us to our sleeper. Dad and I moved into the wheelchair accessible compartment, which had its own bathroom. We gave Mark the compartment upstairs so he could concentrate on his statement to the judge. He spent most of the day writing it. In the afternoon, I joined him and we sat together in silence.

Around 7:30 P.M., an announcement came over the intercom, calling us to dinner. Dad wore his Pittsburgh Steelers Super Bowl cap and a red flannel shirt over black suspenders that held up his jeans. He was emaciated, but he still had his salt-and-pepper hair and his color and his biting humor; he was the best-looking terminal cancer patient there ever was. We were led to a table in the dining car. Its dim lighting, polished silverware, and white tablecloths made it feel as if we were traveling in the 1940s and not in 2006. That was the point, of course, exactly what Dad had wanted, one of the last things he wanted.

"I love the train," he said contentedly.

Mark fetched him a bottle of Ensure, the chocolaty drink that we bought by the case and which had helped keep his weight steady at 106—always 106—50 pounds less than normal.

"Well," Dad said cheerfully, squinting at the menu, "hopefully I won't die before we get there."

2006—THE YEAR OF PLAGUES. DISEASE. PRISON. Divorce. Depression. Somehow, boils and pestilence eluded us. It was the year I decided to go back to the war.

I'm not sure I ever really left. I had spent the fall of 2004 and most of 2005 traveling around Iraq with the U.S. military. At first I went for the adventure, the sense of purpose, to cover the biggest story of them all. After that it got more complicated until, finally, when someone asked why, I just said what I thought I felt at the time, as if it could be neatly summarized, anyway. Certainly, one of the reasons I had gone was to cover combat. Then one day in Sadr City, the Baghdad slum, I was sitting in the back of a Humvee, idling in a vacant lot after a day of patrolling. I was struggling to keep my eyes open when suddenly an orange fireball the size of a two-story building erupted from the earth. It was followed instantly by a deafening explosion and then a gray cloud of dirt and smoke that blotted out the sun. My stomach seized up in pain. I reached beneath my flak jacket, not certain what I'd find, feeling around and realizing it was only a cramp from the sudden clenching of my entire body. Before the bomb went off, five Iraqi soldiers had been lounging in a pickup directly in front of us, swigging water and spitting it back into the dirt. When the smoke cleared, four of the five men were dead, hundreds of marble-sized ball-bearings having ripped through their bodies and the pickup. The bleeding driver was crawling on the ground. I got out of the Humvee and walked tentatively toward the truck. One of the Iraqis, a thin soldier with thick black hair and a wispy mustache, whom I later learned was twenty, was sprawled in the bed of the pickup, his brains dribbling down the left rear panel above the tire. Another, a portly soldier, was killed where he sat in the front passenger seat. Two of the ball bearings were lodged in his forehead.

The next day, I sat for six hours against a wall, smoking for the first time, staring at a tank yard. Then I grabbed my stuff and rejoined the platoon that had been attacked. The men were happy to see me. I wasn't necessarily part of them, but I was part of *it* now, part of the war. And I felt it; I carried it around with me, and I knew that I belonged, that it all made a certain sense that I couldn't really define or place, and that I had never found anywhere else. So I kept coming back, knowing that it was crazy, and maybe irresponsible, feeling proud, feeling guilty, thinking about my seven-year-old son, knowing that the risk wasn't worth it. I felt connected to the people—fellow reporters, soldiers, Iraqis—in the deep and profound way that you read about in books. More than anything, I felt like my work had meaning: to report on America's war. I kept at it all through 2005. Then I came home.

The new year unfolded with my marriage unraveling and my brother at war with the federal government. Mark was a reporter with the *San Francisco Chronicle*. He and another reporter, Lance Williams, had been served with subpoenas ordering them to disclose the name of the source who had leaked the grand jury testimony of Barry Bonds, Jason Giambi, and other prominent athletes implicated in the BALCO steroids scandal. Mark and Lance had used the information to show how Bonds had secretly used steroids to turn himself into the greatest home run hitter of all time. The subpoena had been rumored for years and had become something of a family joke. But we never really believed it. In the spring of 2005, Mark and Lance met President Bush at the White House Correspondents Dinner, where they were being honored for their steroids coverage. "You've done a service," the president and former owner of the Texas Rangers told them.

That was comforting until a year later, when the Bush Justice Department moved to prosecute my brother. Mark and Lance were given six days to turn over not only the leaker's identity but also the grand jury transcripts and "any original packaging." That was not going to happen, and so the only alternative was to fight it in court until the appeals were exhausted.

Mark and his wife, Nicole, sat down the kids, six and eight at the time, and tried to explain what was happening.

"We've got to tell you something," Nicole began. "Dad might have to go to jail."

I wish I could say that I was there for my brother. But I wasn't, not really. I was in another world. I was functioning more or less normally, and yet somehow cut off from my own life. Upon returning from Iraq, my own paper, the *Washington Post*, had dispatched me to Arizona to cover Major League Baseball's spring training. My main assignment, incredibly, was to write about Barry Bonds, who was about to surpass Babe Ruth on the all-time home run list despite the allegations of steroid use that had been exposed by my brother.

Bonds reported to camp late, packing a paunch and his usual headache-inducing charm. He was trailed by a team of videographers collecting footage for a Bonds reality show and two personal trainers, one of whom carried around his bats like a load of firewood. Instead of standing while waiting his turn at the batting cage, the Home Run King would rest on a metal folding chair like some contract bridge player. When he finally spoke, Bonds confessed that, his $18 million salary aside, baseball was "not as interesting" to him anymore.

I should have just headed for the pool right there. But after spending a year watching soldiers and marines toiling in Iraq—the hardest job imaginable—it depressed me to no end. The fact that we were in the desert, this one a playground, didn't help, I suppose. In my more irrational moments, I tried to picture Bonds, geared up and patrolling Ramadi in the 120-degree heat. As I stood in the packed Giants dugout, listening to him prattle on, it occurred to me that there were probably more American reporters covering *him* than there were in all of Iraq.

After that, every day was perfect: blue skies, freshly mown grass, the crack of the bat. Except that I didn't feel like getting out of bed or opening the curtains or doing much of anything, especially writing about Bonds. "What am I fucking doing here?" I asked my brother more than once. I had to admit that I *missed* Iraq. I couldn't relax. As proud as I was of Mark, it felt sort of like a cameo appearance in someone else's movie, and for the first time in my life I felt the pangs of sibling rivalry. That spring, *Sports Illustrated* published excerpts of *Game of Shadows*, Mark's and Lance's book exposing Bonds as a walking pharmacy. That blew the lid off steroids and Bonds. I drove over to the Giants camp to witness the fallout. Bonds emerged from the trainers' room, half dressed, and walked to his locker trailed by a cluster of reporters. (Mark had been dogging Barry for three years, but if Bonds knew that I was his tormenter's brother, he didn't show it.)

"Barry, have you read the excerpts in *Sports Illustrated* showing that you used steroids and, if so, what's your reaction?" I asked.

"I won't even look at it," Bonds replied, not unpleasantly. "For what? There's no need to." Then he walked away.

By opening day, I was in a state. I flew home to San Francisco and confirmed that my marriage, in fact, was over. One day, while arguing with my wife on the telephone, I put my fist through a glass picture frame and tore up my hand. I walked out the door to cover the Giants home opener and never went back. I filed my story and then sat in the press box, numb, staring at the empty stadium, uncertain where to go. I ended up at a studio-sized houseboat in Sausalito, furnished with a couch, a television, a breakfast table, a bed, and various nautical décor, like fishing nets and starfish. I rarely went out. I rarely worked, except to show up at the ballpark to follow Bonds' desultory chase of Ruth, which continued on for weeks.

I spent a lot of time thinking about Iraq, mainly how to get back.

I SLEPT ON THE TOP BUNK ABOVE DAD, MY HEAD ABOUT a foot from the ceiling. Outside, Utah rolled by in the darkness. Dad was out cold, the *thump-thump* of his beloved train lulling him into a deep and satisfying sleep.

That summer Mark and I had finally convinced him to go to the doctor. He'd been dropping weight for weeks, until finally he came back from a train trip to visit friends in LA and could barely get off the floor. Dad went straight into the hospital, ending up at the VA Medical Center, which was perched on a cliff overlooking the Golden Gate Bridge, like a San Francisco retreat. At the end of the week, the doctors filed in to his room. Dad was lying in bed. Mark and I sat on either side of him.

The chief oncologist, a balding, bearded man who exuded cold competence, delivered the fatal news.

That was followed by silence, like the air was being sucked out of the room.

"How long?" Dad asked.

"Four to eight months," the doctor replied firmly.

Mark and I wheeled Dad outside to a bench near the parking lot. It was a cool, cloudless afternoon. Dad, dressed in his blue bathrobe, sat on the bench and lit up a Kool, which seemed both perverse and completely logical under the circumstances. Mark cried and held his hand. I sat in Dad's wheelchair with my arms on my knees, stunned, feeling like it was hard to believe, since Dad, after all, was sitting right in front of us, smoking, just like normal.

I stopped working entirely, not that I had been doing much anyway. After Dad got home, we settled into a routine that, it was hoped, would prolong his life. Dad would spend an hour each morning getting radiated while listening to the Moody Blues, his favorite band. We'd have lunch and hang out; sometimes we'd see a movie. Every other week I had my son, so in the late afternoon I'd make the forty-five-minute drive to pick him up, make dinner, get him to bed, get him off to school, and then drive out to Dad's to do it all over again.

Then, suddenly, Dad started to get better; X-rays showed that the tumor had shrunk, and we started to plan our trip to Idaho, where Dad had old friends. We decided to go in September, hoping that Mark's legal troubles wouldn't get in the way.

One afternoon, Dad felt so good he wanted to hit golf balls. He and Mark went to the driving range, Dad shuffling along with his walker, Mark toting Dad's bag of rusty Gene Sarazen–autographed Wilson's, which he never relinquished to his dying day, even though Sarazen won the Masters in 1935. Mark bought a bucket of balls and they were just about to hit when his cell phone rang. It was his editor: the judge had rendered a decision.

"We lost," Mark told Dad.

"Ah shit," Dad said. "Well, fuck it, there's nothing you can do about it now. Let's hit."

Dad pulled out his Sarazen 3-wood, which looked about the size of a Q-tip compared to the monster clubs of today. In the navy, Dad had been an all-star softball player. Throughout his life, he had the purest arm, the wickedest hook at the bowling alley, the sweetest golf swing. Now, even with his body ravaged by a cancerous tumor, he teed up the ball and whacked it straight as a string as Mark looked on, mouth agape.

"Okay, let's go," Dad said finally.

The judge, Jeffrey R. White, scheduled Mark's sentencing right in the middle of our trip. The *Chronicle* lawyers asked Judge White to push back the hearing, explaining that Mark had plans to take his dying father to Idaho. Judge White was apparently unmoved. The show would go on, and Mark had to be there.

"What an asshole," Dad said, stating the obvious.

Mark decided he would fly home for a day to be sentenced.

Our train pulled into Salt Lake City in the dark around 6:30 A.M. We spent the night, then drove to Idaho, ten more hours on the road. Mark and I were exhausted, but Dad was unfazed, energized, it seemed. Everything was perfect—the hotel, the rental car, his eggs, the crisp bacon, Ensure.

"*Great* breakfast," Dad enthused.

The drive took us through snowcapped mountains and open green fields. We were met near Sun Valley by one of Dad's oldest friends, Jim Toohey, a former marine fighter pilot who flew F-8 Crusaders in Vietnam and later owned a successful Southern California real estate brokerage firm before retiring. Toohey was sixty-eight, just four years younger than Dad. He had a full head of curly brown hair, graying on the sides, and the lean, erect bearing of a man who spent his days hiking, skiing, and doing power yoga. He helped ease Dad into his Subaru and led us down a dirt road.

"And here is your private log cabin," Toohey said, smiling and sweeping his arm ceremoniously.

The two-story cabin had a twenty-foot deck, a cozy living room with a stone fireplace, comfortable couches, and a carved wooden coffee table. Toohey's wife, Jan, another old friend, had stocked the refrigerator with an enchilada casserole, squash pasta, homemade soups, and Budweiser, the only beer Dad ever drank. There were two bottles of wine. Toohey went outside to a huge bin and came back with an armload of firewood that he told us he had chopped himself. He lit a fire and left the three of us alone.

That's how we spent the next couple of days, lounging by the fire, reading magazines, listening to Sinatra, hanging out. Dad shuffled around the cabin in jeans and a pair of insulated red slippers that Toohey had given him, occasionally venturing out on the deck, a constant smile on his face. I went for runs along the base of snow-capped peaks and hiked. It was blissful, really, not only for Dad but for all of us, a respite from cancer and the specter of prison and my post-Iraq malaise. Mark walked the dirt paths around the cabin, lost in thought, practicing his statement to the birch trees and the owls.

And then he had to fly home for his sentencing.

He left at 5:00 A.M., drove three hours to Boise, and flew to San Francisco. He changed into a suit at the *Chronicle* and drove over to the federal courthouse with Lance. Our mother, Ellen Gilbert, and

Nicole met them at the front of the building, along with a phalanx of television cameras and dozens of reporters from around the country wearing T-shirts that said "Sportswriters for Freedom of the Press."

The courtroom was packed. Mark rose before Judge White and read the statement he had written on the train:

> Your Honor, thank you for this opportunity to address the court. My name is Mark Fainaru-Wada, and I have been a journalist for most of my adult life. I got into this business for two main reasons: First, my big brother was a journalist, and I was always tagging along in his wake whenever possible. Second, like many of my colleagues today, I had seen the movie and read the book *All the President's Men*, and it inspired me to become a reporter. Journalism seemed like an honorable, meaningful profession.
>
> Lance and I find ourselves in this position because we were assigned to cover a story to the best of our ability. We aimed to provide our readers with important information that was being hidden from them. A fraud was being perpetrated on sports fans, with athletes using illegal performance-enhancing drugs to manufacture records and achievements that were, at best, deceitful, and, at worst, an illusion. And young athletes who emulated these sports stars were receiving an implicit message: to fulfill their dreams, they, too, would be well served to inject and ingest these dangerous substances.
>
> Your honor, I have great respect for the criminal justice system and understand the concerns about maintaining the sanctity of the grand jury process. I am not above the law, and I appreciate the legal issues under consideration here. I do not wish to spend even a minute in jail. However, I cannot, and will not, betray the promises I have made over the past three years. . . . If I were to break those promises, I would be tossing aside everything that I believe in as a journalist and a person of integrity.

Dad and I sat inside the cabin, waiting for the decision. We had gone to lunch and came back just as the afternoon was turning cold and gray. We had just walked in the door when suddenly, outside the window, softball-sized snowflakes started pelting the deck. It was barely fall, but the snow came down steadily, thumping against the wood, until it began to collect on the ground and in the trees and on the mountains. Dad, giddy and transfixed, put on his windbreaker and his ball cap, rushed outside, and cast his arms to the heavens, yelling and laughing like a kid as I snapped his picture. After several minutes, the snow stopped. Dad walked back inside and sat down by the fire, breathing heavily and smiling. I got him a Bud. Then we lit up a joint and waited.

It was dark by the time the phone rang. Mark got straight to the point.

"We got eighteen months," he said.

People apparently gasped in the courtroom when the judge announced the decision. I could barely think, my head clouded with weed and the apparent inevitability that my brother was headed to jail. I handed the phone to Dad and listened to him swear, raging at Judge White, at "that fucking asshole Barry Bonds," on and on, the expletives followed by stretches of silence, during which Mark assured him that the *Chronicle* planned to appeal and that he wouldn't have to go to jail for a while.

"I love you, son," Dad said before he handed me the phone, disgusted.

MARK WAS BACK IN SUN VALLEY THE NEXT MORNING. He drove up in our great rental car. That night, we took Dad out for a steak and talked about the new reality. It included speculation on how long the appeals process would take (unknown), whether the decision might be overturned (unlikely), whether the case might go to the Supreme Court (Dad's greatest hope), when and where Mark might be incarcerated (unknown), and whether that could be delayed because of Dad's condition (also unknown).

Also on the table was my own growing resolve to return to Iraq. I couldn't shake it. More and more I felt like I had to go back, although when people asked me why I could only respond, "I just feel like I need to."

I hadn't worked in months. Dad was feeling better; the trip, rather than wearing him down, seemed to have rejuvenated him. We talked about taking other trips. Mark and I noticed that Dad's mood, which throughout his life had swung from soaring peaks to the deepest depressions, had remained steady since the diagnosis. He was truly happy and at peace. One day after we got back from Idaho, I overheard him talking on the phone to a friend about how grateful he was, about the incredible generosity he had received from friends and strangers alike.

He paused for effect. Then came the punch line: "You know, this cancer has been the best fucking thing that ever happened to me."

I resumed my life, caring for my son in the morning and at night, my father during the day. It was a continuous routine of driving, shopping, cooking, cleaning, and sleeping. Occasionally I went to see a shrink, on the recommendation of my editors after I came back from the war. My problem wasn't Iraq, she told me. It was that I had been turned into a "crazed housewife."

So I plotted my escape: a ten-day trip back to the war to write about "private security contracting," of which I knew almost nothing.

The day before I left, Dad and I had lunch on the water and he began to cry. "Don't worry, Dad, I'll be back in a flash," I told him. We drove back to his apartment and sat holding hands in a picnic area where he liked to sit and smoke. He started to cry again.

"Are you worried you're not going to see me again?" I asked.

"No," he told me. "I'm just sad that you're leaving."

I asked him if he wanted me to put off the trip.

"Oh, no, son, you need to go back to work," he said.

He walked me out to the car in his blue bathrobe with his walker. He kissed me and told me, "I love you, son." I did the same. When I got in the car and wheeled it out of the parking lot, my father was standing on the sidewalk, smiling and waving goodbye.

WE PROTECT
THE MILITARY

IT TOOK ME LESS TIME TO GET TO IRAQ THAN IT DID. to get to Idaho.

I flew from San Francisco to Washington, DC, then nonstop to Kuwait City to meet up with the private security company that would take me back to the war. The company was called Crescent Security Group, and I had never heard of it until I picked up a book by Colonel Gerald Schumacher, a retired Green Beret who was also a writer and photographer. After the invasion of Iraq in 2003, Schumacher had become fascinated by the proliferation of contractors on the battlefield—security guards, truck drivers, dog handlers, cooks. His book, *A Bloody Business*, was sort of a how-to for mercs (chapter 3: "Becoming a Contractor"). Among other things, it included a forty-page glossary of companies working in Iraq. The entry for Crescent Security Group read:

Crescent Security operates a "Hybrid" Security Company, offering clients a choice of 100 percent Western Security Operators or a mix of Iraqi and Western operators depending upon client requirements. Crescent utilizes modified and up-armored civilian vehicles utilizing the latest technology to provide tracking and communications, ensuring total peace of mind to clients with sensitive cargo movements or VIP escorts.

As it turned out, Schumacher lived fifteen minutes from me in the Bay Area. He was exceedingly generous. He not only introduced me to Crescent, he also drove me out into the Nevada desert to teach me how to shoot an AK-47.

I arrived late in Kuwait, jet-lagged, the desert pitch black. Crescent kept its headquarters at a sandstone villa in a quiet Kuwait City neighborhood, across the street from a mosque. It was a little like basing a paramilitary group in the San Fernando Valley. The company had erected a tactical operations center—computer terminals flashing the latest threat information, satellite phones, Motorola radios, a dry-erase board filled with scheduled missions and a detailed wall map of Iraq—in what probably used to be somebody's family room. Crescent kept its vehicles out back: two dozen Chevy Avalanches and GMC Yukons. The mercs lived separately in dormitory-style rooms with linoleum floors, a single bed, and a wooden desk. The building reeked of transience and greasy takeout; pizza boxes and fast-food wrappers littered the kitchen.

It was still dark when we left the next morning, the muezzin's call to prayer echoing through the courtyard. I rode in one of the Yukons with Scott Schneider, Crescent's director of security. He was stocky, in his midforties, with thinning brown hair, a close-cropped beard, and thick tattooed arms. He wore cargo pants, a black polo shirt with a white Crescent logo, and a black company baseball cap. He could have passed for a scruffy golf pro. We were totally alone. The mercs made the one-hour drive to the Iraq border on their own, they literally commuted to the war. On the way we pulled over at the Al-Ramdalan Supermarket; Schneider, on autopilot, went straight for the Red Bull. I got a cup of coffee. Then we continued north in the

SUV, two middle-aged guys on our way to work. My heart was already pounding. I felt the familiar adrenaline rush, the sudden clarity, like I had high-powered vision. The darkness slowly lifted to reveal an infinite brown desert. The highway was filled with hundreds of tractor trailers, all headed north, the war's supply line.

After eleven years in the army, Schneider had worked as a handyman for the department of public works in Tecumseh, Michigan. He came to Iraq after the invasion to work for KBR, the logistics company. He was pumping gas in the middle of Iraq when he met a colorful Crescent operator named Wolf Weiss, who offered him a job. Weiss was later immortalized in *Rolling Stone* magazine as the "Heavy Metal Mercenary." He had left the marines to become a rock star, ended up working at a Los Angeles tattoo parlor, found God, then landed the job with Crescent as one of the first mercs into Iraq. Weiss had a thick braided pony tail that ran past his shoulders and a wealth of tattoos, including a vividly rendered wolf across his back and the Grim Reaper playing guitar on his shoulder. Weiss personified the mercenary ethos: "When you're getting shot at and returning fire, it's the same, regardless of who you're working for—the adrenaline, the chaos, the sheer horror at times," he told *Rolling Stone*. Then, one night in 2004, Weiss was shot in the head and killed while sitting in his truck during a friendly fire incident with U.S. troops. Schneider took his place.

I was pondering Schneider's steep career path—gas-station attendant to director of security—when we arrived at the border. A sprawling U.S. base, Camp NAVISTAR, stood between Iraq and Kuwait. Schneider pulled up at a dirt staging area the size of a football field. The other Crescent operators had already arrived, and they were standing around in their black shirts and cargo pants, smoking and chatting. The mission that day was to escort twenty-six tractor trailers to an air base near Nasiriyah, about three hours north. The big rigs were already lined up, their engines running, choking the air with diesel. You could see the Indian and Pakistani drivers sitting high up in the cabs, smoking and staring across the border into Iraq. It was a wonder that the whole lot didn't go up in flames.

I went up and introduced myself to the first friendly face I saw: a black guy, about six foot three and 270, a warm smile creasing his bearded face. All the other mercs were white. He wore a black baseball cap with "EMT" stitched across the front in big white letters. As I walked up, one of the other men was teasing him, "You look chipper today."

"Yeah, I talked to my daughter," he said. "She just got her driver's license."

"What does it matter?" his friend responded. "You might be dead."

He introduced himself as Paul Johnson-Reuben. He was thirty-nine, from Buffalo, Minnesota, outside Minneapolis. He said he had hyphenated his last name after getting remarried a few days before he left for Iraq. But most people just called him Paul. He said he had twin sixteen-year-old daughters named Casey and Bree back in Minnesota. He had served in the marines in the 1980s, then the Marine Corps Reserve and the National Guard. Paul had worked almost ten years as a police officer in St. Louis Park, a Minneapolis suburb, until just before the war. He said he had worked for two other security companies in Iraq.

Paul said he was Crescent's medic. Looking at his hat, I asked him where he got certified as an EMT.

"Oh, I'm not really certified," he told me. "But they made me the medic because I've read a lot of books. I just haven't gotten around to taking the tests."

He said it was tough being a medic for Crescent because he didn't have a lot of supplies. I asked him what he was missing.

"Well, like tourniquets," he said.

I thought maybe he was kidding, but he seemed totally serious. What else, I asked?

"Well, morphine, we don't have that," he said. "It's a controlled substance. We can get it but we're not in Baghdad long enough to get anyone to sign for it. You have to fill out a form."

Have you been attacked much lately? I asked.

"In the last month, thirty days, I've been hit over twenty times," he said. "That includes small arms fire, IEDs, including one going off about a foot in front of one of my vehicles, and RPG attacks. Those RPGs were the scariest things I've ever seen. We were going down the road on our way back to Kuwait the other day and I saw something in the air. First I thought it was fireworks. I got on the radio and I was like, 'RPG attack! RPG attack! RPG attack!' Then came the small arms fire, then all these explosions, and then the IED hit."

He said the bomb hit a truck filled with a few of the company's Iraqi employees.

"I thought for sure they were all dead," Paul said. "I don't know how they walked away. They had shrapnel all up in their faces. Afterward we had to torch the vehicle. I had to do it. I just used matches."

When I had thought about private security companies, somehow it hadn't occurred to me that the quality would vary. In my only previous experience, I had hitched a ride through Anbar province one afternoon with DynCorp, one of the largest security companies in Iraq. The operators traveled in South African Mambas, armored trucks that went sixty miles per hour and had V-shaped hulls to deflect mines. The DynCorp operators, nearly all Special Forces veterans, aimed their weapons through circular gun ports that had been built into the bulletproof windows.

This was not DynCorp. Looking around, I began to realize what Crescent meant by "modified and up-armored civilian vehicles." The black and silver Avalanches looked like death-mobiles. The only armor I could detect was a piece of rusted steel that had been welded into the door. It then occurred to me that no one had any guns. When I asked about this, I was told that Crescent kept its weapons in a shipping container on the other side of the border. That's where we would be met by the Iraqi members of the team. No one seemed to know much about them, except that the ex-pats had given them funny, easily pronounceable names like "John Belushi" and "Sammy Davis."

Do you trust them, I asked?

The mercs chuckled.

"No, not really," said one, a lanky former marine named Josh Munns.

A couple months earlier, he said, they had cracked open the shipping container to retrieve their weapons and found that everything was gone: grenade launchers, antitank weapons, M-4s, PK machine guns, dozens of AK-47s, and thousands of rounds of ammunition.

The company had to briefly shut down, and Crescent's owner sent out one of the Iraqis with $50,000 to buy weapons on the black market. The next day, some of the guns came back with the same serial numbers as the ones that had been stolen. Crescent had apparently bought back its own weapons.

I was standing there, listening with growing dread, when Paul, who had walked away, returned.

"Hey Steve, I want to tell you something," he said.

"What's that, Paul?"

"I'm an alcoholic."

He said it so pleasantly and matter-of-factly that all I could think about was how friendly and guileless he was. The tone didn't seem to match the content. One look at Paul and you knew that he didn't have a mean bone in his entire body. He was a gentle giant. But you wondered if he belonged in Iraq.

"I just wanted to tell you that because I didn't want you to think that I left the police department to do this job," he said. "I got a DWI, and the chief came up to me and he said, 'Paul, you gotta stop drinking, and you've got to resign, otherwise you'll end up ruining your whole life.' I didn't want to end up drinking and killing someone."

I asked him if he still drank.

"Oh yeah," Paul told me. "But there's not much time for it here. I would say it's not really under control, but I have better things to do with my time."

I then asked the most logical question I could think of, since we were about to drive into Iraq: "Well, do you drink before work?"

"Oh no," he assured me.

In the military, no one ever moved in Iraq without conducting a premission patrol briefing. Troops gathered informally near their trucks as the convoy commander went over the latest threat information, the route, the procedures for moving through the kill zone in case of an attack.

"Mount up," I heard someone say.

Crescent Security Group apparently had no such procedures.

IF I KNEW THEN WHAT I KNOW NOW. . . .

Crescent was the brainchild of its owner, Franco Picco, a thirty-seven-year-old Italian who grew up in South Africa. After spending two years with the South African military police in Angola, Picco had moved to Kuwait to work for a transport company. From there he took a job with DHL, moving cargo around the Middle East.

As the United States was preparing for war in 2003, Picco saw an opportunity. "Everyone knew when Iraq opened up there was going to be money to be made," he told me in his office one afternoon in Kuwait City. With a Kuwaiti partner, he started his own company, Mercato del Golfo. Picco started moving freight into Iraq as soon as the country opened up.

Within months, Picco found that his convoys needed protection from the insurgents and armed bandits that were proliferating in Iraq. There weren't enough troops to protect the highways, much less individual supply convoys, and so Picco assembled his own private force. He started with one team, led by Wolf Weiss. By the time I arrived Picco's security operation had grown to five teams, with seventeen expats and thirty-seven Iraqis, and he had spun it off into a separate company. Security—not oil or anything else—was Iraq's growth industry. Crescent guarded not only Picco's trucks but also anyone who needed protection and could pay. That included, at various times, the United States government, the Italian military, the Japanese military, and other members of the coalition. Crescent quickly gained a reputation for going anywhere for money. Picco called them "hotshots"—expensive daytrips into the riskiest parts of Iraq, the places the other security companies wouldn't go.

"We protect the military. Isn't that mind-boggling?" he told me. "And I'm talking about escorting soldiers, as well. Isn't that frightening?"

Picco had light brown hair, graying at the temples, and favored pressed, open-collar shirts. He projected an air of bemused gentility; with his thick South African accent, he seemed like he had walked out of the morally ambiguous universe of a Graham Greene novel. Picco didn't seem particularly interested in hiding his motivations. Behind his desk was a dry erase board on which someone had scrawled: *War is inevitable. You cannot cancel it. You can only postpone it to your advantage.*

Picco gave me a quick lesson in mercenary economics. He said he had invested $10 million in Crescent. He was now getting that back every month. "We're turning missions away because we don't have enough space to cover our board," he said. Crescent priced its jobs according to Iraq's geography of risk: $4,000–$5,000 a day to run a team into relatively peaceful southern Iraq; $9,000–$13,000 to travel to Baghdad or the Sunni Triangle. Crescent charged as much as $35,000 a day to run protection in cities like Fallujah and Ramadi, where it was practically guaranteed you'd get hit.

To hold down costs, Picco employed a business model that was adopted by security companies all over Iraq. He paid expats $7,000 a month; team leaders made $8,000. Schneider, as director of security, made ten. The money was paid out in Kuwaiti dinars stuffed into envelopes. The mercs took their pay to exchange houses in Kuwait City, which then transferred the money into their bank accounts in the United States, Britain, South Africa, etc.

Picco filled out his teams with Iraqis who made $600 a month for the same dangerous work. Actually it was more dangerous. The Iraqis manned the PK machine guns mounted in the back of the Avalanches. It had to be one of the worst jobs in the entire war. The Iraqis rolled down the highway for hours, fully exposed, their faces covered with balaclavas to mask their identities and fend off the pelting sand while the expats sat in the air-conditioned cabs, listening to their MP3 players.

Picco seemed to know that he was on shaky moral ground. "Internally, I can't justify it to myself, but the market dictates it," he told me. "You've got so many Iraqis willing to do this work. If I took a twelve-man team made up only of Westerners, that's $84,000 a month. That's not economically viable. You'd be running every single team at a loss."

"To put twelve white people on a team, it's not economically viable," Picco said.

That basic philosophy—Get Yours—permeated the entire company. Crescent's office manager was a twenty-seven-year-old former marine from Salem, New Hampshire, named Chris Jackson. He had gotten out of the service on September 7, 2001, which was probably fortuitous, since his email address was sprochtkf@yahoo. com—"Fuck the Corps" spelled backward, minus a few letters. When he got out of the marines, Jackson attended community college and ran through several jobs—crisis intervention counselor, mortgage broker—and found himself buried under $20,000 in credit card debt. "When I was at that point, I would have sold myself to the Devil," he told me. "I would have come over here and shoveled shit."

Jackson had dark hair and a medium build. He never saw combat in the marines, but he spent a year on the road with Crescent and was almost killed at least three times. One day an RPG (rocket-propelled grenade) blew up right in front of him while he was protecting a convoy delivering pipes to a water treatment plant in Fallujah. For that, he received a $2,000 bonus. Crescent had helped Jackson dig himself out of debt—and then some. Now he seemed obsessed.

"All you're thinking about is the money," he said. "You have $50,000 in the bank and all you're thinking is, 'Another month and I'll have $57,000, another month and I'll have $64,000.' My family hates me being over here. I think that's one reason why I *like* being over here."

Jackson laughed. He said people constantly warned him, "You can't spend it if you're dead."

"Well, if I'm not dead, I'll have a lot to spend," was his standard reply. "The reason I stay over here is I get to avoid real life," Jackson told me.

One of his friends, a schoolteacher, told him that he was in love with his status as a man of danger working in Iraq.

Jackson disagreed.

"I'm in love with the money," he said. "The status is more like a perk."

SCHNEIDER WHEELED THE YUKON OUT OF THE STAGING area and headed for the Iraq border. We were still on the Kuwait side when he spotted a contractor he knew walking across the road. He stopped the truck and rolled down the window. Hot air rushed inside the cab.

"Hey, you want to come with us? You want to go to Iraq?" Schneider asked.

The contractor was wearing Wiley X ballistic glasses—even in Kuwait. He laughed.

"Not for a million fucking dollars," he said.

As we crossed the border, a sand berm with the highway cutting through it, an Iraqi guard stood in the middle of the road with a battered AK, the rifle hanging from his shoulder by a shoelace. Schneider handed him some wrinkled paperwork: the convoy manifest and Crescent's operating license. I sat in the passenger seat, silent, trying to make myself invisible. Ever since I first started going to Iraq, the process of entering and exiting the country had been a constantly changing exercise in bureaucracy, fees, and bribery. Without the right visa you could be held up for hours or shut out entirely. But after a few minutes the guard waved us through. I never showed him a thing.

And then—Iraq, unfolding slowly outside our window; for the first time in nearly a year, I was back. It was like entering the country with an armed tour group: "And here on your left, total destruction." Just beyond the border was the most spectacular junkyard I'd ever seen, acres and acres of trashed and bombed-out vehicles, hundreds of them, baking in the sun. There were charred Humvees, gutted vans, the twisted carcasses of discarded Opels, crushed windshields, rusted engine blocks, glass and debris. "Jeeezus," I muttered. Schneider told me that he once looked over and saw a busted-up helicopter lying on its side.

The operators stopped at the company compound to collect their weapons. They called it "Wolf's Den," in honor of the fallen Wolf Weiss. It was essentially a vast dirt lot with a couple trailers and a row of Conexes, or shipping containers. Schneider returned with his Glock and an AK-47 equipped with a collapsible stock, the better to shoot and drive if he had to. He brought along extra banana clips, which he loaded into a metal rack that had been bolted into the transmission hump, like an extra cup holder. He laid an extra rifle on the floorboard and asked me if I knew how to use it. I told him that I did, since Schumacher, after all, had just taught me, but of course I didn't, not really. Schneider then racked his own weapon—the universal signal for "Start your engines" in Iraq—and off we went.

The convoy lumbered along, the big rigs snaking tightly through the roads of southernmost Iraq. The trucks passed through Safwan, a border town of sad brick houses, half-paved streets, and trash. Usually, kids would stop and wave in Iraq, but the few I saw in Safwan stood on the side of the road, glowering. Schneider told me that Safwan was the seat for a variety of border shakedown scams. The police often hijacked the trailers, seizing the poor Pakistani drivers and tossing them into the Safwan jail until their companies came to ransom them out. It seemed like anarchy: the border police, the militias, the criminal gangs, and the insurgents were indistinguishable from one another. You never knew who you were dealing with, said Schneider. The previous week, the border police had tried to seize one of Crescent's trucks. One of the mercs, a Brit named Andy Foord, had refused to hand over the keys. An Iraqi then pointed a gun at his head, at which point Foord walked way, seething. A day later Foord was back at the border doing business with the people he hated, and who presumably hated him. The tension was constant.

"This is one of those jobs where unless you're doing it you don't know how hard it really is," said Schneider. "It takes a lot out of a person to be a target all the time. It's tough to be the deer."

The convoy hit the junction to Route Tampa and stretched out to its full length, nearly a mile on the open road. All around us was rippling desert, miles and miles of nothing. The team leader, John Young, an army veteran from Lee's Summit, Missouri, was barking out potential threats and items of interest into his Motorola:

"We got a patrol up here, northbound," said Young, referring to a U.S. military convoy that had caused Crescent to slow down.

"Blue Opel sedan, southbound, two pax."

We watched it go by, two passengers.

"There's a box up here in the left lane."

Pause.

"It's empty."

Whenever the convoy passed beneath a bridge, the Iraqi gunners would swivel around to make sure that no one was firing down from behind them, or preparing to dump bricks or a grenade over the railing, as sometimes occurred.

That's how it went for the next three hours as we drove farther and farther into Iraq. After a while, it seemed normal, comfortable even. The only signs of the war were the bombed-out vehicles that littered the desert and, every few minutes, another military convoy. And the mercs, of course. They were all over the highway, different companies driving every kind of vehicle imaginable. There were the armored Suburbans and Expeditions; Ford F-350s, modified with gun boxes that looked like armored lighthouses; and tan armored trucks that looked like boats on wheels. Schneider seemed to know them all. "That's Securiforce," he would say. Or ArmorGroup. Or TMG. Or Erinys. The operators waved in solidarity as they passed.

Crescent, with its low-tech Avalanches and Yukons, was traveling under the auspices of the Italian military, which was withdrawing its forces from Iraq. Nearly every day, Crescent would escort empty tractor-trailers up to Tallil Air Base near Nasiriyah and return to Kuwait with full ones. Italy was one of the most prominent members of the U.S.-led coalition. And yet it had hired an obscure private security company to protect its outgoing materiel, rather than put its own troops in harm's way.

I commented to Schneider on how strange it seemed that private security companies were so embedded in the war, and yet the coalition didn't seem to recognize them.

"Yeah, it's like we're their mistress," Schneider said. "They need us to rebuild Iraq, and they call on us all the time to help them out. But it's like we're taboo. We're unofficial, unacceptable, unacknowledged."

EVEN THOUGH I KNEW IT WOULD BE DIFFERENT, THE transparency of it all—war as a job—still managed to shock me.

Time after time, while traveling with the military, I had witnessed acts of selflessness and bravery, the closeness of men fused by combat and deprivation and the simple continuousness of being together for months and even years. Once in Balad, I wrote a story about a Humvee that tumbled upside down into a freezing canal in the predawn. The three soldiers inside immediately drowned, but one-by-one their colleagues dove in after them, suffering hypothermia and nearly perishing themselves as they tried to wrench the bodies from the submerged vehicle. One air force firefighter hurled himself into the water and never came up. Finally a group of Iraqi soldiers who worked with the Americans dredged the canal with a tool they had welded themselves. It took almost twelve hours, but all the bodies were eventually recovered.

The contractors had their own bond, for sure, but it was different, tempered by the money and the basic fact that any of them could walk away at any time. The sheer turnover—operators came and went, disappearing in the middle of the night, jumping out of their trucks and *walking* back across the border—muddled concepts like loyalty and cohesiveness.

One of the Crescent operators was a twenty-four-year-old former marine from Redding, California, named Joshua Munns. He was lean, about six-foot-four. Josh had been a decent ballplayer, and his father, Mark, a UPS driver, had encouraged him to pursue baseball after high school. Josh chose the marines, telling his dad: "I can't play with things that blow up if I play baseball."

Josh's tour in Iraq had included the 2004 Battle of Fallujah, perhaps the most violent encounter involving U.S. forces since Vietnam. One day, he was riding in the back of a deuce-and-a-half, an open-air cargo truck, when a bomb went off and took off part of his friend's head, which landed in his lap. Mark Munns believed that his son returned from Iraq with PTSD. Josh had trouble sleeping and was moodier than when he left. "It was just a different Josh; you could tell," said Mark. And yet, when Josh left the Marine Corps the following year, he regretted his decision immediately.

"The biggest mistake I ever made was getting out of the military, hands down," he told me.

He took the entrance exam for the Reno, Nevada, police department, where his uncle worked, but narrowly failed the test and had to wait to take it again. In the meantime, he got a job installing swimming pools for Viking Pools of Redding and began to think about re-enlisting in the marines. He went to see a recruiter and asked if he could re-enter as a scout sniper, a combat engineer, or an explosives disposal expert. But he was told that he had to wait until the new fiscal year.

He decided that he couldn't. The drudgery of installing swimming pools was unbearable, and it would be months before he could re-enlist or re-take the police entrance exam. "I couldn't handle the monotony," he said. "A lot of things about civilian life just bothered me. It was just one of those things where you're not getting what you want, and you do something else."

Munns got the job with Crescent through his mom. She was a blond truck driver named Jackie Stewart. When Josh was six, she had left for Portland and didn't see her son again for years. Josh was raised mostly by Mark and his stepmother, Crista. But in recent years, as Jackie got her life back together, she had reconnected with her son. One day she mentioned to him that she had a friend who was working in private security in Iraq. It was Schneider, whom she had briefly dated in high school. Jackie put Josh in touch with Crescent's security director, who agreed to bring him over.

Munns was serious and exuded competence. One day, for a laugh, one of the other Crescent operators persuaded him to pull out his driver's license. The photo showed a goofy, grinning kid with a huge afro of tight brown curls. But with his hair sheered off, standing in Iraq, Josh was all business. He was remarkably blunt. He said he was there to make money for the three-story fixer-upper he had bought back in Redding with his fiancé (the wedding was scheduled for the spring) and to get his adrenaline fix. But it was a poor replacement for the marines, he said. For one thing, the loyalties were different. Josh said he relied on two other mercs, both Iraq war veterans. "I'd take a bullet for them," he told me one morning as we waited to cross into Iraq. "The rest of these people I probably wouldn't. If somebody put a gun to my head and said, 'You got thirty seconds to decide if it's you or him,' I'd probably say, 'All right, go ahead and take him.'"

But it was more than that. Munns couldn't believe what Crescent *didn't* have: sufficient armor for its vehicles, medical supplies, decent weapons. "You don't need it until you need it, and that's a hard adjustment for me," he said. "Because in the marines it's always better to have it and not need it than need it and not have it. We'd carry around a goddamn sink if we had to."

Crescent Security Group was like the Kmart of private security. I could never figure out what the minimum job requirements were. The company had people like Josh Munns—experienced, serious, squared away—and people who had no business being anywhere near Iraq. Crescent hired former cage fighters, tow-truck operators, qualified AARP members, then handed them weapons and sent them out into Iraq. Schneider, I later learned, had pleaded guilty to a domestic violence offense in 1994 and breaking-and-entering and aggravated assault in 1995 in Lenawee County, Michigan. The crimes, misdemeanors, had occurred after he separated from his wife, who after the first offense had obtained a restraining order against him. Three weeks later, around 2:00 A.M. on New Year's, Schneider showed up drunk at her home, according to police records. He peered through the window, witnessed her having sex with another man, and broke down the glass front door. He scuffled with the man, who suffered a broken left forearm, apparently from tumbling down the stairs.

As a domestic violence offender, Schneider was prohibited from carrying a firearm in the United States. The same prohibition was adopted for all Defense Department personnel. But Schneider was somehow able to work in Iraq as Crescent's security director in support of the U.S. military. He carried not only a Glock and an AK but also fragmentation grenades and shoulder-fired missiles.

One email was all it took to land a job as a Crescent shooter. David Horner, a fifty-two-year-old truck driver from Visalia, California, contacted the company after meeting an operator he knew only as "Salty" in the icehouse at Camp Anaconda, the U.S. logistics base north of Baghdad. Horner, who was driving trucks for KBR, had been in the 82nd Airborne—in *1973*. Vietnam was winding down, and he never saw combat. That was the extent of Horner's military experience. He had never picked up an AK-47 until the afternoon a Crescent team swung by Anaconda, loaded his belongings into an Avalanche, handed him his assault rifle, and took him out on his first mission.

"The training was OTJ—on the job," Horner told me. "They had some guys that may have been cooks in the navy; I mean, who the fuck knows? I do know one thing: the experience that people brought with them, it's whatever they said it was. If I had told them that I was fucking Rambo, whatever I said, that's what it was."

Horner felt like he had tumbled down the war's rabbit hole. "The whole thing was just rogue," he said. When he got to Kuwait, Crescent handed him an Italian military ID card that, in fact, the company manufactured itself. Crescent used the fake IDs to get employees—including unscreened Iraqis—onto U.S. military bases, including the Green Zone. "I mean, some of the bases were real slack," Horner said. If anyone asked, he was instructed to say the Iraqis were "Egyptians."

"You'd think on those bases everybody's double-checked and triple-checked, but there was no place those Iraqis couldn't go," he said. "They could have been mapping the whole damn place and we never would have known. They had cell phones, every one of them. And they were on those things *all* the time."

Schneider later tried to tell me that the badges weren't fake, even though the operators openly referred to them as "fake IDs." Picco said it was just "an expression."

One day, Horner was driving north of Baghdad when the convoy approached Al Afem, a small town where Crescent had recently been hit by a roadside bomb. Horner said the Crescent team leader quickly devised a strategy: blast everything in sight. As the convoy roared through Al Afem, the operators aimed their automatic weapons out the windows and emptied magazine after magazine into the town, pausing only to reload. Horner estimated that he went through six or seven clips himself, nearly two hundred rounds. "Personally, I didn't shoot at any building; I shot over the tops of the buildings," he said. "I did not take aim at one person. But I don't know what everybody else did."

Horner said that became Crescent's permanent posture toward Al Afem: shoot and don't ask questions. "We never stopped to see what damage was done: it was just blaze through the town. But, the thing was, I never saw anybody actually shooting *at* us. Not one time. We'd come back and a lot of times we were out of ammo."

"There was just too much cowboying going on," said Horner. One afternoon, he heard a *pop-pop-pop* that rattled his Avalanche. Horner looked in the rearview mirror and saw a white truck veering into a ditch. His Iraqi gunner, he said, had blasted the truck with the PK machine gun. Horner did a U-turn to find out what happened. He found the bullet-riddled truck in the ditch and two wounded Iraqi police officers—one lying in the dirt, the other behind the wheel.

"One guy, he was just screaming in Iraqi and writhing around on the ground," said Horner. "And the driver had a bullet or two in his shoulder."

"Oh fuck, we shot some of our own guys," Horner said he blurted out.

He got on the radio and summoned the Crescent team leader. He asked Horner what happened.

"Man, our Iraqi, I can't understand what he's trying to tell us, but as far as I can tell, we *shot* 'em," Horner replied.

Up the road was an Iraqi police checkpoint. "We didn't know if they would try to get revenge on us or what," said Horner.

"Let's get the fuck out of here," the team leader said.

And so they did, leaving the wounded Iraqis.

Horner said that was the end for him. "There was too much shit going on and I personally didn't feel comfortable," he said. "I wasn't over there to wreck somebody's life. I really didn't know if we made things worse over there. More than likely, we did, was my feeling."

Horner walked into Schneider's office and told him he was out. He asked for his last month's salary. Schneider refused, he said, and told him to leave. Horner said his response was to pull out a knife and thrust it into Schneider's desk, but he still didn't get his money.

In many ways, Crescent was like any company, with its own bitter office politics and familiar cast of characters—the resenters and the self-promoters and the ass-kissers. Except that it all played out with guns. One faction of Iraqi mercs hated another faction of Iraqi mercs. One faction of expats hated another faction of expats. The expats, for obvious reasons, were suspicious of the Iraqis and the Iraqis, for obvious reasons, resented the expats. Most everyone, it seemed, resented Schneider.

Crescent employed an Illinois tow-truck operator named Benjamin Borrowman. Everyone called him "Red" because of his flaming close-cropped hair and goatee. When I asked Red if he had any previous military or law enforcement experience, he boasted, "I have worked with the Secret Service, the FBI, all the city and state governments and police—in towing."

Red said Crescent hired him as a "road mechanic/shooter."

Schneider and others came to suspect him of stealing weapons and alcohol, which Red vehemently denied. One night, Red pulled into Wolf's Den after a mission. Schneider, flanked by several Crescent mercs, emerged from the shadows holding his pistol and forced Red into one of the Conexes, according to Red and another merc who was present. Schneider left him there until morning, letting him out of the shipping container only after Red agreed to write a confession.

Still confined to Wolf's Den, and guarded by two Iraqis with Kalashnikovs, Red plotted his escape. After more than a day, he commandeered an Avalanche and crashed through the gate under a barrage of gunfire. "It was the most exhilarating thing I think I've ever done," he told me. "The gate was closed, chained and locked, with big tubular six-inch piping. Just remembering it I'm getting all tingly. All I heard was gunfire behind me." Red sped the four hundred yards back to the Kuwait border. He screeched to a halt and threw up his arms as the Kuwaiti guards drew their weapons.

"I'm an American and I've been held captive by my security company!" he said.

He was turned over to the U.S. military, which released him. A few days later, he made his way to the Kuwait City airport and flew home to Illinois.

SCHNEIDER VEERED OFF THE HIGHWAY TOWARD TALLIL Air Base, visible in the distance. A herd of camels lumbered single file along the side of the road, smacking their lips, led by stick-wielding men in gray dishdashas and sandals. We reached the front gate and I started to get nervous again. Except for my passport, my only identification was my newspaper ID, my California driver's license and an expired press card that had been issued by the U.S. military in Baghdad over a year earlier. But we were all welcomed inside—me, the Iraqis, the expats. No one even checked my ID. I was with the band.

Inside the base, the operators pointed their rifles into rusty clearing barrels and fired once, the loud *click* telling them the chambers were empty. They then piled back into the trucks and we headed off for a pizza joint that Picco operated on the base.

The restaurant was an oversized white trailer with white plastic tables, plastic chairs, and a front counter where a man wearing a white paper hat took your order. I had just ripped off my flak jacket and grabbed a Fanta when I noticed a Crescent operator I hadn't seen before.

He was young with faint traces of acne on his otherwise smooth face. He had straight, short brown hair, an honest, all-American face, and was built like a college cornerback. Even in his Crescent golf attire, he looked like a Tommy Hilfiger model. He couldn't sit still. He bounced like a pinball from the front counter to the table, to the refrigerator, to the counter, back to the refrigerator.

"You want something to eat?" he asked me.

"I'm good, thanks, I'll grab something," I said.

"You want some pizza? You want a sandwich? They'll make you a really nice sandwich if you ask them. Let me ask them for you."

"No, I'm good. Thanks a lot."

"Don't worry about it, let me get you something. It's free, you know? You don't have pay for it cause our owner, it's his place. We don't have to pay for it."

"No, really, I'll pay," I told him. "But thanks."

We sat down and I asked him where he was from. It was like tipping over a barrel of words. I couldn't write it all down fast enough. In just one breath I learned that he had gone to the University of Florida, that he had tried to be an accounting major, that he had been in Iraq with the army, that he had been traumatized by his parents' divorce, that he had a brother in Buffalo, that his company was fucked, that he wanted to go back to school in the spring. He knew that I was a reporter, but I got the feeling that it would have spilled out exactly the same way no matter whom he was talking to.

The pizza came, and he went and scooped it all up, about a half-dozen boxes for the team. I went over and put a $10 bill on the counter.

"Dude, it's *free!*" he shouted over his shoulder as he walked out the door.

We ate the pizza on the hood of one of the Avalanches in the rutted dirt parking lot. Soon it was time to go. I was still standing there, munching away, when the same kid said to me, "Hey, are you going back to Kuwait?"

"Yeah, back to Kuwait," I said.

"Let's go," he said. "Get in."

And that's how I met Jon Coté.

THE STORIES
YOU TELL

When he arrived in Iraq from the University of Florida in July 2006, Jon Coté had every reason to believe he had signed on with a legitimate company. Crescent Security Group was licensed by the Iraqi Ministry of Interior and the Ministry of Trade. The company held a certificate of membership in the Private Security Company Association of Iraq, which was employed as a consultant by the U.S. military. Before taking the job, Coté visited the Crescent Web site, which displayed the company motto: "Integrity—Commitment—Success."

In fact, Crescent's legitimacy was predicated on certain questionable assumptions, namely that there actually were such things in Iraq as a functioning Ministry of Interior and Ministry of Trade, and associations that went around ensuring *integrity, commitment, and success* for each and every merc. It had been that way almost from the beginning, or at least when U.S. officials began to realize that a loosely knit private army had formed on the margins of the war. Once that happened, the U.S. government promulgated a series of measures essentially designed to codify reality, then get out of the way. One of the first measures was signed by L. Paul Bremer, the head of America's occupation government, on June 27, 2004. Bremer left Iraq the following day. "You are ready now for sovereignty," he told Iraq's new leaders.

Coalition Provisional Authority Order Number 17 made Big Boy Rules the law of the land. It granted mercenaries and other contractors immunity from Iraqi law. The immunity was to remain in effect "until the departure of the final element of the MNF [Multinational Forces] from Iraq," or until the new Iraqi government overturned it. That, everyone knew, was unlikely at least in the foreseeable future.

Never in the history of American warfare had the U.S. military explicitly authorized the use of civilians in combat. But that, too, changed with the stroke of a pen. On October 3, 2005—sixteen months after CPA Order 17, and with at least twenty thousand mercs on the ground according to the Pentagon's own estimate—the Defense Department issued a directive outlining policy and procedures for contractors accompanying the U.S. military, including the use of force. The following year, the authorization to use deadly force was quietly introduced into the Federal Register as an "interim rule."

> Private security contractor personnel are . . . authorized to use deadly force when necessary to execute their security mission to protect assets/persons, consistent with the mission statement contained in their contract. It is the responsibility of the combatant commander to ensure that private security contract mission statements do not authorize the performance of any inherently Governmental military functions, such as preemptive attacks, or any other types of attacks.

Only a few people noticed that the Pentagon had used an obscure defense acquisition rule to ratify what appeared to be a fundamental shift in American war-fighting. They included Brian X. Scott, a U.S. Army veteran from Colorado and the Don Quixote of merc accountability, who protested repeatedly that the government had violated an 1893 law prohibiting the use of quasi-military forces. And the American Bar Association (ABA), which said the interim rule created an actor previously unknown in the annals of armed conflict—the private security contractor—which the ABA described as a "term of art." The most pointed objection came from one Herbert L. Fenster, a lawyer who represented several defense contractors. Fenster filed an eighty-seven-page brief arguing that the new rule represented a "sea change" that enabled civilians "to assume combat roles . . . with only the vague limitation that they not perform 'preemptive attacks.' . . . It seems very doubtful that a statutory (or even Constitutional) basis exists for the Department of Defense so to augment its uniformed force structure with contractor personnel that their combat roles now closely parallel those of Constitutionally and Congressionally authorized forces," Fenster wrote.

Those arguments went nowhere. To withdraw the rule would have been to withdraw reality. Both the military and the State Department seemed content to remain blissfully ignorant of the mercs who were all around them. Whenever I asked U.S. officials a question related to private security, they invariably referred me to the Private Security Company Association of Iraq (PSCAI), which operated out of a small office inside the U.S. Army Corps of Engineers, deep inside the Green Zone.

The head of the PSCAI was a middle-aged former naval intelligence officer named Lawrence T. Peter. He was maybe five foot seven and had a temper that flared whenever anyone suggested that security contractors were anything more than a benign and helpful presence in Iraq. Peter decorated his cubicle with motivational slogans and a vintage poster of a GI holding up a mug with the caption "HOW ABOUT A NICE CUP OF SHUT THE FUCK UP." He once slammed a door and stayed away when I casually remarked that a PSCAI company, Falcon Group, appeared to have assembled a small private army (not security contractors) to defend a warehouse outside Baghdad. It was hard for me to see why Peter was so angry.

He had a good deal. He collected his salary from the security com-panies (he wouldn't say how much) while, at the same time, serving as a $40-per-hour consultant to the Pentagon on private security matters.

The conflicts astounded. While serving as a Bremer adviser, Pe-ter had written CPA Memorandum 17 (not to be confused with CPA Order 17), which, three years later, he proudly described to me as "the extant law for private security contractors in Iraq." Memo 17, among other things, laid out the rules for the use of force. The first sentence, in capital letters, read: "NOTHING IN THESE RULES LIMITS YOUR INHERENT RIGHT TO TAKE ACTION NECESSARY TO DEFEND YOURSELF." The PSCAI had just one other officer—Peter's deputy, H. C. Lawrence "Lawrie" Smith—but its influence was considerable. Smith bragged to me one day that the PSCAI wrote contract language for the military on private security matters. "We don't care what the contract is about, as long as the companies are treated fairly," he explained. The mili-tary later denied that it allowed the PSCAI to write its contracts.

If the government wouldn't regulate the security companies, Lawrence Peter and the PSCAI were more than happy to do so. Pe-ter didn't have the resources or the inclination to conduct inspec-tions or background checks. But if you were in the security business, he was the man to see to obtain an operating license, or a weapons card, or information about a new contract. More than anything, he sprinkled legitimacy over the companies, like stardust. "They'll give a license to anyone who pays them," Geoff Clark, a Brit who han-dled security for a large logistics company, told me one day.

Crescent Security Group paid $25,000 to become a PSCAI member in 2005. The company—with tow truck drivers as shooters and a domestic violence offender as its director of security, with "stash boxes" built into the floorboards of its vehicles to smuggle weapons and liquor, with fake IDs that got unscreened Iraqis onto U.S. military bases—was still a member in good standing when Jon Coté arrived in the summer of 2006. You could see it right there on the Web site, where Crescent displayed the PSCAI logo like the Good Housekeeping Seal of Approval.

Coté was wheeling the Avalanche toward the front gate at Tallil Air Base when we reached a frontage road and were suddenly unable to move. A convoy of big rigs stood in our way. To the left was a chain-link fence that ran the length of the road. To the right was a steep dirt shoulder that sloped down into a vast field of mud.

"Hang on," Coté said with a sly grin. "You got your seat belt on?"

He gunned the Avalanche down the shoulder. The truck slammed into the muck, pitching us into the dashboard, then reared up, the engine roaring, tires spinning. Coté downshifted and the truck lunged forward, bucking us through the mud. To the left were the big rigs; you could see the bedraggled drivers standing in the road, chatting and cooking their lunches over Bunsen burners. As we reached the front of the convoy Coté yanked the truck back onto the hardball.

He laughed and laughed.

I never saw anyone have as much fun in Iraq. It was almost a personal motto: "You don't have to worry about much if you're having a good time," Coté liked to say. His specialty was harmless mayhem: he'd stack mattresses in front of your door to imprison you in your room; steer his Avalanche into places it was never designed for, like Kuwait City sidewalks and malls; play Santa Claus with Iraqi children, handing out trinkets and causing near riots as he stood in the middle of them all, giggling.

Coté said he sometimes felt like he was watching himself *play* himself at war. One afternoon, an IED went off near the front of his truck, close enough to "blow your hair back" but not close enough to cause any damage. Coté, furious, stopped the Avalanche in the middle of the kill zone, leaped out and started searching cars, just him and a couple mercs hunting down insurgents in the middle of the Sunni Triangle. Then he had an epiphany, right there on the asphalt: this is insane, like a video game come to life, and Coté himself was living it. He scrambled back to his truck, but the feeling had lingered.

Coté was constantly in motion, as if moving kept him breathing. He was constantly eating, too, usually rabbit food, like salads without dressing or Lean Cuisine dinners that he kept stacked in his closet back in Kuwait City. Coté used his downtime to perfect his perfect body, prepping it for its return home to the ladies of Gainesville and Buffalo. He posted beefcake previews on his Facebook page, photos that showed only his cut abdomen, or his chiseled arms wrapped around an AK. Coté was something of a narcissist, really, but he was able to pull it off because he was so impossibly nice to everyone he met, inviting them into his frenetic world with his megawatt smile and sharing everything he had— fruit cups, his cell phone minutes, ammunition, and nearly every thought that passed through his complicated head.

He spoke in streams of consciousness, detailed ruminations on his struggles at college, women, the war. I'd sit in his truck, driving through Iraq or Kuwait, occasionally asking a question, listening to him go on. We had nothing but time. That was the job: driving here, driving there, hoping that nothing blew up. That was the war, wasn't it? As Coté wheeled us off Tallil Air Base—home to thousands of soldiers and contractors who lived behind seventeen-foot blast walls and miles of concertina wire, who fed at restaurants and cavernous chow halls where Nepalese servers wearing bowties dispensed five types of entrées, who shopped at a PX the size of Wal-Mart—Coté was talking about money. He said he hadn't noticed it when he was here the first time around with the military, but now it astounded him. It was like you could see it and smell it.

"This place is a money-making *machine*," he was saying as he wheeled us back onto Tampa. "There's just so much of it. It really amazes me: a war, how it *creates* money, generates it, how a war can be profited off. All you have to do is look around: the amount of food and fuel and oil and shit that we use over here. There's so much money over here it's fucking ridiculous. All the companies that work over here are getting rich over here. Not to say that everything they do isn't needed. But I didn't notice how *big* it was before."

Coté said he didn't feel guilty taking a piece for himself. He said he had returned to Iraq to escape his problems back in Florida: his indefinable depression, his indifference to school, his diminishing bank account, and his callow classmates. But someone had to escort supply convoys into Iraq, he said, whether it was the military or him. Without that protection, the poor truck drivers would be overrun in a second. Sometimes you'd hear about the truckers who went into Iraq alone. You could see their charred vehicles all over the desert, and you wondered what became of *them*. "This is an important job, it's a *prestigious* job," Coté told me. He said it was more dangerous than his previous tour with the 82nd. "The war is here; I didn't start it," he said. "I *served* in the war. So I didn't see a big problem with me coming over here and making a little money. If I could do it for my country, why couldn't I come over here and make a little money for myself?"

He said he liked it. He said he felt "lucky." He said it filled a need. The job had allowed him to pause his life, which had spiraled out of control. He said he had regained the self-confidence that he had partied away in Gainesville. "Basically I was looking for a feeling that I didn't have, and this job provided that," he said. "It's a distraction: a distraction from the DUI, how I couldn't find a degree that I liked, how I wasn't getting good grades. And then of course there's the money. I have $30,000 in the bank and I'll be going back to school with a plan. Life-threatening situations have a way of straightening you up."

But the longer we drove, and the longer Coté talked, you could tell that something was terribly wrong. Before he took the job, his friend Mike Skora had painted a picture that, while not totally inaccurate, had glossed over the dark realities of cut-rate private security. Skora had told Coté that the risk was "medium," that the operators spent luxurious weekends riding jet skis on the Persian Gulf, or drinking beer on the boss man's boat. Compared with the army, with its restrictions and endless tasks and just two weeks of R&R on a twelve-month tour, Skora had made it sound like easy time.

In reality, the risk was higher than medium, higher than anyone wanted to admit. And security in Iraq was a full-time job. There wasn't any time for jet skis. It never stopped, because the war never stopped. "That's the worst part of this job: there's no time to think,"

Coté was saying as we rolled down the highway. "You're working every day. Sometimes you should take a step back and take it all in and ask yourself: 'What am I here for? Why am I *really* doing this? Is it *really* worth it?' But you go out and you get hit. You go out, and you get hit. Then you go out again. You just become numb. And you just do it."

IT WAS AROUND 10:00 P.M. WHEN WE CROSSED THE Kuwait border, 11:00 when we walked back into the villa: an eighteen-hour day. I was exhausted, but I wanted to call my dad to see how he was doing. I didn't have a cell phone and my satellite phone wasn't working. Coté offered me his cell. Then he offered to drive me into downtown Kuwait City the following afternoon to pick up a SIM card. We'd been scheduled for another run the next morning, but Schneider informed us that it mercifully had been cancelled.

I couldn't get over the idea of the mercs commuting to the war, then returning to lead normal lives in Kuwait City. And here I use the word "normal" loosely. The mercs did normal activities—like go out to dinner and see movies and troll the Kuwait City malls—but they traveled in the same death-mobiles that they rode into Iraq. The belt-fed machine guns were gone, stored back at Wolf's Den. But the four-foot antennas and the shitty armor and the communications equipment went with them. The antennas would scrape the roofs of covered parking lots as the mercs tried to find spaces for their gun-trucks. Every once in a while an urgent call would come in from the ops room.

"Coté, what's your location?"

"I'm at the food court at the Salhiya Mall."

"Roger that. Pick me up some fries, okay?"

I asked a few of the mercs out to dinner, and they listed our options: Popeyes, Pizza Hut, Hardee's, Chili's . . . Kuwait was the fourth-richest country in the world, the streets so smooth they looked like they were paved every morning, but those were the only restaurants they trusted. I shrugged and picked T.G.I. Friday's, which looked exactly like T.G.I. Friday's.

We sat down at a table: Me, Coté, Paul Reuben, and John Young. Young was a team leader, so he made a grand more than everyone else. He'd worked at Crescent for nearly two years and had made hundreds of runs into Iraq. He seemed like one of those guys who could never go home. It was in his eyes, as blue as a chlorinated pool. They twinkled when he talked about the job, even the very worst of it. The bullet that almost killed him ripped through his flak jacket while he was steering with his left hand and shooting with his right during a firefight near Baghdad's Al Zawra Park. Even after he got a look at the vest—the collar ripped apart by the bullet, exposing the chipped white plate, which easily could have been his neck—the possibility of quitting never crossed his mind.

A few days after I arrived, I took Young up on the roof of the villa to shoot some video of him. He had already shown me the vest and told me the story, and all I could ask was, "Why are you still here?"

Young laughed. "Why am I still here?" He spoke the words wistfully, almost dreamily. "I don't know, really. This is what I do."

Young was forty-four, from Lee's Summit, Missouri, near Kansas City. He had a shaved head and a blond mustache that set off his startling eyes. As a team leader, people sometimes wondered about him. He loved the job, and he loved his men. But he hadn't been in the military since the 1980s, when he participated in the Panama invasion as part of an airborne reconnaissance unit. Young rarely planned his missions, preferring to wing it into Iraq. Skora later told me that Young never learned how to use a GPS: "He was always saying to me, 'Hey, you got to show me how to use that thing one day.'"

Young looked haggard and underfed, and people worried about his health. Coté said that when Young came back from his last R&R in Missouri, he looked worse than when he left. His mom later told me that he'd spent most of his leave in her basement. When it was time to fly back to Kuwait, she took him to the Kansas City airport. A glass partition separates the departure lounges from a walkway where people can wave goodbye. Young normally would make faces and wave to his family, or even come back through security for another hug. This time he sat down with his back to his mother, until finally she peeled away and went home.

Young told me that he'd tried to lead a normal life. He had two children from two marriages: a nineteen-year-old son named John Robert and a fourteen-year-old daughter named Jasmyn. He had worked as a carpenter with his uncle Larry and at one point started a painting business. But Young never loved civilian life as much as he did the military. In the late 1990s, at thirty-seven, he reenlisted. He was still in boot camp when he ripped up his shoulder, and the army wouldn't let him finish. He returned to working for his uncle until the Iraq war broke out, and then he went into contracting.

"I want to have a normal life, I always have, but I've always known that I'm not that kind of person," he said. "I wish I could explain it. I've spent an entire lifetime trying to explain it to myself. I always want the nine-to-five, the family and everything, but I don't know, I really don't know. I'm not saying I'm the best dad in the world, but I *love* my children. I want to see my daughter get married. I want to see my son graduate. I want the normal things in life. But I'm not normal."

Coté ordered a salad. The rest of us had steaks.

In some ways, it didn't seem real to be sitting there, one minute in Iraq, the next at T.G.I. Friday's, the waitress asking me if I wanted a baked potato. It was disorienting.

And then they started telling stories.

Young was escorting trucks to a base at Numaniyah for the new Iraqi army. Reuben was there, too. Coté had the day off, after working seven straight weeks upon his arrival. It was a routine mission, and when the mercs got to Tallil, they decided to move people around. Three Iraqis piled into one of the Avalanches while the expats rode with each other. It wasn't standard procedure, but that way everyone could talk to one another on the long drive north.

Reuben was seated up front, staring straight ahead, when suddenly there was a concussive *whoosh*—like the air itself had punched him in the chest—and the Avalanche in front of him simply disappeared. For more than a minute, no one could see a thing. Black smoke billowed and rose from the highway, rolling over everything like acrid fog. "And then out of the corner of my eye, up against a mound at an old—I don't even really know what it was—it was like this big dirt mound, I saw this truck and it was torn to pieces," said Young. "My first thought was, 'Who the hell left a truck way out here?' It was like 150 meters off the highway. Then I looked again and the truck was smoking, and I saw one of our Iraqis, Mustafa, up against the steering wheel, and I was like, 'Oh my God.'"

Young raced into the desert. He reached the truck and froze. Mustafa was slumped in the driver's seat, moaning, slurping, his hands severed at the wrists, his femur protruding through his pants. In the backseat was an Iraqi called Basheer. He was missing most of his face, but somehow breathing. A third Iraqi called Hassan, seated in the front passenger seat, had also been hit, but his wounds were slight enough that Young was able to wrench him from the vehicle.

"Paul!" Young yelled.

Reuben ran over with his trauma kit while the other mercs formed a perimeter. Crescent had been hit in the middle of nowhere—an empty panorama of green fields, hard-packed dirt, rocks, and scrub. There wasn't another soul around. The Avalanche had been picked up and hurled across the desert until it fishtailed and slammed into the concrete foundation of what looked like an abandoned rock crusher. The driver's side door was wedged against the wall.

Paul looked into the backseat at the faceless Basheer. "I knew there wasn't anything I could do for him," he said. Not even morphine was an option: Reuben, of course, didn't have it. He turned his attention to the driver, Mustafa. He was alive, whispering in broken English, "Paul, I thirsty." Reuben held a water bottle to his lips and examined his wounds. His femoral artery appeared to be slashed. Blood soaked his pants and was dripping onto the seat and the floor. Reuben reached for a tourniquet, but he didn't have any of those, either. He took off his flak jacket and started tearing off fabric.

Whenever the military travels in Iraq, the typical Humvee is equipped with a SINCGARS radio with virtually unlimited range. Mounted on the dash is a blue force tracker—a global positioning system with a monitor that displays a digital map and the locations of other units, with whom soldiers can exchange secure instant messages.

Young had only his cell phone. He grabbed it and tried to call the Crescent ops room in Kuwait City, which would call a logistics command center in Baghdad, which would call the military and request a MedEvac. But Young couldn't get a signal. He walked back and forth, searching for a good spot, screaming, "Can anybody fucking hear me?" He tried to send a text message. Then the phone froze. Young tried to reset it, but he couldn't turn it on or off. Then it went black. The battery was dead.

Young grabbed another phone and switched SIM cards. This time he got through to the Crescent operations manager, Jason Boyle. "Mustafa's bleeding out," Young told him. Boyle, a veteran of the New Zealand military, reached the logistics command center, but he was told that the military wouldn't release a helicopter until it knew what color smoke would be used to mark the landing zone.

Young was livid. "I'm a soldier, okay? You don't send that until you hear the bird coming in. *Then* you pop smoke. That's how it's done." Boyle was screaming at Young to find out what color smoke he had. But Young couldn't hear him, or he didn't know. His phone faded in and out. Boyle pleaded with the military to release the chopper. "They said they could be up in nine minutes, but they had to have certain information," he later told me. "So they just sat there. I was told they were sitting in the fucking helicopter, waiting to go, they just needed the information."

For the mercs, there was another subtext at work: "The military will come out for the military, come hell or high water," said Boyle. "It doesn't matter if people are shooting. With us, I mean, they're not gonna risk everything for us."

Reuben, an amateur medic covered in sweat and blood, struggled to keep Mustafa alive. In the backseat, Basheer had died. Paul wrapped the makeshift tourniquet around Mustafa's thigh. But he had trouble tightening it; the fabric was slick with blood and he had nothing to tie it off. Mustafa remained conscious, stuck in the mangled vehicle, life oozing out of him. "That guy was *brave*," said Paul.

Finally, after forty-five minutes, the sky began to thump, and the MedEvac appeared. A U.S. Army medic clamped a tourniquet around Mustafa's thigh. Mustafa and Hassan were then loaded onto the helicopter and flown to a combat support hospital in the Green Zone.

"I really thought Mustafa was gonna live," said Paul.

He was finishing up his steak.

"They told us he died fifteen minutes after he got to the hospital. He bled out."

THE IMAGES STAYED WITH COTÉ, AS THEY DID WITH ME. That was the thing: once it was inside your head, there was no getting it out. There were the stories you saw and the stories you heard, and after a while they were all one nightmarish slideshow. Once in Mosul, I heard a story about an army sniper who had blown off an insurgent's head with an M-14. After the kill, his team went down and scooped up a piece of skull and brought it back to the base in a Ziplock bag to show around. I didn't see it, but I saw it. I can see it still.

There were so many ways to die in this endless war.

A story I saw:

In Mosul one afternoon, riding blind inside a Stryker, the army's twenty-two-ton attack vehicle. The ramp went down, and I walked out into a world of zombies: soldiers staggering in the middle of the road, their faces bloody masks, civilians dead in the rubble. At first I thought it was a bomb. Then I looked closer. Another Stryker had collided with an armored personnel carrier filled with plainclothes Delta Force operators. It was curfew, and broad daylight; there was no one else on the streets. But they had collided head on.

A story I heard:

In Hawija, a little-known killing field that soldiers caustically referred to as the "Sister City of Fallujah," reservists were using the back of a Humvee to knock down a metal door. The driver gunned it and crushed his own platoon sergeant, a concrete factory worker from Lewiston, Montana, whom everyone called Big Daddy. He bled to death in the road, the driver frozen in his seat, unable to comprehend what he had done, damaged forever, you had to believe.

Coté told me the worst one of them all. We were driving back from Tallil in the dark. By then I was spending most of my time with Coté. He was great copy, and he made me feel safe, him and his friend Josh Munns. They were young, competent, barely removed from the military, both with recent tours in Iraq. They convinced me that as long as we stayed south of Tallil, we were fine. Crescent had made dozens of runs as the Italian military continued its outsourced withdrawal from Iraq. The Tallil run had become routine. The mercs said they could do it in their sleep.

Coté drove in a T-shirt with the window down. I wore my flak jacket. The sky was crammed with stars, and you could feel the warm night and smell the desert. As usual, Coté had his MP3 player on shuffle, and hip-hop and rap songs droned softly in the background. Coté tapped the steering wheel and bobbed his head as he drove.

After the bombing, he was telling me, Crescent had sent him north to collect the remains of Basheer, the Iraqi who had lost his face. The body had been transported to Tallil, and Coté's team was assigned to take it back to Basheer's family. They lived in Basra, but because that city was so dangerous, Crescent had arranged a hand-off beneath an overpass on Tampa.

It was almost noon, already scorching, the inferno of southern Iraq in mid-August, when the team reached the air base. The mercs grabbed some lunch, then went to pick up the body. It had been packed in ice in a metal casket. The soldiers were apologetic. "It was like if I gave you a package and there was no labeling on it, so you don't know which end is up," said Coté. "That's kind of what happened when they gave us this box. They didn't know which end was up or the bottom or whatever. They were like, 'We're really sorry, but we don't know how they packed this.'" The mercs asked for Basheer's possessions. A soldier handed them a plastic bag containing a ring and some blood-soaked Iraqi dinars.

The mercs strapped the box to the back of one of the Avalanches. By then, the temperature had climbed to 120 degrees. It was a three-hour drive back to the meeting place. The convoy pulled off the road at the Basra turnoff. The mercs parked the gun-trucks beneath the overpass and waited in the shade. Basheer's family arrived thirty minutes later: a half dozen cars carrying some twenty-five men, most of them dressed in white dishdashas and sandals.

At the sight of Basheer's casket, the men began to wail. They beat their chests with their fists, crying and screaming Basheer's name. The screams echoed beneath the overpass, making it sound as if there were two hundred mourners. The mercs grew nervous; they wondered if the grief and outrage might suddenly be turned on *them*. They quickly retrieved the casket and strapped it to the roof of a white Caprice. "We were all trying to get the thing on there as fast as we could," said Coté.

Then, suddenly, Coté became stricken. At the end of the casket was an open drip valve. In their haste, the mercs had placed it directly over the windshield of the Caprice. After three hours in the heat, the ice inside was almost melted. A stream of crimson water ran over the windshield. Coté turned away, dizzy. "I'm like, '*Fuck this, this is really fucking sad,*'" he said. "Basheer's brother was screaming his name as loud as he could, and it was echoing and echoing. He's beating himself with his fist, and all these other guys are crying. And then they just put a sheet over him and took off."

The mercs drove back to Kuwait in silence. Coté replayed the scene over and over inside his head. "I started putting myself in that situation. What if that was *me* in that box?" He knew the image was there to stay: he saw windshield wipers running over bloody water as the procession pulled away. "That kind of mental picture, it's not something you want to have in your head," he said. "The screams from his family, it just rips your heart out."

When they arrived at the villa, Coté sat down in his room with Skora. He was less than two months into the job.

"I don't know, man. I don't know about this," Coté said.

"Just stick around for a while," said Skora. "I'm sure it'll get better."

So Coté stayed.

"DUDE, YOU GOT TO GET THE FUCK OUT OF HERE. You gotta go back to school."

It was me talking to Coté. We were on the way to a back-room Kuwait City jeweler in one of the Avalanches. Coté had hired him to make a butterfly-shaped ring for his mother's birthday. She loved butterflies, he said, because they were so free, like the two of them. Coté had a complicated relationship with his mom. He partially blamed her for his parents' divorce, which occurred when he was a junior in high school, shattering him and his older brother, Chris. At the same time, he said he understood her need for freedom and space. He planned to give her the ring when he went home.

After the jeweler, we went over to one of the gleaming malls where Kuwaitis spend their millions. Coté looked like an alien, wandering amid the robed men and covered women in his tight white T-shirt and extravagantly torn jeans. There was a bookstore, with a selection of English titles, and I bought him a paperback copy of *Bright Lights, Big City*, figuring that the story of partying and self-destruction might resonate with him.

Journalism, as a profession, demands a delicate balance of intimacy and distance. But I guess the balance shifted for me, and suddenly I found myself giving Coté advice. I didn't really think much about it. Crescent, as a going concern, was not even remotely safe; anyone could see that. Coté had his whole life ahead of him.

I couldn't take another grim American dining experience, so after the bookstore I had dragged him to a Lebanese restaurant on the mall. We sat on couches, eating plates of grape leaves and lamb. Coté professed to like it.

"This company is a fucking mess," I told him. "I know sometimes you don't feel it, but you have everything in the world going for you. You don't belong here."

Sometimes Coté would say it didn't really matter if something happened to him, because he didn't have a wife, or kids, or anyone he was responsible for. I don't think he ever totally believed it; it was one of those things you say to help you make sense of how you feel at the time. He didn't say it this time.

He said he had already been thinking about it and had decided to go home. He said he was planning to go back to school with a new major. He said he was thinking about something like exercise physiology.

"I think maybe I'd like to be a trainer, you know, like an athletic trainer for a college team, something like that," he said. "Something outdoors. I know I can't sit at a desk all day. I know that."

I wasn't sure if he meant it, but later when I got home I called his voice mail in the States. The recording announced to his friends that he was coming home for good. Coté also emailed his Sig Ep fraternity brothers, telling them that he was coming back to school and asking them to reserve a room for him in the house for spring semester. Then he called his friend Shiva Hafezi and asked if she could pick him up at the airport.

The night before I left Kuwait, I decided to shoot some video of Coté. He sat on his bed in his room at the villa, leaning against the wall in a black T-shirt with an orange alligator and the words "UNIVERSITY OF FLORIDA BLOOD DONOR." I was asking him the standard questions: why he had come to Iraq, the appeal of the job. I asked him if it was more or less dangerous than he thought it would be.

"More," Coté said, without hesitation.

Then I noticed the shadows on the wall behind him.

"You know, I'm looking at the shadows on your back, and it looks like you have wings," I said.

"No it doesn't," said Coté.

"Yeah, it *does* kind of," I said, laughing.

Coté turned his head to look, but of course then the shadows moved, so he didn't see them.

NOW YOU ARE
GOING TO DIE

ON THE NIGHT OF NOVEMBER 15, 2006, COTÉ WAS
wired. He had a mission the next day, but he couldn't sleep. He
walked down the hall to see if Mike Skora was awake. Skora had
just come back from R&R with his family in Chicago, and he was
still shaking off the jet lag. It was nearly midnight in Kuwait, but
Coté, as always, was hungry, so he and Skora decided to drive to
McDonald's in the Avalanche. Coté ordered a salad. Skora had a
Big Mac, in keeping with his general philosophy that whatever
meal he was eating might be his last, so what did it matter?

They returned to the villa around 2:00 A.M. Coté was still
wound up, primed for mischief, so he and Skora grabbed a mattress,
carried it through the hallway like giggling burglars, and propped it
up in front of Paul Reuben's door. Then they went back to Skora's

room, where Coté explained to his friend why he had decided to give up the merc life.

In college, Coté had always felt old. Not even his relationships with his fraternity brothers had come close to the bonds he had forged in the military. It was America's postmillennial wars that had infused his life with meaning and given him the adrenaline rush he craved.

Coté had come back to Iraq to chase that feeling, and the money, of course. But now it was over. "I'm young," he told Skora. "I'm missing college. I can't do this anymore." Skora, who was thirty-four and still addicted to the life, suggested that maybe Coté needed to move on to another company, one with better conditions and higher pay. But Coté said no, he was done. It wasn't just Crescent. He was ready to go home.

The next morning, Skora had the day off, but Munns woke him up around six, anyway. The mattress was still in front of Paul's door; any moment he'd walk right into it. Skora walked Munns and Coté out to the Avalanche. Coté mentioned that he wasn't feeling well, and Skora told him he should try to beg out of the mission. It was only Tallil, Coté said. He'd be back for dinner. Munns suggested that they all go to Chili's that night, their favorite restaurant. Then Paul, groggy and irked after having to burrow through the mattress to get out of his room, appeared next to his truck. "I know that was you guys fucking with my door," he said, and everyone laughed.

"Hey, you gotta come with us," Munns told Skora.

"Nah, I got better things to do," Skora replied.

He turned around and went back to bed.

An hour later, Coté, Munns, and Reuben were gathered in the dirt staging area on the Kuwait side of the border. Young was there, too, along with three other Crescent operators: Bert Nussbaumer, a twenty-five-year-old Austrian who had recently joined the company; Jaime Salgado, a thirty-two-year-old veteran of the Chilean army; and Andy Foord, a thirty-five-year-old British school teacher turned merc.

Foord had never been in the military. His varied employment history included teaching kindergarten and high school and running convoys through restive areas of Sri Lanka for Save the Children, the humanitarian organization. Foord had worked for three other security companies in Iraq; he came over to Crescent after his previous firm, Lloyd-Owen International (LOI), lost its only contract and promptly folded. "Crescent wasn't the worst company in Iraq by a long shot," Foord told me

Foord had a reputation as a skilled operator with a short fuse. At Crescent, he made team leader but was later demoted. Schneider, among other things, blamed him for ratcheting up tensions between a faction of Iraqis that Crescent had hired from LOI and some of the company's pre-existing Iraqi employees. "The LOI Iraqis were supposed to help out and fill in; they weren't supposed to be the primaries," said Schneider. "But instead of going with the primaries, Andy would take the secondaries. A lot of the primaries wouldn't even know about it. They'd show up for work and have no work."

Foord acknowledged that he rarely used the original Crescent Iraqis, many of whom he mistrusted. But he said but never misled them into thinking they should report for work. As team leader, Foord ended up firing several Iraqi employees, accusing them of stealing weapons and ammunition. One was a former Iraqi weight-lifting champion named Qusay; the expats sometimes called him "Mongo." One afternoon, Qusay got into a heated argument with Nussbaumer at Tallil Air Base. It had taken both Foord and Salgado to subdue the massive Iraqi, who drew his finger across his throat and yelled at Nussbaumer: "You are a dead man!" Foord fired Qusay on the spot.

I was never able to get near the Iraqis long enough to hold a meaningful conversation. On the road, they traveled outside, exposed and buffeted by the wind. At the border, they melted back into their lives. But they, too, clearly had grievances. On some missions, they simply refused to get in the back of the trucks to man the PK machine guns. The expats usually didn't argue; Young, for one, said he wouldn't force the Iraqis to do something he wouldn't do himself. But it was a sign of the fundamental inequality, the deepest flaw in Picco's business model. To me, it was like the occupation in microcosm: for the Iraqis, it was their country, but they were second-class citizens. The resentments the arrangement fueled were endless and, ultimately, fatal.

The border, too, had turned into a kind of mini war, the whole multitude of combatants coming together at the berm. Everyone spoke the same language: money and brute force. One afternoon, the border police hijacked a truck belonging to another security company called Castlegate. Instead of paying the ransom, one of the company's operators walked into the police station holding a grenade. The truck and its driver were promptly returned. The story made the rounds among the mercs as an object lesson in the art of negotiation in southern Iraq.

"It got to the point where every time we went across we were expecting something to happen," said Skora.

Crescent crossed the border at eleven that morning with a convoy of thirty-seven empty big rigs. The seven expats stopped at Wolf's Den to collect their weapons and the rest of the team. But only one Iraqi showed up. His name was Wissam Hisham, a paunchy interpreter who had been given the nickname "John Belushi" because of his vague resemblance to the late actor.

The mercs tried unsuccessfully to reach the other Iraqis by cell. "It wasn't the first time they hadn't shown up," said Foord. "That usually means they don't want to run that day. The team made a decision just to roll with it and hopefully hook up with the Iraqi team later." Picco later insisted that the Iraqis, in fact, had been there. First he told me there were eleven waiting guards. Then he said seven.

Foord was livid.

"There was only one—John Belushi," he told me. "Not eleven, not seven, just Belushi."

Salgado, the Chilean, grew alarmed. He turned to Nussbaumer and said, "Bert, we can't go up there like this, all alone."

But the big rigs were already rolling across the border. To turn around the immense convoy—part of it already in Iraq, part of it still in Kuwait—would have been a logistical nightmare. "It was stupid and dangerous," said Salgado. "John Young, I don't know if he had talked with operations, but he said we had to go to work. So we just geared up and left." Foord said Young, the team leader, informed the Crescent ops center of their predicament. "John, I know he had a long conversation about how there was no Iraqi security," Foord said.

Ultimately, no one balked. It was Tallil, after all, the merc milk run.

Crescent thus entered Iraq with seven operators to protect a convoy that stretched nearly one and a half miles. Later, I was talking to Cameron Simpson, the country manager for ArmorGroup, which handled more nonmilitary convoys than any other company in Iraq. He said ArmorGroup had a strict rule of thumb: the company used no fewer than twenty operators to protect no more than ten tractor-trailers, a ratio of two shooters for every big rig.

When I told him about Crescent's ratio that day—seven operators for thirty-seven semis—Simpson shook his head.

"It's insane," he said. "I don't know how you could sleep."

THE CONVOY TOOK FOREVER TO SNAKE THROUGH THE border. The last of the big rigs were still at Safwan junction when Coté, who was riding point with Munns, radioed that a police checkpoint was blocking the northbound lane.

Young was traveling with Reuben behind Coté, directly in front of the convoy. He announced that he was going to lead the convoy into the southbound lane, going against traffic to get around the checkpoint. It was a common tactic, since the Iraqi police often spelled trouble: it might be a shakedown, or worse. Some insurgents posed as Iraqi police. Some insurgents *were* Iraqi police. You never knew. After passing the checkpoint, Young led the convoy back across the median into the northbound lane. He announced that he was picking up speed.

The trucks began to spread out. Coté barked out the procession of oncoming traffic. Two familiar Humvees went by, Patriots 1 and 2, the U.S. Army's version of the Highway Patrol. Foord, more than a mile back at the rear of the convoy, could see the tan armored trucks come into view, the gunners perched in the turrets. The Humvees rumbled past and disappeared.

A few minutes later, Coté announced another checkpoint up ahead, this one beneath an overpass called Bridge 3. A vehicle was blocking the road, Coté told them, and this time there was no way around it. The convoy was being stopped.

Foord, still at the rear, pulled over near a roadside picnic area. He parked the Avalanche sideways in the middle of the road, giving himself a clear view of any potential threat coming from the south.

Suddenly, Young came over the radio. He called out to Nussbaumer: "Bert, get your ass up here with John Belushi as fast as you can!"

Foord was still trying to figure out what was happening when an unmarked white pickup roared up beside him. Foord didn't see it until it was right on top of him. The truck screeched to a halt near the driver's side door. It was packed with armed men wearing dark green and black camouflage uniforms and ski masks. Some wore the red berets of the border police. On the roof of the truck, propped up with a bipod, was a PK machine gun.

The men surrounded Foord, their weapons drawn. The driver identified himself as a police officer. He reached inside Foord's window, snatched the AK-47 from his hands, and ripped the radio mike from his flak jacket. Foord sat motionless. Out of the corner of his eye, he saw the passenger-side door open. One of the masked gunmen leaned inside the cab and pointed a Kalashnikov at his head. He was so close that Foord could smell his body odor. Foord thought he saw the man's finger tighten around the trigger. He instinctively threw his head back. In that instant, there was a deafening blast, and then a split second when Foord wondered if he was still alive.

Then he hit the accelerator.

The Avalanche peeled out, Foord tearing north up Tampa. Behind him, he could hear the sledge-hammer sounds of automatic weapons aimed in his direction. His rear window exploded, and he could hear bullets pinging off the inside of the cab and the skin of the truck. Salgado, who was parked about fifty yards north, watched in horror and then took off after Foord in his Yukon while the gun-men scrambled to get back in the white truck.

Foord roared up the side of the long convoy, Salgado trailing be-hind him. As they neared the front, Foord could see a new Chevy Lumina blocking the road. He thought he could squeeze past, but before he tried, Coté and the interpreter John Belushi stepped in the middle of the road and flagged him down.

It was a moment of surreal confusion. Foord was running for his life. Coté, meanwhile, was asking him what the shooting was about. Coté told Foord that they needed to cooperate, that it was a routine checkpoint and the police were merely checking papers. Young was also walking around, urging calm according to Salgado.

"They're fucking shooting at me; they're trying to kill me!" shouted Foord, still in his truck.

"No, no, stay calm, we have to cooperate with them," Young replied, according to Salgado.

Moments later, several armed men descended on Foord. They yanked his Glock from its holster and dragged him from his truck. They did the same with Salgado. If Young and Coté had believed that the checkpoint was routine, that perception was now gone. The mercs watched, stunned, as Belushi, Crescent's own interpreter, stormed up to Foord, stuck a chubby finger in his face and accused him of shooting one of the masked Iraqis. Foord protested that he couldn't have; his weapon had been seized. But Belushi refused to hear it. He was screaming at Foord in English, shaking his fist.

"Now you are going to die, motherfucker! Now you are going to die!"

Belushi shouted to the gunmen in Arabic, at which point "sev-eral of the men in ski masks moved forward and prepared to shoot me, one of them with my own pistol, two with their AKs," Foord recalled. He stood frozen. But before they could shoot him, a small man wearing a black leather jacket stepped between them and ap-peared to issue orders. Instead of shooting Foord, the gunmen hustled him to the side of the road. The other operators—Coté, Munns, Young, Nussbaumer, and Salgado—were also forced to kneel with their hands behind their backs. Several masked men

The Crescent Kidnapping

On November 16, 2006, dozens of armed men ambushed a convoy of 37 trucks protected by five private security vehicles near Safwan, in southern Iraq. The gunmen kidnapped four American guards and one Austrian.

Composition of the Crescent Convoy

At the head of the line: "Point vehicle," whose two American guards acted as scouts, and the "lead vehicle," with the American team leader and another American. All vehicles kept in constant radio contact.

Alongside the convoy: The "floater vehicle," which moved alongside wherever needed. It carried the Austrian guard and the Iraqi interpreter.

The trucks Thirty-seven tractor-trailers followed in a single line.

At the rear: The "close rear vehicle" followed by the "far rear vehicle," which carried one guard each.

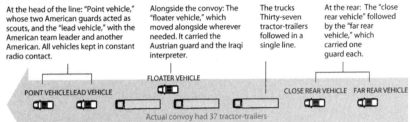

FLOATER VEHICLE

POINT VEHICLE LEAD VEHICLE

CLOSE REAR VEHICLE FAR REAR VEHICLE

Actual convoy had 37 tractor-trailers

Crescent's Five Security Vehicles

Point vehicle
Jonathon Cote (driver), Joshua Munns

Lead vehicle
Paul Reuben (driver), John Young

Floater vehicle
Bert Nussbaumer (driver, Austrian), Wissam Hisham (Iraqi interpreter)

Close rear vehicle
Jaime Salgado (Chilean)

Far rear vehicle
Andy Foord (British)

All guard vehicles usually carry one or more armed Iraqi guards, as well. But on Nov. 16, the Crescent convoy did not pick up any Iraqis at the Kuwait-Iraq border as they usually did, except for an interpreter.

The convoy was headed to Tallil Air Base to pick up equipment from the Italian military.

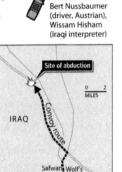

Site of abduction

Convoy route

IRAQ

0   2
MILES

Safwan   Wolf's Den

KUWAIT

TURKEY

Mosul

SYRIA

Tigris

Baghdad

IRAN

JOR.

IRAQ

Euphrates

SAUDI ARABIA

Tallil Air Base

Detail

Basra

KUWAIT

0   200
MILES

The Ambush: 12:30 p.m.

● Gunmen   ● Captured guards   Graphics below are not to scale

1 Convoy leader Jon Cote sees a roadblock manned by what he believes to be Iraqi police. He halts the mile-long convoy just short of Bridge 3.

2 The floater vehicle with the interpreter is ordered to the front of the convoy.

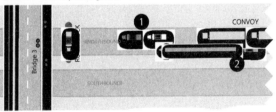

CONVOY

Bridge 3

NORTHBOUND

SOUTHBOUND

3 Dozens of men from the roadblock — some in Iraqi police uniforms, others wearing camouflage clothing and ski masks, and several in civilian clothes — disarm the guards from the first three vehicles. They order the guards to kneel by the side of the road, except for Cote and Hisham, the interpreter. They talk with the armed men, who claim to be checking their weapons and licenses.

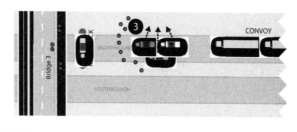

 4 In the rear of the convoy, Andy Foord, in the last security vehicle, blocks the road to force following northbound traffic onto southbound lanes.

5 He is approached from the front of the convoy by 10 armed men in a white pickup truck. Foord is disarmed, and one gunman shoots at him but misses.

6 Foord speeds to the head of the convoy followed by Salgado in the close rear vehicle.

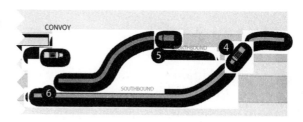

 7 When Foord and Salgado of the two rear vehicles arrive at the roadblock, Cote flags them and tells them to cooperate.

 8 At this point all the security guards are handcuffed or bound, except for the Iraqi interpreter, Hisham, who appears to be cooperating with the attackers.

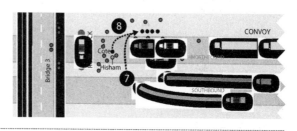

 9 When all seven guards are secured, the attackers appear to receive a phone call that seems to unnerve them. They scramble to put all captives into their vehicles. Foord and Salgado, still restrained, are left behind because there is not enough room for them.

 10 About 1 p.m.
Gunmen speed away with their hostages. They also take with them 9 Iraqi drivers, who were released shortly after the ambush, and 19 trucks, several of which are later recovered.

11 Two U.S. Humvees arrive from the south. The troops free Foord and Salgado and take them back to the border. A Crescent crew later takes the remaining trucks back to the border.

SOURCES: Staff and eyewitness reports

BY DITA SMITH, GENE THORP, TODD LINDEMAN AND CRISTINA RIVERO — THE WASHINGTON POST stood over them and pointed pistols and AKs at their heads. Paul had been separated from the group. He was squatting in front of one of the big rigs, almost as if he were striking a yoga pose. Every few minutes, one of the masked men would come over and slap him in the back of the head or push him face-first into the pavement with the muzzle of an AK. "At no time did I see any provocation for this abuse and can only assume that he was being singled out for this treatment because of his color," Foord later wrote in a statement to British investigators.

As they knelt beside the highway, the shaken operators took in their surroundings. Body armor, Motorola radios, ammunition cartridges, and their personal effects littered the highway. Two white Toyota Land Cruisers were parked beneath the bridge. Standing next to the SUVs were at least four men dressed incongruously in suits. In addition to the dozens of camouflaged gunmen, there were two or three men wearing blue uniforms and dark blue body armor, the word POLICE emblazoned across the front. On top of the overpass, two gunners had belt-fed machine guns trained on the area. Foord and Salgado estimated there were thirty to forty attackers in all.

The man in the black leather jacket barked out an order and several of the masked men scurried away. They returned with handcuffs and began to secure the operators' hands behind their backs. But there weren't enough handcuffs for all seven. The gunmen resorted to cloth tape and, finally, a cigarette-lighter power cord to tie up Paul.

The man in the black leather jacket then held up several sets of car keys before the bound Crescent operators. In fractured English, he appeared to be asking which keys went with each vehicle. They all looked alike, though, and, besides, the mercs couldn't point. The man in the black leather jacket finally gave up and walked away.

Bound and kneeling, the Crescent expats seethed as they watched Belushi, smoking and walking among their attackers. He wore brown pants and a black flak jacket thrown over his black Crescent polo shirt. No one touched him. No one spoke harshly to him. "The motherfucker was just walking around free," Salgado said.

That's when the mercs realized it was an inside job.

"It was Belushi," Foord told me. "It was fucking Belushi who set us up."

EVEN THEN, NO ONE COULD TELL IF IT WAS SIMPLY A brazen and elaborately staged robbery—in broad daylight, on Iraq's main supply route, which was controlled by the U.S. Army—or something worse.

With the operators bound by the side of the road, Belushi walked over and started talking to Josh Munns. He told him that Foord had shot one of the masked gunmen in the leg. Munns turned to Foord and asked if it was true. Foord said again that he had been immediately disarmed. He told Munns that he hadn't fired a shot.

Salgado, who had witnessed the initial confrontation with Foord at the rear of the convoy, thought perhaps one of the gunmen had been hit in the barrage as Foord tried to flee. But he didn't know. Salgado said he thought the attackers initially planned to hijack the convoy and steal the trucks, but that somehow it had escalated. "I think maybe they were just going to scare us, or they were *trying* to scare us," he said. "But it got out of hand. It's hard to say why. But it seemed like something happened."

Young, keeping his voice low as he addressed the team, asked if any of the operators had pressed the dashboard "panic button"—a device that alerted the logistics command center in Baghdad that a convoy was under attack. Munns said he hadn't. Salgado said he didn't have one in his Yukon. Foord said he had pressed it, but he wasn't sure if it was working.

The man in the black leather jacket appeared again, shouting, and several of the gunmen scrambled over to the operators. They pulled them up by their arms and began to load them into the trucks. Salgado was placed in the front passenger seat of his own Yukon. Foord was shoved in the backseat next to a cooler on the left side of the same SUV. He winced as the door was slammed on his hands. Two camouflaged gunmen stood watch over the two men: one at the front of the Yukon, the other at the rear.

Inside the truck, Salgado whispered, "Andy, do you know who these people are?"

Foord said he thought they were police, maybe militia.

"No, look closer," said Salgado.

Foord looked at the gunman who was standing in front of the truck. He had turned away and was still wearing a mask, but Foord could see that he was solidly built. A tight black T-shirt covered his bulging biceps and his broad back, which tapered down to a slim waist and well-defined butt. Foord was still checking him out when a voice called out from behind the Yukon: "Qusay! Qusay!" The gunman turned, and Foord could see his enormous upper body, the body of a serious weight-lifter.

In that moment, Foord said he realized that the man who held him captive was the same man he had recently fired, the ex-weight-lifting champion called Qusay. Salgado later said that he, too, was "100 percent" certain of the man's identity. Still whispering, Salgado pointed out four other men he believed to be fired Crescent employees. Foord felt sick. He was now certain he'd be executed. There was little evidence to suggest otherwise: every few minutes, the man they believed was Qusay would aim his rifle at Foord's head, then jerk it back as if he had pulled the trigger.

Foord and Salgado sat in the Yukon, silent, the air thick with dread. They could see the big rigs being driven off in groups of three and four. In the middle of the chaos, men in red berets were darting back and forth to one of the Land Cruisers parked beneath the bridge. The windows were tinted, but Foord and Salgado could see the men open the door to consult with a silhouette inside. They both concluded that the man inside the Land Cruiser was the leader of the operation.

And then, suddenly, Salgado's cell phone began to ring.

The gunmen had taken everything—his Chilean passport, military IDs, $2,000 in cash that he was carrying to buy a PlayStation for his seven-year-old son, Bruno, at the Tallil PX. But somehow they had missed the phone. It was buried deep in his front pocket, and now it was ringing and ringing. "I knew that if they heard it they were gonna kill me right there," he said. Salgado, frantic, his hands cuffed behind him, contorted his body, twisting and turning, trying to make it stop or muffle the sound. Finally, after more than a dozen rings, the phone went silent. When I later asked Salgado how the ringing had gone undetected, he laughed and said in Spanglish: "*Solo suerte, mi amigo.* Just plain fucking luck."

Later he checked the phone log; the call had come in from the Crescent ops room at 1:50 P.M.

As they sat inside the truck, Foord and Salgado could see the gunmen herding some of the truck drivers into groups. Every few minutes, one of the men in suits came over to ask them to identify the keys for the Yukon. When they couldn't, the men hurried off, shouting at each other in Arabic. Soon people were running. Salgado heard the words "*Amreeqi! Amreeqi!*"

"The Americans are coming," Salgado whispered to Foord.

The cavalry was on its way.

The gunmen tore out. Tractor-trailers, pickups, Land Cruisers, the Lumina, an Avalanche for which the gunmen had apparently found keys—all began to head north. Foord and Salgado watched the vehicles pulling away, first with relief, then alarm, and finally terror as they thought about what might happen next. A white pickup crammed with gunmen pulled up beside them. The masked men were spilling out of the windows, waving their guns and yelling. The two gunmen who were guarding them squeezed inside the truck.

Salgado closed his eyes. "I was just sitting there, waiting for the blast in the back of my head," he said. Instead, the next sound he heard was the pickup driving off.

Salgado opened his eyes to an empty wasteland. In the shadow of the bridge, Route Tampa was littered with debris. The area was filled with a vast and eerie silence, as if a tornado had just come through. Salgado looked down the highway, to the big rigs that hadn't been stolen. They were parked in a jagged line that stretched as far as the eye could see. And in the distance, standing next to them, were their paralyzed drivers, uncertain what to do or where to go.

Foord and Salgado yelled to the driver of a big rig parked just a few feet away. They could see him sitting in the cab, traumatized, staring into space. Foord and Salgado yelled out and asked him to come down and set them free. The driver stared through the windshield, ignoring them, unwilling to believe that it was over.

Foord managed to get his door open. He walked over to his truck and searched for a knife that he kept hidden under his seat. It was gone, along with the microphone for the radio. The satellite tracking system had also been disabled, literally ripped from the console. Foord ran from truck to truck with his hands taped behind his back, trying to find something to cut himself loose.

As he searched, Foord began to realize that he and Salgado were alone. The trucks contained none of the other operators. Coté, Munns, Reuben, Young, and Nussbaumer were gone. Foord, unable to free himself, ran back to the Yukon and told Salgado. They could only assume that the gunmen—unable to find the keys, in a hurry to get away before the Americans arrived, the last truck filled beyond capacity—had left them behind.

Salgado and Foord looked back down the highway. The truck drivers were filing toward them now in groups of two and three, straggling up the road like disaster victims. There was nothing Foord and Salgado could do except wait. Foord looked past the wandering drivers, past the line of idle trucks. Suddenly, on the horizon, he saw two vehicles approaching. He looked closer and saw that it was the two U.S. Army Humvees that patrolled Route Tampa, Patriots 1 and 2, slowly making their way up the side of the convoy.

The cavalry had finally arrived.

FOORD WALKED OUT INTO THE MIDDLE OF THE ROAD. Unable to raise his arms or show his hands, he turned around and waited for the Americans to come to him.

The Humvees stopped beside him. The soldiers, covered in body armor and Kevlar helmets, piled out, their index fingers extended next to the triggers of their M-4s. Foord quickly explained that he was part of a security convoy that had been ambushed, and that five contractors—including four Americans—were missing. One of the soldiers produced a knife and cut him loose. Foord went back to the Yukon. Salgado was in handcuffs, so Foord fished Salgado's cell from his pocket and called the Crescent ops room. He told Jason Boyle that Coté, Munns, Reuben, Young, and Nussbaumer had been seized. Also missing were nine Pakistani truck drivers and nineteen of the thirty-seven big rigs. Boyle told him he would scramble a team.

Until then, Crescent had been largely in the dark. The company was nothing if not consistent, and it quickly became known that it had failed to register the convoy with the Logistics and Movement Coordination Center (LMCC) in Baghdad.

The LMCC was a ground-traffic control center for convoys and a lifeline when they came under attack. Registration was a routine procedure; it took five minutes. But during an ambush it could be critical. When a convoy pressed the panic button inside the trucks, a klaxon sounded in an air-conditioned trailer in the Green Zone. The satellite tracking system displayed the registration number and the convoy's location on a giant computer screen. The LMCC could immediately coordinate a response.

Foord had managed to press the panic button, but when the klaxon sounded in Baghdad, no one could figure out its origin. Because the convoy wasn't registered, it showed up as a mysterious blip on the screen. Boyle later told me Crescent didn't register the Tallil run because it was assumed that the Italian military, which held the contract, would respond to any emergency. "And, as we found out, the Italians were bloody useless, they didn't help at all," he complained.

As I understood it, the logic of ignoring the most basic precaution was that Crescent was counting on the Italian military to come to its rescue, even though the Italians had already outsourced their own security to Crescent to avoid putting their troops in harm's way.

When Foord's call came in, Skora was sitting in his room at the villa, waiting for Coté and Munns to come back. Another Crescent operator knocked on his door and said he was needed in the ops room. "You gotta get the vehicles ready," Boyle told him. "You gotta go to the border right now."

No one was panicking just yet. At first glance, it seemed like another border shakedown. Skora figured that soon they'd hear from the Iraqi police, telling Crescent how much it had to pay to get the operators and the trucks back. There would be a negotiation with Picco, arrangements would be made, and soon Coté would be walking back into the villa, joking about it, ready to go to Chili's.

Still, Skora could already feel the guilt washing over him. What were the words he had used to recruit Coté? Medium risk? He felt queasy as he thought about what he would tell Coté's parents. He was hopeful that it wouldn't come to that.

Coté and Skora had met in the 82nd Airborne while they were both stationed at Bagram Air Base in Afghanistan. Coté, a model soldier, had been plucked from the line to be a sergeant major's driver. Skora was a staff sergeant at headquarters. Despite their differences in rank (Coté, at the time, was a private first class), they had hit it off.

One afternoon, they were hanging out at the PX when a couple civilians pulled up in a Suburban. The men were bearded and casually dressed and carried tricked-up M-4s. Skora and Coté struck up a conversation. The men said they worked for a company called Blackwater and they made $15,000 a month.

"It was like a fifteen-minute conversation that changes your life," said Skora.

The contractors recommended a Web site where they could find jobs, and when Skora got out of the army the next year he posted his CV. He got a job immediately. Soon he was recruiting Coté, who four months after his arrival had now disappeared.

Skora and the rest of the Crescent team crossed the border, grabbed their weapons at Wolf's Den, and sped up Route Tampa to the scene of the ambush. It was just a few miles up the road. By the time they arrived, the U.S. military was escorting the remaining big rigs back to Kuwait. The British military, which controlled southern Iraq, was investigating. The nine missing truck drivers had already been found, alive and unharmed, the attackers having unloaded them just up the highway. But Cote, Young, Munns, Reuben and Nussbaumer were missing.

As the mercs pulled up, Foord and Salgado were standing in the middle of the highway—Foord fuming, Salgado in a semidaze, the silver handcuffs dangling from one of his wrists. The two men had walked back down the road to look for the spot where Foord had initially come under fire. The spot wasn't hard to find. The asphalt was strewn with shell casings, four pools of blood, and long skid marks where Foord had quickly made his escape. The two men scoured the area, hunched over, plucking brass from the highway. Before long they had collected twenty-two shells.

Foord described the ambush in broad strokes for his colleagues: the fake checkpoint, the shooting, Belushi, the handcuffs, the confusion over the keys, the multitude of Iraqi security forces and former Crescent employees who took part. It was hard to believe: the brazen daylight attack had taken place just a few miles from the Kuwait border and a massive U.S military installation filled with thousands of troops.

The mercs were still standing in the road when, suddenly, a white Toyota Land Cruiser flew past. The vehicle belonged to yet another security company, Securiforce International. Behind the SUV, in hot pursuit, was a pickup filled with what appeared to be Iraqi police. Hours after Crescent was ambushed, it turned out, a Securiforce convoy had also come under attack at the border. One of the company's vehicles had bolted back into Kuwait, but another took off to try to escape the police, who, of course, were also the criminals.

Skora stood watching, on the very spot where one of his best friends had just been seized. He could hear shooting, and when he looked closer he saw that the Land Cruiser had bullet holes in the rear window.

"Let's get the fuck out of here," someone said.

Skora and the Crescent team had brought extra keys for the Avalanches. The mercs started the vehicles and headed south toward Kuwait. It was disturbing to turn back: they had been able to retrieve the trucks but not the men who had occupied them. Most of them had been in the military, and the thought of leaving a brother behind, even in the private military, was abhorrent to them. The mercs crossed the border to the safety of Kuwait, knowing that their colleagues were still out there, somewhere in the abyss of southern Iraq.

YOUR BLOOD

After leaving Crescent, I had flown up to Baghdad to interview other private security companies. I was planning to stay a few days before returning to California, where my father was still managing terminal cancer like an extended holiday—vacationing in Idaho, hitting golf balls, taking long lunches, and entertaining friends. I called him one night and he told me about an excursion he had taken the day before to one of his favorite bars, about a mile from his apartment. After a couple beers, he had decided to *walk* home, an ordeal that had taken an hour or so.

"Dad, are you crazy?" I asked him.

Mark hadn't even known about it until he walked into Dad's apartment and found him sprawled on the couch, weaker than ever.

"I just wanted to get out," Dad told me. "It was great."

His voice was raspy and far away, and you could hear him struggling to talk. Right then I decided to go home. I told him so.

"That's great, son," he said weakly.

"Okay, Dad, hang in there. I'll see you in a couple days."

I walked back to my room and lay down on the bed. It was late in Baghdad, after curfew, and every few minutes you could hear the crackle of gunfire, the thrum of low-flying Black Hawks coming and going from the Green Zone down the street. I wanted desperately to be home, but I still had to get an exit visa, fly from Baghdad to Amman and then fly another sixteen hours.

Late the next morning, after getting my visa, I convoyed to the airport in an armored Jeep Cherokee. We had our own mercs, of course, a team of Iraqis the newspaper had hired as the violence in the country intensified. Like everyone, our security had evolved with the war: more expensive armored trucks, more sandbags, more shooters, more guns. It was a fact of life in Iraq; after a while, the sight of an AK-wielding male was no more surprising than seeing a palm tree or a street vendor or a cat. Mercs were part of the country's new landscape, like the blast walls—so ubiquitous and permanent that artists turned them into urban canvases—and the miles and miles of concertina wire.

I passed through the concentric rings of airport security—five checkpoints, by my count, just to reach the ticket counter, eight to board the plane—flew on to Amman, checked in to the Sheraton, and went to bed early to make my 6:00 A.M. flight. I got up at 3:30 and checked my email. There was an urgent message from my brother, telling me to call home. I called him from the road to the airport. It was still dark.

"He's fading," Mark said.

"What do you mean?"

"He can't talk. He's comfortable. Something happened. We think he might have had a stroke."

That morning, Mark told me, he had come by Dad's apartment to make breakfast. Usually the door was open, the screen unlocked, and you'd find Dad on the couch listening to a cable TV station that streamed classical music. This time the door was closed. Mark knocked. When no one answered, he left, figuring Dad was still asleep. He came back thirty minutes later. After a wait that seemed like an eternity, Dad opened the door. He staggered backward and fell into the couch, his expression vacant.

Mark called the hospice nurse. She came over, examined Dad and told Mark, "You might want to say goodbye."

Mark murmured into Dad's ear, but then, after they got him into bed, he seemed to stabilize. He couldn't talk, but he was comfortable, aware. Mark sat with him throughout the day, feeding him ice chips and stroking his forehead.

"He can hear you," Mark told me. "But he can't talk."

He held up the phone to Dad's ear.

"Dad, I love you," I said. "I'm on my way home."

The phone was silent.

"Dad, I'm so proud of you. I'm gonna see you soon, okay?"

"He heard you," Mark told me. "Don't worry. It'll be okay."

I told my brother I loved him. I said I'd call when I got to my connection.

I boarded the plane and broke down in my seat. There were still four hours to Frankfurt, another twelve to San Francisco. There was no phone on the plane, and so I sat, surrounded by strangers, wrecked with sadness and guilt.

I raced off the plane in Frankfurt but there wasn't a phone in sight. I was routed onto a train, which emptied out into a security line that seemed to stretch forever. My flight was scheduled to leave in an hour; it took me thirty minutes to get through the line. On the other side was a pay phone. I punched in the number, and then my credit card, and then the expiration date. The phone rang twice and picked up, but I couldn't hear anything. "*Mark!*" I yelled into the phone. I dialed again—number, credit card, expiration date—and the phone rang again, once, twice, a dozen times. I slammed down the receiver and went to the gate. My plane was boarding. There was another phone in the waiting area. I dialed it and Mark picked up.

There was a pause but I could hear Mark breathing.

"He just passed," my brother told me.

I slid down the wall into a squat. I can't remember what else Mark said. Eventually we just held the phone in silence. Soon the waiting area was empty. They were closing the doors.

"I gotta get on the plane," I told him.

"What do you want me to do?" he said.

I asked him to leave Dad in the apartment until I got home.

He was still there when I walked in thirteen hours later. A makeshift hospital bed had been set up in the living room. Dad was lying on his back, half covered by a blanket. His mouth was slightly open, his body tiny and cold, the cancer having taken a third of him before it finally took his life. Dad had gotten a haircut while I was away, and I remember thinking that it looked good. The room was cold and smelled like cigarettes. The walls were covered with drawings the kids had made and clippings from Mark's unresolved battle with Barry Bonds and an Amtrak poster I had picked up in Washington. There were unframed pictures of Dad and his family, his oldest friends, and maybe a dozen or so books stacked in milk crates and cardboard boxes. Dad never had much, but by the end of his life he had rid himself of nearly every possession except the ones that were most important to him.

I sat for an hour or two, thinking about everything and nothing. I got up a few times to kiss him on the forehead, grabbed a Bud out of the refrigerator and drank it sitting next to him. Then I called Mark. He came into the room and stroked Dad's hair.

"You're cold, Dad," Mark said.

A few minutes later, two men from the mortuary showed up and, with compassionate precision, they put Dad on a stretcher and loaded him into a white van. Mark and I walked back into the apartment and sat in silence. That has to be the world's emptiest feeling, right? The person you love, who was just there—a presence from your earliest memories—you can smell him and hear his voice, only he no longer exists.

The next time we saw Dad, he was handed to us in an olive green shopping bag with twine handles, like the ones you get at Macy's or Nordstrom's. I was surprised at how heavy he was.

A few days later, Mark and I cleaned out the apartment. It took only a few hours, including the furniture. The stuff we didn't pitch we loaded into my car and dropped off at Dad's favorite thrift store. We had lunch, mostly in silence. Then I drove home.

When I turned on my cell phone, there were urgent messages asking me to call the office. My editor quickly got on the phone. He apologized, then asked me the name of the security company I had been traveling with the week before.

"Crescent Security Group," I told him.

"That's what I thought," he said. "Listen, there's a story on the wires that Crescent was ambushed in southern Iraq. Five of their guys are missing."

I felt light-headed, like when a plane suddenly loses altitude. I was holding the steering wheel, screaming into the phone in the middle of the freeway.

"*What?*" I said. "Do they say who's missing?"

He said the names hadn't been released.

I raced home to call Coté in Kuwait City. I got a recording, first in Arabic, then in English: "The person you are trying to reach is unavailable or out of the coverage area."

CHRIS COTÉ HAD JUST SUITED UP FOR HIS WEEKLY hockey game at the Pepsi Center in northeast Buffalo when one of his teammates said, "Hey, there's some hot blonde looking for you." He walked outside the locker room and saw his stepsister Samantha standing in the hallway, crying and holding her phone.

"Jon's missing," she told him. "You need to call home."

Reception was weak inside the rink, so Chris ran in his skates to the front of the building. His stepmother, Nancy, answered the phone. She told him that a woman from the State Department had called to say, almost matter-of-factly, that Jon had gone out on a mission and didn't come back. He was listed as missing. Chris went numb. He didn't know what to do. He realized there was nothing he *could* do. He decided to play and then deal with it after he got home. But the thoughts followed him onto the ice, through the game, into his green Nissan as he drove back to the stately brick house where he lived with his family in Getzville.

Chris Coté was 361 days older than his brother. People sometimes mistook them for twins. After a while, they started to go along with it.

"You guys are so cute. Are you twins?" some girl would coo.

"Yeah, we are," one of them would say.

Chris thought it might as well have been true, he and Jon were so close. In many respects, they were opposites. Chris was slightly shorter than Jon, quiet and introspective. He exuded responsibility and caution: in high school, he decided to hold *himself* back a year to improve his chances for college. He was handsome, with short brown hair and soft blue eyes, but unlike Jon, who radiated heat, his features seemed muted by his shyness and reserve. As a teenager, Chris would complain to his mom, "How come every time I bring a girl home she ends up liking Jon?" She told him he had to sell himself, to put himself out there, but it never came naturally. Jon, in turn, saw Chris as his responsible other half. After he enlisted, he signed letters to his brother "Your frivolous twin, Pvt. Jonathon Coté" or "Your Blood." Chris kept Jon out of fistfights and hauled him home drunk from parties. He was Jon's caretaker, his best friend, his designated driver for life.

The boys were marine brats. Chris was born on February 15, 1982, in Okinawa, Japan, Jon at the Long Beach Naval Hospital in Southern California. Their father, Francis, was a career chief warrant officer who served in an artillery unit in the Gulf War. Francis was born François Louis Côté, in Sayabec, a village of southeastern Quebec. When he was five, his mother was killed in a traffic accident. His father, a doctor, was killed three years later; a drunk driver plowed into him as he was crossing the street. Now orphaned, Francis, his three younger brothers and one younger sister were taken in by their uncle Benoit and aunt Ilda, who lived across the border in Buffalo.

With his parents dead and Ben, a truck driver for Consolidated Freightways, frequently away, Francis developed a kind of superhuman resourcefulness. Seemingly he could do anything: rewire a house, cook, build furniture from scratch. Once, after his Honda Accord was rear-ended, throwing it out of alignment, he hacked the car in half and welded it back together with a new rear end. While still in the Marine Corps, Francis earned degrees in computer information systems and business management. When he got out, after twenty years and a day, just long enough to collect his pension, he landed a job as a program manager for IBM.

Francis imposed the double-barreled discipline of the U.S. Marine Corps and the Roman Catholic Church on his two sons. On weekends, Chris and Jon installed ceramic tiling or chopped firewood by the truckload. Francis sometimes would confine the boys to their rooms, forcing them to memorize prayers they were too young to understand. Lanky in his youth, Francis grew into a stocky bear of a man, with an impressive sweep of graying hair. He was a benevolent dictator. In the summers he and his brothers took their boys on "man trips" inspired by *Raising a Modern-Day Knight*, the Robert Lewis book on raising boys with Christian values. Francis would sit around the campfire, imparting lessons on integrity and compassion and sexual responsibility. Francis had once considered the priesthood as a profession; his boozy Christianity was the kind that gives allowances for swearing and drinking and laughing. But his faith was rooted in a fundamental belief: there was nothing in this world you could count on—not the roof over your head, not the food on your plate, not even your parents' existence. Only God could sustain you.

Then, when Jon and Chris were in high school, their parents divorced. Looking back, you could see it coming. Their mother, Lori, was the daughter of a strapping Buffalo native who ran an auto upholstery business called Vic's Auto Home Trim Shop, and his devoutly religious wife. Lori was a free spirit, expressive and emotional, and she chafed under the military discipline that Francis imposed on their lives. But, for Chris and Jon, their world had suddenly disintegrated. In the upheaval that followed—Lori struggling to cope, Francis usually out of town on business—the boys ended up on their own, high school juniors sharing their own apartment on North Forest Road. It drew them even closer. Chris solidified his role as Jon's guardian. Together they went through a joint existential crisis: Literally, they had lost their faith. They refused to go to church or pray.

"It just turned our lives upside down," said Chris. "I mean, if you devote yourself to your religion and you punish your children for not memorizing a stupid fucking prayer, and you make a promise to

God to be with this woman *for better or for worse* and you can't make that work—I mean . . . where was God in all of this?" He turned it over and over in his head, standing in the shower, allowing the water to wash over him, "wondering what my life was about."

Then Jon joined the army. Lori moved to Hollywood, Florida, to live with a cousin near the beach. Francis married Nancy, who had dark blond hair, a wicked sense of humor, and a no-nonsense authority that she applied as head of the Drug Enforcement Administration's (DEA) Buffalo division. They moved into Nancy's two-story house in Radcliffe Estates, a Getzville subdivision of broad lawns and winding streets, along with Samantha, her beautiful teenage daughter, and her redheaded son, Max, a music prodigy. Chris got a job at a Yamaha dealership and moved in, too. He and Jon called it "Nancy's House," but somehow it worked. Their family, if not their faith, was restored.

Now Chris, his mind reeling, walked into the warm house, the heat pumping against the gathering winter, shoes piled up next to the door. Everyone was gathered around the television, waiting for the latest update on CNN, which was broadcasting stories about the kidnapping but not the names of the missing men. The phone was ringing off the hook. Nancy, whose nineteen-year-old stepson was killed in a car accident during her first marriage, had sent out an "urgent prayer message" after getting the call from the State Department. She had been planning to tell Francis when he got home from a business trip that night, but he had pulled over to the side of the road and read her urgent message on his Pocket PC. That's how he found out his youngest son had been kidnapped.

Chris sat down to watch. There was hardly any information: how it happened, whether the men were even alive. Nancy, who bore witness to the worst of humanity in her job as a DEA agent, silently assumed that within a couple days they would hear that Jon was dead. There was no ransom demand, no word from the kidnappers. Crescent was a black hole. The Cotés knew that Jon worked in private security, but from the beginning everything about his company had been vague: who owned it, where it was located, its relationship with the U.S. government. They didn't even know whom to call.

Then Chris was jolted by a thought: his mother. He needed to call her before she found out some other way. He walked down to the basement and took a moment to steel himself. A voice ran through his head, as if narrating it somehow confirmed reality: "Now I have to call my mother and tell her that her son has been kidnapped in Iraq."

"Mom, I need you to try to sit down somewhere," he said.

Lori gasped. "*What? What?* Oh my God. Is this is about Jonathon?"

"Yes, it's about Jon."

Chris persuaded her to calm down long enough to break the news. Lori burst into tears, sobbing, hysterical, until Chris, too, was crying.

The calls were repeated, over and over—in Austria, in Kansas City, in Minneapolis, in Redding. I was calling, too, frantically trying to find out what had happened, not yet certain who had been taken, still reeling from my dad, from the fact that I had traveled on the same road one week earlier. Finally, I reached Mike Skora in Kuwait. He gave me the news: it was Coté, Munns, Reuben, Young, and Bert Nussbaumer, the Austrian. All were missing. The Crescent villa was crawling with British intelligence, FBI, and DEA agents, Skora said. But no one had any idea where the men were.

Skora told me what was known about the ambush. The main question was why none of the Iraqis had shown up for work, and why the convoy had still gone into Iraq undermanned. Skora had been calling one of the Iraqi operators, a guy they called "Sammy Davis." But the phone only rang through.

AFTER THE KIDNAPPING, THE BRITS TOOK FOORD AND Salgado to a military base to give statements. Foord, the schoolteacher, provided eleven typed pages of dramatic prose ("He then kept screaming at me, 'You are going to die motherfucker, now you are going to die!'") Salgado, writing in strained but comprehensible English, wrote a single page. The men were then flown by helicopter to the British military headquarters at the Basra airport. The Brits were employing an unmanned drone in the search for the hostages, and they put Foord and Salgado in the ops room to help. "At one point they thought they found the trucks that were ours," said Salgado. "But then the camera zoomed in and it was someone else's."

Basra, Iraq's second-largest city, had long been cited by the coalition as a haven of stability in postinvasion Iraq. But the kidnapping—the single largest abduction of Americans since the start of the war—exposed a different reality, one of unremitting chaos. The audacity of the operation—and the apparent involvement of some of the same Iraqi security forces that formed the bedrock of the U.S. strategy in Iraq—was breathtaking. "The scope of this hijacking took a significant amount of coordination," Major General William B. Caldwell IV, the U.S. military spokesman, told reporters in Baghdad. "It was very well planned and orchestrated and deliberately conducted."

The ensuing days were filled with the kind of confusion and imprecision that marked nearly every violent confrontation in Iraq. Caldwell told reporters that, during a raid in Safwan, coalition forces killed two gunmen who were apparently involved in the kidnapping but had been unable to locate the hostages. Basra's provincial governor said two of the missing contractors—one dead and the other severely wounded—had been located by police. The chief of operations for the Basra police force contradicted the governor and said the five hostages were being held by "a criminal gang." The police invited the media to view some *two hundred* suspects who were rounded up in raids just twenty-four hours after the kidnapping. The forlorn men sat on the ground outside the Basra police station, blindfolded, broiling in the sun. One of the suspects was in a wheelchair, his legs amputated at the knee.

That evening, a man wearing a white headscarf around his face appeared on Al Alam, an Iranian-run satellite news network. He announced in Arabic that he was from a group called the Mujahedeen of Jerusalem Company, which he said had abducted the Western contractors. He demanded the withdrawal of American forces from Iraq and the release of all prisoners held by the coalition. The hostages did not appear in the video.

The Mujahedeen of Jerusalem Company was widely described as "a previously unknown group."

Since Crescent was now radioactive, Picco sent a convoy from one of his other companies to retrieve Foord and Salgado from the Brits. When the two men arrived in Kuwait City, they found the villa almost empty. Between the kidnapping and the steady exodus of alienated mercs, Crescent had been reduced to a shell: the front office, led by Picco, Schneider, and Paul Chapman, Picco's deputy; the ops room, anchored by Jason Boyle and Chris Jackson; and a few shooters like Skora, who vowed to stay until his friend Coté came walking through the door.

There was one new guy. His name was Raul Correa, and he was a forty-five-year-old novelist-cum-merc from Providence, Rhode Island. Correa had been in the 82nd Airborne from 1980 to 1983, enlisting to avoid jail. In his early thirties, after a period of alcohol and drug abuse, a suicide attempt, and a brief stay at a Providence psychiatric hospital, he entered a support group where he learned about a Columbia University scholarship program for older students. He got accepted, studied English, then moved on to Columbia's prestigious School of Arts, where for his master's thesis he wrote a military coming-of-age novel called *I Don't Know but I've Been Told*.

The book, narrated by a nameless paratrooper who loves a Panamanian prostitute and hurls himself from planes on mescaline, was published in 2002 to good reviews ("If he writes another book, stand at attention!" *USA Today*). But it didn't sell. Correa, heartbroken, thought he might not write another book until, at the depths of his despair, he got the idea to go to Iraq as a modern mercenary and write about the experience. One minute he was teaching Proust to Columbia undergrads, the next he was holding a Kalashnikov in Hilla.

Correa hadn't picked up a weapon in twenty years. "And, lo and behold, I got hired five different times," he told me. The mercs called it "the Circuit," hopping from contract to contract, from company to company: Custer Battles, SOC-SMG, Aegis (twice). Near the end of 2006, Correa was surfing the Internet when he came across Crescent, which, even on the company Web site, looked to him like "a bunch of meth-addict hillbillies." But Correa wanted more trigger-time; he felt it was essential to the authenticity of his book. He sent off an email and, two hours later, Crescent offered him a job.

Correa was waiting for his ride at Anaconda, the giant logistics base in Balad, when he heard that his new employer had suffered a setback: a catastrophic attack that caused the disappearance of five men who were doing exactly the same job that he had been hired to do. Correa found the news disturbing on a number of levels, the least of which was his now-uncertain employment. He emailed Crescent, expecting to hear that his services were no longer needed. On the contrary. "They said they were really shorthanded, what with the kidnapping and all. They said that if I still wanted to come they'd love to have me, but I had to get myself to Kuwait." Correa thought about it for a day. Then he caught a military flight to Kuwait. He took a cab to the Crescent villa.

"I was probably not in the best state of mind," he later acknowledged.

Correa brought a novelist's sensibility and his own rich experience in psychoanalysis to the Crescent asylum. He was struck first by the eerie presence of Salgado and Foord around the villa. The men were like haunted souls who had stared deep into the abyss, only to be rescued by some giant hand that had returned them to the material world. Foord lived "off site" with his family, but Salgado spent most of his time in his room, trying to find a way home. The kidnappers had taken all of his documents, including his Chilean passport. He couldn't get out of Kuwait. Correa would walk by his room and find him downloading porn, or blasting speed metal or Skyping his wife, who could be heard crying, hysterical, pleading in Spanish. "To me those guys should have been under psychiatric evaluation, not because they seemed crazy, but because of what they'd been through," said Correa. "I saw Andy's vehicle, and he really should not have been alive."

Crescent was out of the convoy business, at least for the time being. After the kidnapping and the Securiforce shootout of the same day, the U.S. military had shut down the border to contractors. But

Picco was still running his restaurants, and he needed mercs to move food around Iraq or "some cook who might need his visa stamped in Basra," said Correa. To avoid having to cross the border, some of the mercs were living in trailers on Contractors Row at Tallil Air Base. Other times they flew across with the military. Correa had come without a rifle, so Schneider arranged to buy him a used AK from a Basra arms dealer who met them beneath an overpass on Tampa one afternoon.

After the kidnapping, Crescent, understandably, had jettisoned most of its Iraqis. The company replaced them with a half dozen unemployed Nepalese who had wandered by the trailers at Tallil looking for work. Correa's new team also included a helicopter mechanic and two shooters whose previous experience was as gate guards.

Skora was the team leader. Correa asked who the assistant team leader was.

The question was greeted with silence.

"Well, we were kind of thinking that *you* would be," someone said finally.

"I was like, 'You're out of your fucking tree,'" said Correa.

Picco was desperately trying to keep the revenue spigot flowing. One day, he told Skora that he was entertaining an offer to take a group of businessmen into Iraq, fully armed, at $50,000 a head. The proposal, as Skora and Correa understood it, was part safari, part merc fantasy camp.

Skora talked Picco out of it.

Life went on. Around Thanksgiving, a couple weeks after the kidnapping, the Crescent staff was invited to a party in Kuwait City. The mercs went downtown and had suits made for the occasion. Correa, as the new guy, was left behind in the ops room to answer the phones "in case the families" of the hostages called, he said.

There was no news about them. The expected ransom demand had not materialized. At the same time, no bodies had turned up, and no one had released the kind of snuff video for which Iraq had become infamous. It was baffling. After nearly four years of war, kidnapping in Iraq had developed into a cottage industry. Hostages were often bartered between groups, killed for political purposes, used to extract money, or all of the above. Sometimes people disappeared forever, but it wasn't the norm.

After about a month, the British military came up with a plan to flush out the Crescent employees who may have been involved in the kidnapping. The idea was to summon the Iraqis to a meeting at Wolf's Den, ostensibly to give them their monthly pay. Once inside, the Iraqi guards would be given a weapons-cleaning demonstration, a ploy to get them to disable their AKs. Then the Brits would pounce.

Correa and Skora felt certain it would be a bloodbath, that the Iraqi police or someone else would storm the compound and slaughter them. There was only one way in and out of Wolf's Den. It would be the O.K. Corral, only with automatic weapons.

A half dozen Iraqis showed up, none who had been identified by Foord and Salgado. As the men waited for their pay, they broke out a soccer ball and started kicking it around the sandy compound.

Correa and Skora hit the ground. Dozens of British soldiers and plainclothes Americans materialized out of nowhere, weapons drawn. They pushed the Iraqis into the dirt and flex-tied their hands behind their backs. Most of the Iraqis were scowling at Skora, who had run countless missions with them, and had personally invited them to the meeting. The soldiers fitted the Iraqis with earmuffs, blacked-out goggles, and, finally, hoods. They were loaded in armored vehicles and driven away.

The expats were terrified; now they had to make the three-hour drive back to Tallil. Ever since the kidnapping, Crescent was a marked company. No longer road warriors, the mercs had scraped the stickers from the Avalanches and drove around Iraq anonymously. Usually they went "counterflow"—mercspeak for driving against traffic. It was a harrowing way to travel, but no one could sneak up on you.

After the snatch-and-grab, Skora pointed his truck north and tore up the southbound lane of Tampa at a hundred miles per hour. When an oncoming vehicle got too close, Correa, riding shotgun, popped off a round or two. "We just fired warning shot after warning shot," Correa said. "I mean, imagine driving from Providence to

Maine going 100, 110 miles an hour in the wrong lane on I-95. And anytime someone gets close to you, you shoot.

"I really thought I was going to die with that fucking company," said Correa. The final straw came a few weeks later. One afternoon he and Skora were waiting for a car to clear the road. Correa could see two Iraqi men sitting in the front seat. They didn't appear to be a threat, but they wouldn't move. Finally Correa decided to squeeze off a couple warning shots. In that moment, the car lurched forward. Correa thought he saw the windshield explode.

He was certain he had killed the two men. As Skora rolled past the shattered car, Correa saw only shards of glass where two innocent people had been. He buried his head in his hands. Schneider was riding behind them, and as he viewed the wreckage he joked over the radio: "Well, *somebody's* not happy."

"Oh, my mind went places," said Correa. "I was thinking, 'If this is true, I won't come back from this.'"

"Dude, you didn't kill them," said Skora.

But Correa was certain he did. After a sleepless night, he walked up to Schneider and asked him what he had seen. Schneider laughed at him.

"You didn't fucking kill them," he said. Schneider told Correa he saw the two men, angrily shouting next to the blasted car.

Correa eventually became convinced that he hadn't killed anyone, but it was hard to shake. More than anything, the shooting had forced him to confront not just his actions but his presence in Iraq, the reasons why he was there. It wasn't a pretty picture. He thought about his hollow life, and his art, and how he was using another country, another people, to satisfy, what, a primal urge?

That's what continued to haunt him. "When you put a gun in your hand and you go into someone else's backyard to satisfy that sort of urge, it has moral repercussions," he said.

NEW YEAR'S APPROACHED AND STILL NOTHING.

For the families, it was its own form of torture: wrapping one's mind around the infinite possibilities of evil, pushing those thoughts aside, half asleep, waking to the same nightmare. Within days of the kidnapping, the families had been surrounded by the rituals of loss: prayer vigils, candles, flowers, cards. In Gainesville, a giant yellow ribbon appeared on Coté's fraternity house. But Coté hadn't vanished or died; he was still out there, somewhere. That's what was most chilling.

Sometimes I woke up in the middle of the night, thinking I heard the phone. I'd come running out of bed, my heart racing, looking for my cell in the dark. When I found it, and no one had called, I couldn't fall back to sleep. As a news story, the kidnapping had quickly faded, giving way to some new atrocity out of Iraq. Did anyone even read it anymore? It was the imagery that stayed with you, that made it real, but there was so little of that—in the papers, on television, in the endless testimony on the Hill. Once, our security guys were waiting outside the Green Zone when a suicide bomber blew up a restaurant. The bomber's mustachioed head landed on the sidewalk, fully intact. I knew this because our guys came back with pictures in their cell phones and passed them around. But no one saw that. Another time in Kirkuk someone detonated a "head bomb"—that is, explosives packed into a severed head. That didn't make the news, either.

Early one morning, when I couldn't sleep, I wrote in my journal: "The abstractions are what keeps Iraq going, the absence of real facts and pictures and descriptions." I meant the abstractions of violence, bloodless and impersonal, never how it really was. I was still in California, my late father behind me in his green shopping bag. I was thinking about Coté and the other hostages and the horrible things that might be done to him, but never known or said. "The fact that there is not a single fact about them makes it easier for everyone because, of course, they have not really vanished," I wrote in my journal. "At best, they are being kept in a concrete room, blind-folded maybe, maybe being fed, held by people who want to sell them. At worst, somebody took an electric drill to their bodies, attached electric wires to their genitals, imitating Abu Ghraib, cut off their heads with a dull knife while they were still alive and filmed them."

I remembered once writing about an American soldier who

picked up a suicide bomber's severed arm and yelled out, "Anyone want to arm wrestle?" Someone edited it out of my story. It was too graphic, I suppose. I never asked. Another time I wrote a passage about a soldier who straddled the leg of a sergeant to keep him from seeing the baseball-sized hole that had been blown into his ankle. That didn't make the paper, either. When you deal in abstractions, of course, you never have to confront reality.

"In our own way, we are sanitizing the war, and perpetuating it," I wrote to myself.

JUST AFTER CHRISTMAS, IN BAGHDAD, A YOUNG American reporter named Hannah Allam set up an interview with Ahmad Chalabi, the notorious exile, whom many people blamed for manipulating the Bush administration into war. Chalabi, who seemed to have more lives than a cat, had since fallen out of favor with the Americans, but he had reinvented himself as a Shiite political operative, allied with the militia leader Muqtada al-Sadr.

Allam had become Baghdad bureau chief for the Knight Ridder newspaper chain at twenty-five; she stayed in that job after Mc-Clatchy Newspapers acquired Knight Ridder in 2006. An Oklahoma native with a sprawl of dark curly hair, she had spent most of her childhood in the Middle East and had two brothers in the Marine Corps. As Allam's interview with Chalabi was winding down, the discussion turned to which side was more brutal: the Shiite militias or the Sunni insurgents.

Chalabi insisted that the Sunnis, led by Al Qaeda, were the most destructive force in Iraq, the Shiites more benign. "Look, they aren't beheading foreign hostages," he said.

"Yeah, well, I'll believe that when the bodies of those poor Crescent guys are found," said Allam. Most people suspected that the hostages were being held by Shiites because they had been abducted in Shiite-dominated southern Iraq.

"There are no bodies," Chalabi told her. "They're alive."

Allam, startled, asked him how he knew. But Chalabi wouldn't elaborate. Allam insisted that if he had information he owed it to

ABOVE: After serving as a U.S. Army paratrooper, Jon Coté said private security gave him the opportunity to escape the problems of civilian life and save money for college. "If I could do it for my country, why couldn't I come over here and make a little money for myself?" he asked. (*Courtesy of the Coté family*)

BELOW: Jon Coté, during his tour in Afghanistan with the 82nd Airborne Division. Coté joined the army two months before the September 11 attacks. He made sergeant in three years and was honorably discharged in 2005, a decorated veteran of two wars. (*Courtesy of the Coté family*)

Paul Reuben, a former suburban Minneapolis police officer, served as Crescent's medic but complained that the company lacked basics such as tourniquets and morphine. (*Steve Fainaru*)

John Young, a Crescent team leader, participated in the U.S. invasion of Panama in an airborne reconnaissance unit. An injury cut short his attempt to reenlist in the army in his late thirties, and he applied for jobs in private security after the start of the Iraq war. (*Author's collection*)

Mike Arrighi, a former Richmond, Virginia, homicide detective, worked security in Iraq for several companies from 2004 to 2007. He warned that U.S. military oversight for the industry was virtually nonexistent: "We could hire the Rockettes and give them guns, and they wouldn't know." (*Courtesy of Mike Arrighi*)

The charred Chevy Suburban torched by Triple Canopy team leader Jake Washbourne following an incident south of Baghdad. Some members of Washbourne's unit alleged that he shot up the vehicle to make it look like an insurgent attack. (*Courtesy of Mike Arrighi*)

Jake Washbourne, the Triple Canopy operator known as "J-Dub," in Baghdad. Washbourne fired into the windshield of a taxi on Baghdad's airport road, apparently for amusement, according to three of his colleagues. (*Courtesy of Isireli Naucukidi*)

Isireli Naucukidi, a cava farmer and former Fijian soldier known as "Isi," was the first to report a questionable shooting incident involving his team leader, Jake Washbourne. (*Courtesy of Isireli Naucukidi*)

Shane Schmidt (left), aka "Happy," and Charles Sheppard (above), aka "Shrek," members of Triple Canopy's Milwaukee team, in Baghdad. Schmidt and Sheppard waited two days to report that their team leader, Jake Washbourne, fired unprovoked shots into a taxi. The two sued the company after Triple Canopy fired them. (*Courtesy of Shane Schmidt and courtesy of Charles Sheppard*)

The author's father, Bob Fainaru, relaxing in Sun Valley, Idaho, one day before his youngest son, Mark Fainaru-Wada, was sentenced to eighteen months in prison for refusing to divulge the source who leaked Barry Bonds's grand jury testimony. (*Author's collection*)

Franco Picco (right), owner of Crescent Security Group, with an Italian soldier. Picco formed Crescent to protect his own supply convoys and later expanded it to provide security for other coalition allies, including the Italian military. "We protect the military. Isn't that mind-boggling?" he said. (© *Gerald Schumacher Spectrumquest*)

Crescent filled out its teams with Iraqis who earned significantly less than their American colleagues and were forced to man PK machine guns while exposed to the elements and possible attack. The inequities fueled tensions within the company. (© *Gerald Schumacher Spectrumquest*)

Scott Schneider became Crescent's director of security despite a domestic violence conviction that prohibited him from carrying a weapon in the United States, a prohibition that was also adopted by the U.S. military. (© *Gerald Schumacher Spectrumquest*)

Scott Schneider (left) and Wolf Weiss of Crescent Security Group leave the scene of a roadside bomb that did not involve the company. Schneider took over as Crescent's director of security after Weiss, the "Heavy Metal Mercenary," was killed in a friendly fire incident. (*Courtesy of Crescent Security Group*)

Jon Coté (top) and Paul Reuben during a break in Iraq.
(*Courtesy of the Coté family*)

John Young holds the flak jacket that saved his life when
a bullet ripped through the collar during an attack in
Baghdad. (*Steve Fainaru*)

Josh Munns, who fought in Iraq with a marine sniper platoon, returned after growing bored with his job installing swimming pools in Redding, California. He got the job with Crescent through his mother, who knew the company's director of security. (*Courtesy of Mark Munns*)

Wissam Hisham, an Iraqi interpreter known as "John Belushi," turned on his Crescent colleagues during a kidnapping on MSR Tampa, according to two operators who were left behind. "It was fucking Belushi who set us up," said one. (*Courtesy of Jaime Salgado*)

Qusay Ali Hussein, a former Iraqi body-building champion whom the Crescent expats called "Mongo," was identified as one of several former Crescent operators who participated in the kidnapping. (*Courtesy of Jaime Salgado*)

Iraqi gunners manning machine guns on Main Supply Route Tampa. Crescent fired several Iraqi employees who were suspected of stealing weapons and personal items. Resentments over the firings and pay disparities were believed to play a role in the kidnapping. (© *Gerald Schumacher Spectrumquest*)

Raul Correa (left), a novelist and former paratrooper, joined Crescent after the kidnapping, which had left the company shorthanded. "I really thought I was going to die with that fucking company," he later said. Mike Skora, who recruited Jon Coté, vowed to stay with Crescent until his friend was found. (*Courtesy of Raul Correa*)

One of the $200,000 Rock vehicles purchased by ArmorGroup International, a British private security company. As violence increased and bombs became more powerful, the security companies, like the military, increased manpower and added expensive armor in what was effectively a parallel surge. (*Steve Fainaru*)

BLACKWATER
I'm sorry, I can't hear you over the sound of how awesome I am

An image that made the rounds among contractors in Iraq. Blackwater, in the words of one merc, was "universally despised" for its arrogance and disdain for outsiders. (*Author's collection*)

Jack Holly, as director of logistics for the U.S. Army Corps of Engineers in Iraq, assembled a small private army of a half dozen security companies to protect reconstruction materiel. Holly was among the first to warn that the aggressive tactics of Blackwater Worldwide, a State Department contractor, were undermining the U.S. mission in Iraq. (*Courtesy of Victoria Wayne*)

Major General Hussein Kamal (left), head of the Iraqi Intelligence Directorate, with Matthew Degn, an American senior intelligence adviser to the Ministry of Interior. Kamal and Degn sent memos up the U.S. chain of command and issued repeated warnings that Blackwater was out of control and undermining U.S.-Iraqi relations. (*Courtesy of Matthew Degn*)

Blackwater grew to become the most prominent security company in Iraq, protecting the U.S. ambassador and other prominent diplomats under a contract with the State Department. After a series of shooting incidents, including one that took the lives of seventeen Iraqis at a Baghdad traffic circle, the State Department's oversight of Blackwater came under scrutiny. (© *Scott Peterson, Getty Images*)

The Crescent hostages, as seen in a video delivered to the Associated Press. FROM TOP, LEFT TO RIGHT: Jon Coté, Paul Reuben, John Young, Josh Munns, and Bert Nussbaumer. (*Associated Press*)

Paul Reuben's twin brother, Patrick, a Minneapolis police officer, with Paul's twin daughters Bree (middle)
and Casey. Bree and Casey spoke with their father
shortly after a devastating bombing and pleaded with
him to come home. (*Courtesy of Ben Garvin*)

Jon Coté with his mother, Lori
Silveri, in Hollywood, Florida.
(*Courtesy of the Coté family*)

The Cotés pose for a picture after the annual family hockey game at Buffalo's Pepsi Center. From left to right: Nancy Coté (stepmother), Christopher Coté, Max Shroyer (stepbrother), Francis Coté, Samantha Shroyer (stepsister), Jon Coté. (*Courtesy of the Coté family*)

Eight hundred people packed the Nativity of the Blessed Virgin Mary Church in Williamsville, New York, for Jon Coté's funeral on May 2, 2008. The crowd included more than a dozen members of Coté's army platoon, several fraternity brothers from the University of Florida, and friends and relatives from throughout the country, but not a single representative of Crescent Security Group. (*Courtesy of the Coté family*)

the families of the hostages to make it known, at least to the U.S. government. "Put yourself in those families' places," she told him.

Chalabi pulled out a laptop and turned it on. Allam's jaw dropped.

On the screen was a video: Young, Coté, and Nussbaumer, their hands cuffed in front of them, standing against a backdrop of gold drapes. The three hostages wore white short-sleeved undershirts, loose gray pants, and socks. The video zoomed in on each of their faces before they spoke. Young blinked rapidly.

"My name is John Young," he said calmly into the camera. "I'm forty-four years old and I'm from Kansas City, Missouri. I work for private security in Iraq. I'm asking people in my country to please help me and my friends out of Iraq and to pressure the government to remove troops from Iraq."

Coté looked like he may have been beaten. The area around his nose appeared swollen and there were red blotches on his face. He spoke slowly:

"My name is Jonathon Coté, I'm from Gainesville, Florida, and I work for a private security company. I'm asking the American people to put pressure on the government to leave Iraq to help me and my friends get out of here."

Nussbaumer spoke third in heavily accented English. 'I'm twenty-five years old, Vienna, Austrian citizen. I want you to get me and my friends out of Iraq."

The video then cut to Munns, who stood alone. He wore the same loose clothing as the others and did not appear to be hand-cuffed. He spoke against a white backdrop, different than the gold curtains of the previous scene.

"My name is Josh Munns, from California, USA. I was in the U.S. Marine Corps in Haditha and Fallujah"—a reference to Sunni Arab cities wracked by fighting between U.S. and insurgent forces.

The video cut quickly to Reuben. Unlike the other hostages, he wore a blue track suit with orange stripes across the shoulders. Reuben had turned forty on November 24.

"I'm Paul, I'm thirty-nine years old, or forty, I'm not quite sure of today's date," he began. "I'm from Buffalo, Minnesota. I'm married, I have twin daughters—they're sixteen—and I have a stepson that's sixteen. And I'm asking America to release us by getting our troops out of America."

Reuben turned his gaze to his right and smiled nervously as someone appeared to correct him. He laughed.

"I'm sorry, out of Iraq."

The camera zoomed in for a close-up and the video ended with a tight shot of Reuben's smile.

The video was time-stamped 14-4-2006, an indication to Allam that the captors hadn't set the timer properly or had changed it. It was impossible to tell when the video was filmed.

Chalabi initially told Allam she couldn't publish the information. He said the captors had provided the video weeks earlier hoping that he would serve as an intermediary in negotiations with the Americans. But he wanted nothing to do with it. When I reached him more than a year later, Chalabi told me that he had been reluctant to get involved because of how he would be perceived: "It is always a problem to get involved in a kidnapping case, especially when it's for profit." He said he was concerned that the Americans might question his motives and possibly try to implicate him. "From experience it's much better to keep away from such things," he said.

By then, some U.S. officials were accusing Chalabi of having links to Iran. I asked him if he might have turned over the video more readily if his relationship with the Americans had been better.

"Perhaps," he replied.

"There was an opportunity," Chalabi told me later. The kidnappers were clearly trying to communicate and possibly negotiate the hostages' release. But, since Chalabi himself had refused to get involved, the opportunity was slipping away.

Allam appealed to him to release the video, even if he wouldn't go the authorities. "I just imagined my mom in Oklahoma not knowing what had happened to my brothers in such a situation," she said. Chalabi finally agreed to let her record the audio and take notes. "I felt sympathy for the families," he told me. "I thought that the best way to get the maximum benefit was to put it out through the press."

Allam watched the video nearly three dozen times. She asked

Chalabi if he had any additional information about the kidnappers. He said only that the group was Shiite.

Allam went back to write her story. She and her editors agreed that the families should be notified before the story and audio were released, so she emailed the digital recording to the U.S. embassy. She was still writing when an FBI agent called on her cell phone and asked if she would meet in the Green Zone to discuss the video. Allam and her editors were concerned that she might be drawn into the case, but ultimately she agreed.

Two agents picked her up at the bottom of the 14th of July Street Bridge inside the Green Zone. One of the agents sat up front, the other in back with her. They began to ask questions, trying to gain information about the video's origin. There wasn't much she could say. She had made a promise to Chalabi, who at the time still didn't want to be revealed as the source.

When the questions were exhausted, Allam said she had a question for them: what did they know about the Mujahedeen of Jerusalem Company, the group that had originally taken credit for the kidnapping.

The agents said they had never heard of it. They asked her if it was Sunni or Shiite.

Allam was stunned. "I couldn't fathom that the two lead agents on the case had not investigated the group that claimed responsibility for the abductions, even if it was a previously unknown group," she said. "Perhaps they were bluffing to get more information, but I truly don't think so. It became apparent to me within five minutes of talking to them that their investigation had not even taken them out of the Green Zone."

Allam went back and finished her story. About a half hour later, the phone rang. It was one of the agents, asking her if she had mistakenly grabbed his cell phone in the back of the car. She hadn't, but Allam thought his tone was almost accusatory, as if she might have grabbed it purposely.

"I was thinking, 'Damn, brother, if you can't keep track of your own phone in the backseat of your own car, how the hell are you going to find these guys?'"

SCOPE OF
AUTHORITY: GOD

EIGHT DAYS LATER, A VIDEO WAS DELIVERED TO THE offices of the Associated Press in Baghdad. This one was more sophisticated than Chalabi's. The video opened with a red, white, and black map of Iraq next to a tasseled copy of the Koran. The map and the Koran parted to reveal the words "The National Islamic Resistance in Iraq: The Furkan Brigades. This kidnapping operation was executed in the Safwan district of Basra."

In a creative flourish, the credits faded to reveal John Young, seated on the ground with his legs crossed and his hands folded over his lap. This time Young wore a gray-collared sweat suit, white around the shoulders. The video was dated 21-12-2006. It was time-stamped 10:20:27, the seconds ticking as the video rolled. After identifying himself as "John R. Young" and confirming the date, "21 December 2006," the Crescent team leader took a deep breath and said, "I'm well. My friends are well. We've been treated well."

The video then cut to Coté, who was also seated. His appearance was jarring. No longer a fresh-faced kid after thirty-five days in captivity, he was unshaven, and his unkempt beard and hair made him look ten years older. He wore an odd yellow polo shirt with four uneven rectangles that looked like hazy photographs. Coté fidgeted and he blinked. This time he gave his hometown as Buffalo, not Gainesville. "Um, I'm being treated well," Coté said. "Um, I can't be released until all the prisoners from the American jails and the British jails are released." Coté was taking a nervous breath when the video cut to Nussbaumer.

There were now three videos: one in which the group called the Mujahedeen of Jerusalem Company claimed responsibility for the kidnapping but didn't show the hostages; a second in which the hostages were shown but no one claimed responsibility; and now this one. What did it mean? The National Islamic Resistance in Iraq: The Furkan Brigades was also unknown. Was the group related to the Mujahedeen of Jerusalem Company? Did that group ever hold the hostages? Were the groups one and the same? Or had one group sold the men to another? Even the demands had shifted. In the first video, the Mujahedeen of Jerusalem had called for the removal of U.S. troops and the release of the prisoners. In the one delivered to Chalabi, the hostages asked only for the removal of the troops. In the third video, the men called for the release of all prisoners.

It looked like the men had been separated. In Chalabi's video, Young, Coté, and Nussbaumer were together, Munns and Reuben apart. In the latest video, Young, Coté, and Nussbaumer still appeared to be together: according to the time stamp, they were filmed within nine minutes of each other. But when the video cut to Munns, the backdrop was different, and ten hours had passed. Reuben was filmed twenty-four hours after Munns. He appeared standing up against a backdrop of floral wallpaper. His hair was short and he looked healthy. "I just want my family to know that I'm doing well," he said.

After the kidnapping, I wrote a four-thousand-word article on the missing men. The *Post* decided to withhold it to avoid publishing any information that might bring them more harm. At home in California, I was surrounded by their words and their images: on video, in my recorder, in my notes, in my head. Soon they were in my dreams. People would tell me how lucky I was, that I had dodged the ultimate bullet, or even that my father had saved me, his final act, by bringing me home early. I don't know. I was lucky, for sure. But Iraq to me was always a separate reality. It turned all of us into philosophers and fatalists: if it didn't happen to you, it wasn't supposed to, drive on.

Once I was on a patrol in Balad on my mother's birthday. It was late, the road dark, the warm night filled with the smells of apple trees and date palms. Then, around midnight, the road exploded. The Humvee in front of us was lifted off the ground. Fist-sized chunks of asphalt hurtled toward us, suspended in the headlights like a meteor shower, cracking the bulletproof windshield as we careened into a ditch. In the first Humvee, the turret gunner was screaming, "My face! My face! I can't see!" In the one I was in, the gunner was pouring rounds into the orchards, and hot brass was falling down into the cab.

Then suddenly it was silent. No one was seriously hurt; the screaming gunner was bloodied and deafened but otherwise fine. The soldiers were patting their Humvees, murmuring, "Good job, baby, good job."

When we returned to the base, I called my mom on my satellite phone and wished her a happy birthday. I acted as if nothing had happened, and I felt that, in a weird way, it *hadn't* happened, at least not in her world. A few hours later, we went out on the exact same run. When we reached the bomb site, the sun was up and there was a six-foot crater in the middle of the road.

After the Crescent kidnapping, people would say to me, "You're not going back, right?" I wasn't sure what to say. There was nothing to say, because I already knew that I was. I told myself that it was because of the story, and that was true. I felt like I had seen "a hidden part of the war," as Coté had put it, one with its own rules, its own language and subculture, its own secret battles. To me, in many ways, it summed up what Iraq was about: War without pretext. War without ideology. War without planning. War as a paycheck. But I knew that deep down I also went back because I was like them, searching.

GROUND ZERO FOR THE PRIVATE WAR WAS LOCATED within a series of tan concrete buildings inside Baghdad's Green Zone. It was the compound of the U.S. Army Corps of Engineers' Gulf Region Division. The Corps oversaw the $58 billion reconstruction of Iraq, a program of historic ambition that had become synonymous with waste, corruption, and greed. No one argued that it was easy, though: The Corps was trying to rebuild Iraq in the middle of a multipronged war.

The Corps was a military organization made up primarily of engineers, water-treatment experts, and electricians. For muscle it turned to the mercs. From 2004 to 2007, the U.S. military paid $548 million to just two British companies, Aegis Defence Services and Erinys Iraq, to protect the Corps on reconstruction projects. That was over $200 million more than was originally budgeted. Aegis gained notoriety in late 2005 when a video appeared on a Web site purportedly run by company employees, showing Aegis mercs strafing civilian vehicles to the soundtrack of the Elvis Presley song "Mystery Train." A later version of the video contained laughter and the voices of men joking with one another during the shootings. The military investigated but announced in June 2006 that it would not seek criminal charges. In 2007, the Corps renewed Aegis's contract for $475 million—the largest security contract in Iraq. By then, the military had privatized security on dozens of U.S. bases throughout the Iraqi theater and had launched a pilot program to outsource security on military convoys. The theory was that the policy freed up troops to fight insurgents. Aegis even protected the general in charge of all U.S. military contracting in Iraq and Afghanistan. "I'm kind of practicing what I preach here," said Major General Darryl A. Scott. As I interviewed him in the Green Zone, an Aegis operator sat outside his door. "I'm a two-star general, but I'm not the most important guy in the multinational force," Scott said. "If it's a lower-priority mission and it's within the capabilities of private security, this is an appropriate risk trade-off."

Aegis had barely existed at the start of the war. It was founded by a swashbuckling former British lieutenant colonel named Tim Spicer, whose résumé looked like it was written by Frederick Forsyth (in fact, Forsyth, author of *The Dogs of War,* was reportedly an Aegis shareholder). Spicer had done mercenary work in such exotic locales as Papua New Guinea and Sierra Leone. In the Papua New Guinea adventure, his former outfit, Sandline International, took $36 million from the impoverished island-nation to put down a rebellion. Instead, Sandline's presence provoked riots and, ultimately, a coup, according to a detailed account in *Corporate Warriors,* the P. W. Singer book about the rise of the private military industry. Spicer was briefly jailed on a weapons charge that was subsequently dropped. The next year, Sandline was hired to forcibly "reinstall" the elected government of Sierra Leone, which had been overthrown. Spicer later cast the mission as a blow for democracy and human rights. But in fact he had been hired by a fugitive financier who hoped that the reinstated government would grant him diamond and mineral concessions. The operation erupted into a full-blown British scandal amid allegations that Spicer violated a UN weapons embargo. The Brits even gave the scandal a Forsyth-worthy name: "the Sandline Affair."

"Tim Spicer is a mercenary," said Robert Young Pelton, an adventure journalist who wrote about him in *Licensed to Kill,* his book on hired guns in the war on terrorism. "Didn't anyone Google him?"

But Spicer and Aegis were merely part of the Corps' vast private army. Without that army, reconstruction—and thus the war, in many respects—would have ground to a halt. The Corps' private army had a private commander. His name was Jack Holly. He was a barrel-chested, cigar-chomping former marine colonel who served as head of logistics for the Corps of Engineers in Iraq.

Holly had been a respected logistician in the marines. In civilian life, he kept a neatly trimmed salt-and-pepper beard and wore a uniform of khakis, pink-checked shirts, and tennis shoes. His presence was no less commanding. Holly was loud and opinionated, with a personality that matched his immense operation. By early 2006, his network had moved 31,100 vehicles, 451,000 weapons, and 410 million rounds of ammunition, as well as computers, baby incubators, school desks, and myriad other items, all over Iraq.

Holly employed a half dozen security companies to protect this materiel. He allowed Lawrence T. Peter, the director of the Private Security Company Association of Iraq (PSCAI), the industry trade group, to sit in on his daily planning meetings. Peter worked across the hall from Holly in an office inside the Corps' Logistics Directorate. But Holly didn't see a conflict. Private security was so integral to his operation, and the military and the State Department were so absent when it came to regulation, the PSCAI had merely stepped into "the void that had been left by the U.S. government's failure to recognize the problem," he reasoned.

Holly was offended by the word "mercenary"; he felt that it devalued the work. "I don't tolerate the word 'mercenaries'; I think it's disgusting," he told me. "Yeah, they're working for a living. They're working to buy their wives things or take their kids places that they couldn't afford when they were on active duty. I try to tell people, 'Have you ever thought that maybe private security is paid a fair wage and the military is not?' People think it's like Amazon, like you order it up and it comes the next day. But it doesn't happen that way here. It only gets to you here if somebody bets his life on its delivery. That's the fundamental issue: nothing moves anywhere in Iraq with betting your life."

Holly had watched the industry evolve since 2003, and to him it was pure capitalism. "There's very few people here because of apple pie, mother and the American flag. I mean, this was not created out of the mist; this was the American business model. There was supply and there was demand, and the supply and demand created a price." Holly thought the price was worth it, because the security companies relieved soldiers and marines from work that he thought was beneath them. "When you see the number of people I've had killed, the American public should recognize that every one of those people represents an American soldier or marine or sailor who didn't have to go in harm's way. I've always had this vision of George C. Scott, talking about shoveling shit in Louisiana. Well, I don't want a mother to know that her son was on a convoy coming up from Kuwait and he got killed guarding Frappuccino that was going to the fuckin' U.S. embassy. To me, soldiers and marines have a mission to do certain things, and on other things you can out-source risk."

Holly knew the risk better than anyone; he knew he was at the center of what was essentially a parallel war. On May 8, 2005, one of his convoys—Convoy 1047—dropped off 500 pairs of pants, 2,000 plastic whistles, 100 AK-47s, 250,000 rounds of ammunition, and other items at Al Asad Police Academy in Anbar. On the way back, Convoy 1047 came under attack by small-arms fire, rocket-propelled grenades, and two roadside bombs. The after-action report told the whole awful story:

> Of the twenty men on Convoy 1047, thirteen were killed or were missing. Due to the fighting, the IEDs, and rockets, some of the bodies were so mutilated that it was impossible to determine how many actual bodies were on hand, or if some were taken hostage. Six separate sets of remains were recovered; four other bodies were rigged with booby-traps of IEDs. While still under fire the Marine officer in charge elected to destroy the IEDs by shooting M-1 tank rounds into a pile of corpses. . . . The precise match of identity and the remains of some of these people will never be known.

Convoy 1047 belonged to a British firm, Hart Security, which at the time traveled in unarmored trucks. One month later, another Hart convoy came under attack. In the middle of the firefight, the Hart team leader called Holly's ground-control center on his cell phone and said he was running out of ammunition. There was nothing Holly could do. As the convoy was overrun, the team leader left his phone on. Holly listened by speakerphone. "We listened to the bad guys for almost an hour after they finished everybody off," he said.

It was a turning point in Holly's private war, an escalation. Holly vowed that he would never again use unarmored vehicles. He went to his primary shipper, Public Warehousing Co. (PWC) of Kuwait, and ordered a change. PWC replaced Hart with another British company, ArmorGroup International, which had turned its fleet of Ford F-350s into combat vehicles. The modified trucks went into the chop shop and came out with advanced armor plating and steel-reinforced gun turrets that supported belt-fed machine guns. Other companies followed suit, ramping up production of an array of armored trucks of various styles and colors, until Iraq's supply routes resembled the postapocalyptic world of *Mad Max*.

Holly generously offered me a tour of his world.

"What you are going to see is a parallel and totally separate system, and it's almost unknown," he told me. "It's not even recognized and well known by the military."

AS MY TOUR BEGAN, ARMORGROUP WAS PHASING OUT some of the Ford F-350s and replacing them with armored "Rock" vehicles. You could see the trucks around the company villa: they looked like giant armadillos on four wheels. ArmorGroup had invested $6.8 million in the Rocks, which were built on Ford F-550 chassis and cost $200,000 apiece. The trucks had twin gun hatches, a V-shaped hull to deflect roadside bombs, and a steel skin able to withstand armor-piercing bullets. In short, they were perfect for urban combat in Iraq. Chris Berman, who helped design the Rock for North Carolina–based Granite Tactical Vehicles, told me that was the point: "With two belt-fed machine guns in there, that's enough to chew up most people."

The Rock symbolized a new phase in Holly's war. The thin line between the military and the security companies was evaporating. The year had begun with President Bush announcing a "surge" of some twenty thousand additional troops to secure Baghdad. The security companies, out of public view, had launched their own parallel surge, boosting manpower and adding expensive armor such as the Rock as violence increased. It was strategic: the insurgents didn't differentiate between public and private forces. In 2005, one out of every eighteen private convoys came under attack. By 2007, it was one out of every seven.

"The military are very conscious that we're in their battle space," said Cameron Simpson, ArmorGroup's country manager. "We would never launch into an offensive operation, but when you're co-located, you're all one team, really."

ArmorGroup protected one-third of all nonmilitary convoys in Iraq. The company was like a case study in how the mercs had metastasized since the beginning of the war. When ArmorGroup first arrived, in 2003, the company fielded four teams with 20 shooters who drove around in soft-skinned Mitsubishi Pajeros, essentially jeeps. It now had 1,200 employees in-country—the equivalent of nearly two battalions—240 armored trucks, and 30 mechanics. ArmorGroup was a publicly traded company, with 9,000 employees in thirty-eight countries. And yet half of its $273.5 million in revenue in 2006 was derived from Iraq. The company ran as many as twenty-five convoys a day. Its daily rate was $8,000 to $12,000, but the price fluctuated depending on several factors, most notably risk.

"It's a monster," said Simpson, chuckling. He was as amazed as anyone: "Every time I discuss how it was at the beginning, arriving here with a suitcase and $1,000, and there was no one else around, to what it is today, I mean, it's just incredible." He gave me a tour of the company headquarters, a sprawling complex of sandstone houses near the Green Zone. We strolled past the charred husk of a barely recognizable truck that Simpson said had been recently destroyed by a roadside bomb. There were teams quietly coming and going; you could see them rolling out in the F-350s with the ubiquitous warning on the back in Arabic and English: STAY BACK 100 METERS.

After Crescent, I couldn't get over the professionalism of the operation. It was the same deadly game, but everything about Armor-Group was understated. The operators, including Simpson, were well groomed and polite; in their khakis and dark blue polo shirts, you could have replaced the guns with books and turned them loose at Oxford. "People call us 'the school boys' because of the way we dress and the way we act," Simpson said. "We try to be conservative and not over the top, as best you can in this environment." Most shockingly, the company obeyed the law. A lot of people considered it an oxymoron: Iraqi law. Not even the U.S. government put up the pretense of following it. ArmorGroup plastered stickers on its trucks, identifying itself as a licensed security company. It turned over personnel and weapons data to the corrupt Ministry of Interior. When I asked why, when most other companies didn't, the answer floored me: "If you come to someone else's country and don't abide by their laws, it's just the height of arrogance," said Sammy Jamison, ArmorGroup's convoy manager. "We may not always like it, but we will comply. We can't ask the Iraqi people to respect the rule of law if we don't do it ourselves." It was probably the most reasonable statement I heard during my three years in Iraq.

But the company's ethos obscured a fundamental reality: it was the most dangerous work in the county. There were three basic types of merc employment: static security (protecting places); private security detail, or PSDs (protecting people); and convoy protection. The latter was a death trap; some of the most hardened mercs I knew wouldn't get anywhere near it. The big rigs were like lumbering targets for ambushes and IEDs. In 2006, ArmorGroup ran 1,184 convoys and was attacked 450 times, once every 2.6 missions. The company had lost 30 employees since the start of the war. Only three *countries* in the twenty-five-nation coalition—the United States, Britain, and Italy—had sustained more combat-related deaths.

Often ArmorGroup would fire back. One of the company's shooters told me a story about a convoy that came under attack three separate times on a two-mile stretch north of Baghdad. One bomb exploded near the team leader's truck, but the convoy kept going. Then another bomb exploded near one of the big rigs. As the convoy continued to move through the kill zone, it came under small-arms fire. The ArmorGroup team responded with a blizzard of automatic weapons fire.

"We were still moving, so whether you've hit anybody or not, it's very hard to say," he told me.

ONE MORNING I TRAVELED OUT OF BAGHDAD WITH YET another security company, Threat Management Group (TMG). By then, I couldn't keep track of them all. The PSCAI, the merc trade association, listed 177 active companies on its Web site. But those were only the ones that people knew about. They came and went all the time; some based their existence on a single contract, and if they lost it, or it ended, the company itself might disappear. TMG had started out as the security arm of Public Warehousing Co., Holly's main shipper. PWC (later renamed Agility) spun the company off to capitalize on the soaring market for security. TMG traveled in SUVs with Level B6 armor—the best available—and F-350s with gun boxes that looked like miniature lighthouses. The team leader, Joseph Chong, a forty-five-year-old Fijian army veteran, had been in Iraq since late 2003, after answering an ad that he saw on TV. Chong was supporting eight kids and said he made four times as much as he did when he was working as an operations manager in Fiji's Sports Ministry.

Our destination was the Abu Ghraib warehouse complex outside Baghdad, the way station for billions of dollars of materiel that Jack Holly shipped around Iraq. The warehouse was built on the site of a former Iraqi tank factory, about a mile or so from the notorious prison. It had acquired a variety of colorful nicknames, including "Fort Apache," the "Isle of Abu," and "Rocket City," for the rockets and mortars that frequently rained down.

The Isle of Abu had everything but a moat: When you pulled up, you half expected a drawbridge to descend from the towering blast walls. There were miles and miles of concertina wire, and, on all sides, guard towers draped with jungle netting to conceal the Kurdish guards manning belt-fed Dshka machine guns. Inside, sixty-four concrete buildings stood on a one-and-a-half-mile-long and half-mile-wide patch of mud and standing water. Fear and loneliness clung to the place like dew. For their meager entertainment, the handful of Agility expats who lived there had built a small fishing pond and a driving range, but I imagined that it would be like hitting golf balls from an oil platform, the compound was so cut off from the world. The Iraqi employees lived in a barracks-style dormitory with Ping-Pong and foosball, only because it was too dangerous to go home. Over the front door, someone had stenciled the word INMATES in small black letters.

Before I visited, people told me, "You won't believe the security." It was true. After a variety of security breaches at the warehouse, Holly had brought in the A Team: Falcon Group. It was a Kurdish security company with ties to the KDP, one of the main Kurdish political parties, and its military wing, the Peshmerga. The Kurds had a reputation for ruthless efficiency. The previous year, I had watched them consolidate control over the northern city of Kirkuk through a campaign of abductions and repatriations reminiscent of Saddam. Falcon Group had surrounded Abu Ghraib Warehouse with a battalion of five hundred guards. They wore identical camouflage uniforms, carried AK-47s, and shot to kill. One year earlier, I was told, insurgents attacked a passing U.S. military convoy on the highway outside the gates. Guards opened fire from one of the towers and killed two of the insurgents—the public and private wars colliding.

I asked if I could see the commander of the Kurdish force, and, after a few phone calls, I was led through the mud to a nondescript building, down a dingy hallway, to a small office where sixty-one-year-old Leon Sharon, of Ft. Lauderdale, Florida, sat behind a desk smoking a cigarette. Sharon, like his troops, wore a khaki uniform with a "Falcon 6" patch identifying him as the company's field commander. His office was also his bedroom. An American flag covered the window, filtering the afternoon light. There was a cigar-filled humidor on his desk and, behind him on a shelf, cartons of Marlboro Reds stacked next to a leather-bound copy of the Koran.

Sharon had a grizzled, intelligent face from chain-smoking and four decades of military service, including Special Ops. After he retired, he had gotten into the private military business, including a stint with the Steele Foundation in Haiti, where the company provided bodyguards for President Jean-Bertrand Aristide until 2004, when Aristide was whisked out of the country in what he described as a coup and the Bush administration described as a rescue.

Sharon said he had gotten an email from a friend one day, asking him if he'd be interested in a job commanding five hundred Kurdish guards in Iraq. Sharon responded, asking about the work, the scope of authority, exactly how much power he'd have over the unit.

He got back a one sentence reply: "Scope of authority: God."

"Send ticket," Sharon replied.

"It's an isolated site here," he told me. "You have five hundred men, they're yours, you do what you gotta do.

"When you have this many men, you don't manage it as you do a corporation, you manage this very much in the military style," he said. "My men aren't carrying potatoes; they're carrying AK-47s. If that makes it seem military in nature, so be it. It's not pilferage we're worried about here. It's people storming the walls, it's people blowing up convoys, it's the amount of indirect fire that comes in. It's a very different security environment than you will find in the rest of the world."

Sharon didn't seem like he was hung up on the terminology. He referred to Falcon Group as a "private military contractor," which was further than most would go. When I asked him the standard question—Are you a mercenary?—he merely shrugged.

"Everybody works for a living; obviously, everybody gets paid," he said. "If getting paid for your work makes you a mercenary, then everybody is a mercenary, to some degree.

"All of us have come out of the military. We may have left the monastery, but we're all still monks in our own way. . . . You're not talking about the dregs of society, you know. You're talking about people who had a fine military career behind them and continued on. You know, if I was a plumber I'd be laying pipe in Miami for some rich bastard over there. I'm not a plumber. This is what I do."

Sharon offered to take me on a tour of the complex in his truck. We drove across the compound to one of the guard towers. We climbed up to the top, next to the machine gun, and looked out over the walls. You could see exactly what Sharon was facing. The neighborhood was right on top of him, and you didn't want to stand up there for very long. Sharon was embedded in the heart of the insurgency, with millions of dollars in strategic material stored inside his warehouse. Every day, the trucks went in an out, vulnerable to attack. Sharon said the complex sustained 4–6 KIA and 6–8 wounded every month. The attacks were so constant that a small field hospital had been erected inside the main warehouse.

I asked Sharon if I could take his picture. He declined.

"It's not a game," he said. "People get killed here trying to go home. People trying to come here get killed because they work here. People on convoy escort get killed because of the materiel that we're shipping out of here. Truck drivers get killed because they get caught up in these ambushes. And you have security personnel who end up caught up in the mix. And the work has to go on as normal."

Somebody had to do it, said Sharon, and if it wasn't the military, then who?

"The whole face of private security changed with Iraq," he said, "and it will never go back to how it was."

Sharon was about to turn sixty-two. I asked him when he was planning to go home. He just grinned.

"Last man here, please leave the key under the door," he said.

"I WILL JUST TELL YOU THAT BLACKWATER STICKS IN my craw," said Holly. We were sitting in his office late one night in the Green Zone. Sometimes I just sat and listened to him talk, or hung out while he and the other "log dogs," the logistics hounds, screened pirated movies on a wall in the courtyard. Holly would sit in his favorite beach chair, sipping coffee, his cigar smoke rising into the warm night. Holly had been in Iraq since the beginning. He had endured the entire alphabet soup of failed American agencies: ORHA and the CPA, IRMO and the PCO. His strong opinions had been forged by blood and experience and toil. I don't know how many people listened to him. I know that if they had listened to him more, they would have saved themselves a lot of trouble, and maybe fewer people would have died.

It was Holly who pointed out to me the fatal flaw in America's mercenary experiment (although of course he wouldn't have called it that). It had to do with the ad hoc nature of it, the way it was set up at the beginning. When security in Iraq broke down, and it became clear that no more troops were coming, a desperate—really a survivalist— scramble broke out for armed protection. Government agencies, private businesses, humanitarian organizations, the media, and, yes, the military, went looking for hired guns. The economics of it were fascinating. Demand was so high in those early days that the price for a "tier I operator"—an elite merc with Special Forces experience—rose as high as $2,000 a day. Over time, the "market for force," as political scientist Deborah Avant called it, reached a kind of equilibrium. It turned out that there was an endless supply of people willing to pick up a gun and thrust themselves into the middle of a war, and the price fell to about $500–700 a day. But armored vehicles were less plentiful—they were harder to produce than mercs, and less mobile. The war had created a shortage of them, and so the price of armor shot up. "It's a sad commentary," said Holly. "But people's lives are more acceptable to lose than vehicles that cost $200,000 or $300,000 each."

But the real problem was how to keep track of them all, to keep the mercs on their leash. In the military, the command structure is rigid and vertical, from the lowliest grunt up to (theoretically) the commander in chief. All are subject to a highly developed legal process, the Uniform Code of Military Justice. In America's private army, the Contract reigned supreme. Whoever issued the Contract was king. There were thousands of private security contracts written up in Iraq, maybe tens of thousands; no one really knew, especially the military. Many of them were buried under layers and layers of subcontracts, or were handled privately. The result was a lawless void, Big Boy Rules, mayhem, really. By 2007, the military had brought charges against dozens of soldiers and marines in Iraq, including sixty-four servicemen linked to murders. Not a single case had been brought against a security contractor. Part of it was the law: CPA Order 17 had given the mercs immunity from the Iraqi legal process. To charge them with the crime would have required the application of an obscure civilian contractor law, the Military Extraterritorial Jurisdiction Act (MEJA), or to place them under military law. Neither had been tested, practically or legally. But it was more than that. Even if the laws were in place, who exactly would enforce them?

It was Blackwater that really chafed at Holly. I don't know which he had more contempt for: the company or its employer, the U.S. State Department.

Blackwater, largely because of Iraq, had become the Kleenex of corporate mercenaries: most people couldn't name any of the hundreds of other brands out there. Founded as a law enforcement training facility in 1997 in rural North Carolina, the company had parlayed the global war on terrorism to become one of the largest private military providers in the world. The company employed more than a thousand people in Iraq, operated in nine countries, and kept a database of more than twenty thousand former soldiers, Navy SEALS, marines, and law-enforcement personnel. Blackwater had surveillance blimps, a 183-foot ship, a fleet of planes and helicopters, and the Grizzly, which it marketed as "the world's only Armored Personnel Carrier intended to counter the most lethal threats in the modern urban combat environment."

If the Iraq war had an official sponsor, like the Olympics, it would have been Blackwater. By the end of 2007, the company had made a billion dollars off the war. It was the most prominent member of a triumvirate of companies (the others were DynCorp and Triple Canopy) that held what some mercs called the "MOAC," or mother of all contracts. Its real name was the Worldwide Personal Protective Service (WPPS), a $3.5-billion diplomatic security program run out of the State Department. Blackwater had started in Iraq protecting L. Paul Bremer, the viceroy for the occupation government, and had continued as the security provider for all subsequent American ambassadors and diplomats.

Blackwater became famous on March 31, 2004, when four of its operators were ambushed while escorting kitchen equipment through Fallujah. A mob shot and burned them, mutilated the bodies, and hung two of the charred corpses from a bridge over the Euphrates River, where they remained for hours. One week later, the marines attacked Fallujah in one of the major turning points of the war.

Holly begrudged Blackwater neither its success nor its sacrifice. What infuriated him was its impunity; the State Department allowed the company to do whatever it pleased. After the Fallujah incident, for example, the military, which hadn't even known that Blackwater was operating in the city, spent millions to create an operations center to monitor armed civilians on the battlefield. The system, embedded in the Green Zone, was called the ROC (Reconstruction Operations Center). It tracked companies using the same kind of transponders that Holly used on convoys. Except that Blackwater, the catalyst for the ROC's creation, refused to participate. The State Department didn't require it. The military still had no idea where Blackwater was at any given time.

"Blackwater is very arrogant," said Holly as we sat in his office. "They're secretive, and they're secretive because that's the way the State Department wants it. If the ambassador told them they had to play ball with their DoD counterparts, Blackwater would do it. But that won't happen. I think it's self-fulfilling. It's like, 'We don't let people know what we're doing. We're the State Department. We're Blackwater.' So they don't come down the street and say, 'Well, we had an incident today' or anything like that. They don't say shit."

Later, people would debate whether the savagery of Fallujah—the grotesque images seared into memory—informed what Blackwater ultimately became. It was one thing for Crescent, a small company that operated totally off the grid, to maraud over the Iraqi countryside, accountable to no one. But Blackwater was part of State; the company reported directly to the U.S. embassy's Regional Security Office. Even the merc trade group, the PSCAI—which Blackwater helped fund—admitted that the company was untouchable. The PSCAI's deputy director, H. C. Lawrence Smith, told me: Blackwater "has a client that will support them no matter what they do." The PSCAI's director, Lawrence Peter, said: "They're Blackwater employees but it's almost as if they're deputized to the State Department." The company's reputation spanned all of Iraq. Inside the Green Zone, Blackwater routinely ran vehicles off the road, or pointed their rifles at bystanders, regardless of their nationality. "They're universally despised in the Green Zone," said Mike Arrighi, an American security consultant who arrived in-country in 2004. "That's not an overstatement: 'Universally despised' is probably a kind way to put it." Blackwater's founder, Erik Prince, a former Navy SEAL, reportedly was devoutly religious. But his operators were known for brawling and whoring. A friend of mine described her disgust as two Blackwater mercs, shortly after introducing themselves, proposed a two-on-one sex act that involved one of the men ejaculating on the other.

Outside the Green Zone, Blackwater terrorized the Iraqi population. Ann Exline Starr, an American who worked as a CPA (Coalition Provisional Authority) adviser, first traveled in Iraq with a military escort. The soldiers often drank tea and played cards with the Iraqis, trying to cultivate relationships. But as security deteriorated, she was assigned guards from Blackwater and DynCorp. The change was startling. The contractors moved aggressively, sometimes pushing people around. "What they told me was, 'Our mission is to protect the principal at all costs. If that means pissing off the Iraqis, too bad.'" It struck Exline Starr as totally contrary to the U.S. mission in Iraq, the reason she was there in the first place.

On February 7, 2006, a Blackwater convoy was moving rapidly through the northern city of Kirkuk when it came up behind a taxi on a two-lane road. What happened next was described by Rizgar Ali, Kirkuk's Provincial Council president, and several witnesses. The sixty-five-year-old taxi driver panicked, they said, and either failed to move or made an erratic turn that Blackwater perceived as a threat. The mercs opened fire. They killed the driver, Nidham Qadir Muhammad, a twenty-six-year-old passenger named Khalid Mahmood Nadir, and Shihab Ahmad, a thirty-nine-year-old schoolteacher who was standing on the side of the road.

Kirkuk was governed by the Kurds, the most pro-American of Iraq's divided sects. But the local population reacted with fury. Hundreds of demonstrators descended on the U.S. consulate. A cousin of one of the victims said the crowd wanted to burn the building to the ground but was turned back by representatives of the Kurdish political parties. Khursheed Muhammad, the taxi driver's son, said, "Now, every time I hear that someone targeted Americans and killed them, I feel happy." Rizgar Ali, one of the most influential Kurdish politicians in Iraq, said the shooting left the Americans "hated and ostracized" in the Kirkuk region. He said he sent "official letters to the American and British consulates and met them in my office to find out who the murderers were. They didn't do anything or give me clear answers. They only said, 'The ones who did it were from the Blackwater company.'"

When I asked Blackwater about the incident, the company didn't respond. Neither did the State Department. For months, I wrote emails and made calls asking State basic questions about how it regulated Blackwater and other security companies. When the response finally came back, in the form of an email from an anonymous press officer, this was as specific as it got: "State Department personnel, including contracting officers, routinely meet with private security contractors both on the ground in Iraq and in Washington, DC, and coordinate with other U.S. federal agencies and the Iraqi government with regard to compliance issues."

Many people marveled at the irony that the State Department, an agency created to promote diplomacy, was seemingly oblivious "that the very profile of its mission was at odds with its aims," as one frustrated security official put it. Part of it, certainly, was Blackwater's success rate: not a single State Department employee had been killed under the company's protection. But the price for that protection went well beyond the steep bottom line on Blackwater's contract, and it was a price that was rising. One afternoon, I was interviewing an Iraqi security official at the Ministry of Interior. When the conversation turned to Blackwater, he almost shook with anger.

"They are part of the reason for all the hatred that is directed at Americans, because people don't know them as Blackwater, they know them only as Americans," he said.

"Blackwater has no respect for the Iraqi people. They consider Iraqis like animals, although actually I think they may have more respect for animals. We have seen what they do in the streets. When they're not shooting, they're throwing water bottles at people and calling them names. If you are terrifying a child or an elderly woman, or you are killing an innocent civilian who is riding in his car, isn't that terrorism?"

It was the spring of 2007, and the price would continue to go up. Way up.

AFTER THE THIRD VIDEO, RADIO SILENCE FELL OVER the Crescent hostages.

The families waited, but there was no formal ransom demand, no further videos or communiqués from the Mujahedeen of

Jerusalem Company or the National Islamic Resistance in Iraq: The Furkan Brigades.

I decided to take a trip down to the port at Umm Qasr in southern Iraq with Agility, Jack Holly's shipper, and the company's security wing, Threat Management Group. My main purpose was to check out security at the first stage of Holly's operation: the point at which the reconstruction materiel originated. But I also knew that I would be within a few miles of where the kidnapping occurred. There was no information coming out of Baghdad, and I thought perhaps I might hear more as I got closer to the border.

The five-hour trip was uneventful, with not a shot fired in anger. Along the way I chatted with Mike Weber, who served as Agility's project manager. We sat in the backseat of the SUV, wearing flak jackets and talking about the private war. Weber had spent a career in the military, retiring as a colonel, but he, too, was staggered by it. TMG, he said, would soon be acquiring "Level B7" armored trucks that cost $300,000 to $500,000. Seemingly there was no end to it. Weber speculated that as the United States pulled out of Iraq, the private army might actually grow. "It's almost like you could draw down the mission and do it all with private security," he said.

As we got closer to the port, I realized that we were retracing the steps of the missing men. It was eerie and depressing, the desert empty and forbidding. At one point we had to stop and wait for a herd of camels to cross the highway. Finally we reached the port. The heat felt like someone was pressing down on your head with an iron. We were met by a smiling young woman in her thirties wearing a bright pink polo shirt and khakis. She had flaming red hair that fell over a worn leather shoulder holster containing a Walther P99 semi-automatic pistol. She shook my hand and handed me a water bottle.

"I'm Molly Ringwald with a gun," she told me cheerfully.

Traci St. Denis ran the place for Agility; technically, she was site manager. She had a husband and a job as a firefighter back in Latham, New York, near Albany, but after a reserve stint in Iraq, where she ran convoys, she found it wasn't enough. If there was anyone in Iraq who was more enthusiastic than Coté, it was St. Denis. In 2006, she had a heart attack on the job and came back two months later. "I feel fortunate to be here," she told me. "I'm selfish that way. I like feeling good about my job." St. Denis wrote a blog called "My Life in Iraq" for the *Albany Times Union*. With her beaming smile, red hair, and enthusiastic prose, she could have been writing from St. Bart's. "To answer your question, yes, I am crazy (or nuts, strange, devoid of all senses, you fill in the adjective)," she informed her readers when she decided to go back after the near-fatal heart attack.

The port at Umm Qasr matched her personality: borderline insane. The week before I got there, dueling Shiite militias had engaged in a shoot-out on the Dubai ferry, which now sat docked and bullet-riddled in the harbor. The militias battled constantly over the lucrative port; mortars frequently landed on the docks and in the water. Agility had walled off the reconstruction materiel in a fortified enclave. It all sat on an enormous dirt lot—toilets, generators, boats, trailers, school desks, light fixtures—surrounded by blast walls, razor wire, guard towers, and, of course, more than a hundred Fijian and Iraqi mercs.

The security manager was an acerbic Brit named Geoff Clark. He'd spent sixteen years in the British military before retiring to the private sector. Private security was a mixed bag in Iraq, he told me. "The military doesn't like us, but they tolerate us as a necessary evil because they know that if it wasn't for us, they would need another twenty-five thousand to fifty thousand troops on the ground here." The private army, meanwhile, was wildly uneven, he said. "You've got some who are very professional, and others who I wouldn't let protect a cup of piss."

Clark reserved his greatest contempt for Crescent. He knew the company from being around the border. "They were a bunch of clowns, the whole lot of them," he said. "It wasn't really the guys. It was the company's operating procedure that was a total joke." The kidnapping was one of the least-surprising events to occur in Iraq, he told me.

I asked him if he had heard anything about the hostages. He said he hadn't, not lately, but he presumed they were all dead.

"There was a rumor that one of the bodies turned up," Clark told me. "They said it was skinned."

HOSTAGE AFFAIRS

THE PHONE RANG NEXT TO FRANCIS AND NANCY COTÉ'S bed around 3:30 A.M. Nancy was closest to it, and the sound shook her awake, filling her with dread.

It was Picco, Crescent's owner, calling from Kuwait. Francis was sitting up now and Nancy handed him the phone. The sound of Picco's thick South African accent hit Francis in the gut. But Picco told him he had good news. Or, rather, he was "expecting good news." He said he had sources who had seen the men alive. He said he couldn't be more specific. But he left the impression that their nightmare would soon be over. "We thought they were coming home," said Francis. Picco delivered the same promising message to each family.

Francis and Nancy waited for another call. It was difficult to work or sleep. Days passed, then weeks, and then months. But they never heard from Picco again. Over time, Francis and Nancy wondered if it had even been real. The call had been so cryptic and fleeting, almost like a dream. Francis thought about contacting Picco in Kuwait, but he figured that if there was more news he would have heard about it, and so the optimism, the first in months, evaporated like mist.

It was easy to forget that it was business. Except that once the mercs went missing, the money stopped, too. Picco had simply cut them off, as if they had taken unauthorized vacations, or several months of undocumented sick leave. He told the families that he was holding three months' pay for each employee pending their release. For Coté, a college student, it didn't mean much. But Reuben paid child support for his teenage daughters (Bree had gotten pregnant while he was in captivity) and supported a wife and a teenage stepson. "*Three months?* Oh my God," gasped his wife, Keri, upon hearing the news. Young also paid child support for his teenage daughter and helped support his nineteen-year-old son, who was attending community college near Kansas City. Josh Munns' house, the Redding fixer-upper that he was planning to occupy with his fiancé, had been in escrow when he was abducted. The deal fell through shortly after.

By January, Keri was threatening to sue Picco for her husband's back pay. Exactly where she would sue Crescent—which was based in Kuwait, registered in the Virgin Islands, and operated in Iraq under a contract with the Italian government—was unclear. Picco finally agreed to wire $3,500 to each family, exactly half a month's salary. If the men turned up dead, he said, their beneficiaries would receive $300,000. Crescent had absolved itself of responsibility. Picco later told me that he fired Schneider when he learned after the kidnapping that his director of security had a domestic violence conviction. When I caught up with Schneider, he blamed the missing men, who he said were adequately trained and equipped. "We pretty much catered to them. We spoiled them," he said. "You know, basically the operators screwed up. I mean, you hate to speak ill of people, but the way the situation transpired, they just made mistake after mistake."

The families were left with only rumors and tantalizing clues. In March, four months after the attack, British forces stormed a house in Basra and found a list of four hostages with their contact information. Three of the hostages were Coté, Young, and Nussbaumer. Handwriting analysis confirmed that the men had written the information themselves, suggesting that their captors were planning to contact the families directly. An unexpected name also appeared on the list: Ronald J. Withrow, of Roaring Springs, Texas. Withrow was a thirty-nine-year-old computer specialist who, seven weeks after the Crescent attack, had disappeared at another fake checkpoint near Basra. He had not been heard from since. The Brits found what appeared to be Withrow's flak jacket and some Iraqi police uniforms. The mysterious kidnappers now appeared to hold six foreigners, including five Americans.

Were there more?

Bits of information were spun into elaborate theories. Some people speculated that the hostages were being held in Iran because the first video had been broadcast on Iranian television, which was thought unusual. There were reported sightings of the men at Iraqi police stations, on Basra sheep farms, in Safwan safe houses, even in Kuwait. Crescent was paying informants all across Basra, and they often provided tips. "A lot of the information would come in at the end of the month," said a former Crescent employee. "That's when they got paid." One day, FBI agents visited Francis and Nancy looking for Jon's shoes. It turned out coalition forces had detained a man wearing American-style military boots inscribed with the name "Coté." The FBI wanted to make a forensic comparison. But nothing more was heard.

The families felt powerless, desperate, their lives suspended. The State Department had assigned a representative from the Office of American Citizens Services and Crisis Management to keep them informed. Her name was Jenny J. Foo, and at first she called each family once a week from her office in Washington, DC. After several months, Francis organized a Monday conference call so that Foo could update everyone at the same time.

But there wasn't much to report. Foo would discuss why U.S. authorities refused to distribute leaflets asking for information about the hostages ("too dangerous") or tell the families that the FBI was pursuing leads she wouldn't describe ("unfortunately they didn't pan out") or offer words of comfort ("that must be so hard"). Foo was cheerful and compassionate, and she appeared every week without fail. But the families soon realized that she was a functionary, her primary role to placate them, and their frustration only grew. The FBI, not the State Department, was running the investigation out of Baghdad's Green Zone, and that, too, was confounding. It was the largest kidnapping of Americans since the start of the war, and yet the probe was centered 350 miles from the crime scene, nowhere near the region where the hostages were thought to be held. Agents would spend ninety days in Iraq, then hand off the case. The CIA, the Brits, the U.S. military, and the Austrian government were also involved, but even Foo had to acknowledge to the families, "They tend to be territorial. They're supposed to be coordinating . . . but they don't always do that."

"Jenny, why can't the government just *tell* us whether our boys are still alive?" Sharon DeBrabander, Young's mother, asked her one morning.

By then, Foo knew everyone's voices.

"Sharon, we just don't have the answer to that question," she replied. "I'll tell you one thing: if it was a congressman's son they would have answers," Sharon said to me one day.

It was terrorism in full. Sometimes in Iraq, people would talk about the things that could happen to you, a fixation on the "grim perversities of smut and death," as the writer Chris Hedges called it, and debates would break out: was it worse to be beheaded or blown up, to lose your arms or your legs? But, to me, this was the most terrifying fate imaginable: to be erased, disappeared, leaving your family and friends to fill in the blanks of your existence, neither alive nor dead, forever wondering.

The families clung to anyone who claimed to have information about their loved ones. In Minneapolis, a gun shop owner named Mark Koscielski announced that he was opening his own investigation in response to what he called "the inaction of our US Government/FBI." Koscielski was an old friend of Reuben's; he had provided the tricked-up M-4 that Reuben carried with him into

Iraq. For years, Koscielski had fended off attempts to shut down his downtown store, Koscielski's Guns & Ammo, while at the same time working up a frothing contempt for the federal government.

Koscielski spoke with a speech impediment, and he filled the families' heads with conspiracy theories and grandiose plots. One afternoon, he called me in California and said he was planning to travel to Kuwait, and then Basra, to gather information and negotiate the hostages' release with $150,000 he claimed to have raised. He asked me if I wanted to go. I laughed and politely declined, telling him that I didn't think it was a good idea for two Americans to wander into one of Iraq's most dangerous cities alone. But soon Koscielski was informing the FBI about his plans. When the head of the Minneapolis Joint Terrorism Task Force warned him not to go, Koscielski employed the word "fuck" in its many grammatical forms. Before long, he was in Kuwait.

His first three days were "a total waste due to the fact that no one . . . would accept American Express Travelers' Checks," he wrote in a six-page trip report to the families. Once Koscielski figured out how to exchange money, he set out to meet with "my contacts," who he identified only as James, Ricky, and Abel. They provided startling revelations, such as the Iraqi police were "a bunch of fucking thieves" and a gang called "Ali Baba" was behind the kidnappings. Koscielski apparently didn't realize that Ali Baba was the generic Iraqi phrase for "bad guys." Koscielski ended his trip interviewing random people in the departure lounge at the Kuwait City airport. He walked up to them and announced, "I'm here from America, looking for information on these five guys and here are their pictures." He never made it into Iraq.

Upon his return, Koscielski notified the FBI that he had no intention of sharing the critical information he had gathered. Koscielski wasn't much of a speller, and he wrote: "I have seen what you have done with pass info. Not a FUCKING THINK!"

By the brutal summer of 2007, the families decided to defy the U.S. government and go public.

The State Department and the FBI had warned them that speaking out might endanger the hostages. Or that criticizing the U.S. government was exactly what the kidnappers wanted; it would hand them a victory. But the families figured they didn't have much to lose. There had been no evident progress in the investigation, no more videos, no ransom demands, no "proof of life," not even bodies, which at least would have given them closure. In Buffalo, Kansas City, Redding, and Minneapolis, the families began to hold press conferences and grant interviews, hoping that public pressure might prod U.S. officials to pursue the case more aggressively.

With the surge of American troops into Baghdad, the Iraq war had entered a new phase. The mercs, of course, were critical to the campaign, but their vague status was never more apparent than when they got killed or wounded or disappeared. The system couldn't handle it; it wasn't set up for that. In a way, it had a perverse logic: the mercs fought by their own rules, and so they died by their own rules. But there was a whiff of shame about how the military and the State Department ignored them so assiduously. It was as if by not counting them—in life or in death—no one had to acknowledge that America had been reduced to relying on a private army to prosecute a war that had entered its fifth bloody year.

The disparity was striking, because the sacrifice of the American soldier still inspired soaring poetics and led commanders to move mountains. On May 12, six months after the Crescent ambush, a U.S. Army patrol came under attack on a dark road near Yusifiyah, a farm town south of Baghdad. Three American soldiers were abducted during the attack. Four soldiers and an Iraqi interpreter were killed.

The army sent four thousand Americans and two thousand Iraqis to scour the palm groves and high grass along the Euphrates River. Three more Americans were killed during the search. On day eleven, the body of one of the missing soldiers turned up on the riverbank. On day twenty-three, insurgents affiliated with Al Qaeda released a video announcing that the two others had been killed. Still the army persevered. U.S. troops took thumbprints and retinal scans for more than a thousand people. When locals were reluctant to accept cash for tips, fearing they'd be targeted, the soldiers poured water over the money and scrunched it together to make it appear old. "I'll find 'em," vowed the battalion commander for the missing soldiers. "I ain't stopping till they kill me or send me home."

Here were two groups of Americans missing in Iraq. One was composed of active soldiers, paid directly by the U.S. government. The other was composed mostly of retired soldiers and marines who were paid indirectly by the government through private contracts. Gerry Schumacher, the author of *A Bloody Business*, was a retired Special Forces colonel who had spent twenty years as a Green Beret. The difference between how the U.S. government treated soldiers and mercs appalled him. As the families began to speak out, Schumacher complained to the *Orlando Sentinel* that he believed the government had "written off" the Crescent hostages.

"It is very unfortunate that when contractors get captured, the amount of effort to recover them is minimal compared to what you see if an American soldier gets captured," Schumacher said.

The article ran beneath the headline HOPE FOR UF STUDENT CAPTURED IN IRAQ FADES. It quoted Francis Coté, who told the newspaper that the effort to find his son no longer appeared to be "a priority."

Shortly after, Schumacher got an email from G. Alexander Crowther, PhD, the principal adviser to the Office of Hostage Affairs in Baghdad, which was responsible for overseeing kidnapping cases for the U.S. embassy. Crowther wrote that he was "saddened" by Schumacher's criticism, which "demonstrates that you have not talked to anyone working hostage issues here at the US Embassy in Baghdad, especially the fine FBI professionals who have recently risked their lives in Basra working this very case."

"We are working this case just as hard as we work all of the cases that we get here," Crowther wrote. "We all work hostage issues 7 days a week. Some are U.S. citizens, some are Iraqis, some are from other countries. Some are contractors, some are military. Each and every one of them gets the full attention of the entire hostage community here at the Embassy."

Schumacher wrote back: "Are you suggesting that the effort to locate the CSG personnel is in fact comparable to the recent efforts (including massive door to door searches) to locate the missing . . . Army soldiers?"

As summer arrived, the *Washington Post* was still withholding the long article I had written the previous November. By then, the *Post* was one of the few papers in the country that hadn't printed the hostages' names. Every couple months, my editor and I would debate whether the article should be published. The bottom line was always the same: how would the kidnappers respond to the mercs' own words, or the videos I had taken the week before the kidnapping, or a four-thousand-word deconstruction of Crescent's ideology of greed? How would we feel—how would we respond—if bodies started turning up? I was on my way to Baghdad, and we agreed that I would discuss the article with U.S. security officials.

As always, the Green Zone was a hive of merc activity. One checkpoint was manned by Nepalese Gurkhas with Global Risks, a British company. AK-toting Peruvians, employed by Triple Canopy, manned the air-conditioned kiosk where visitors passed through a metal detector before entering the U.S. embassy. Even the press officer who greeted me, it turned out, had worked for DynCorp. It was always slightly demoralizing to enter the embassy building, wrinkled and drenched, to meet the dry people who worked in air conditioning all day. The press officer ushered me to an ornate dining room the size of Madison Square Garden, where I bought an iced mochaccino from a gourmet coffee cart. We then ventured deeper into the former palace of Saddam Hussein, one marbled corridor after another, until finally we arrived at our destination.

The office consisted of four plywood walls hammered together in the middle of another room in the middle of the cavernous palace. It was like being inside a Russian nesting doll. Tacked to one wall were photos of some three dozen people—all missing in Iraq, I was told. I spoke with an American official I was forbidden to quote or identify. He grimly explained that lives were at stake. He wanted to assure me that the government was doing everything it could to find the Crescent hostages, whose names he then mispronounced or forgot entirely. When I outlined the substance of the article we planned to publish, including the allegations against Crescent, he seemed unfamiliar with the basics of the company. As he walked me out, the official suggested that I might want to think about turning his fascinating story into a book when he left Iraq.

Maybe he knew more than he let on. Really, could there be any more difficult task than investigating a kidnapping in the middle of a war? But I left feeling the Crescent hostages would never be found. It was never clear to me why the Justice Department rotated agents in and out of Iraq every ninety days or why the investigation was never located in Basra, where the crime occurred. One U.S. official told me that, because of the security risks, an assignment to Basra was voluntary, and few people were willing to go.

But the message was clear enough: private contractors, even Americans, did not merit the same resources as U.S. troops or official U.S. government employees.

That night, I called Francis in Buffalo. He told me the families had begun to take matters into their own hands. For months, the families had been trying to get the State Department or the FBI to distribute leaflets in southern Iraq. The leaflets became a symbol for what the families perceived as official U.S. government indifference. Francis finally had his brother André print up thousands of leaflets with photos of the missing men (the president of the Muslim Public Affairs Council of Western New York translated them into Arabic). He persuaded an American shipping company to fly them to Amman for free. Now, he told me, he was trying to line up a cargo plane to drop them over Basra.

The families had also hired a private investigative firm, using $20,000 they had collected at fund-raisers. The company was assigned the task that had eluded the FBI for nearly a year: to seek "proof of life" and bring the hostages home, alive or dead.

No one was more frustrated about the pace of the government's investigation than Nancy Coté. A career drug enforcement officer, she was just the fiftieth woman to join the DEA when she started in 1980. She had worked dozens of major drug cases, including the investigation into New York City kingpin Leroy "Nicky" Barnes. She had risen to become the number-one agent in her hometown, Buffalo.

From the beginning, Nancy had been outraged by the lack of urgency surrounding her stepson's case. She worked her contacts inside the law-enforcement community, trying to maintain interest, reminding everyone that one of the missing Crescent hostages was the son of a DEA agent.

In the late summer, the government quietly changed its tactics. The DEA, prodded by Nancy, decided to put its own man on the case. It was an unusual arrangement, since the FBI technically still had jurisdiction, and the DEA rarely handled kidnappings. The deal was for one man, one case. Only the Cotés would know he was DEA; the other families of the hostages were kept in the dark.

The agent was a twenty-year veteran of the drug wars who was rotating into Iraq on his second tour for the Justice Department. The new arrangement meant that he wouldn't be constrained by the ninety-day rotations, or the FBI's insistence on running the case out of the Green Zone. He arrived in Baghdad in the summer of 2007, and he didn't stay long. Soon he was at Ground Zero, entrenched in southern Iraq, working leads and informants.

He would stay there so long he became known as Joe from Basra.

ON THE ONE-YEAR ANNIVERSARY OF THE KIDNAPPING, I traveled to Parkville, Missouri, for a fund-raiser held by the family of John Young. The date, November 16, nearly coincided with the anniversary of my father's death: November 10. The two events would be forever intertwined for me, and I felt in a way I was commemorating both. It was hard to believe it had been just a year, given everything that happened. My brother had narrowly escaped jail when the federal government came up with the leaker of Barry Bonds' grand jury testimony on its own. Prosecutors had dropped the subpoena ordering Mark to testify and were now going after Bonds for perjury.

My flight to Kansas City was late, and the fund-raiser had already started when I pulled into the dirt parking lot of Veterans of Foreign Wars (VFW) Post 7356 on the Tom Watson Highway. It was a rambling white building with a small wooden porch on which people were dropping cigarette butts into a gray plastic receptacle, almost like a parking meter. Inside, about a hundred people were scattered around a long room with a low ceiling. A man was auctioning off small items—puppies, electric air pumps, lawn mowers—to raise money for "our hero John Young, who's still missing in Iraq."

I ordered a beer and asked the bartender to point out Young's mother, Sharon DeBrabander. We had spoken several times but had never met. She was standing in the middle of the room, wearing a floral print dress and clutching a half-smoked pack of Basic cigarettes. I walked up to introduce myself and was knocked back by her eyes, which were crystal blue, exactly like her son's, and mournful. We shook hands and agreed to talk after the auction was over; she led me to Koscielski, who, she said, had flown down from Minneapolis.

Koscielski, the gun shop owner turned investigator, was standing on the porch smoking a cigarette with Shannon McCullough, a former Crescent operator from Ohio. Koscielski was fifty-four, taller than I had imagined, about six foot three, with a wide round face and receding brown hair. He wore old jeans and a faded shirt beneath a parka. McCullough was stocky and wore a Bluetooth headset, which stayed in his ear the entire night. There was a winter chill in the air, and after Koscielski dropped his cigarette into the gray bin, we went back inside to talk in a wooden booth.

Although the hostages hadn't been found, the case had lifted up the Crescent rock to reveal the full range of the company's misbehavior in Iraq. The U.S. military, for reasons that weren't yet clear, had finally started to pay attention, and between the kidnapping and the scrutiny, Crescent was crashing and burning. In Iraq, a skeleton crew of Mike Skora and a few other mercs was holed up at Tallil Air Base while military investigators cracked open shipping containers and pored over weapons logs. In the United States, I had heard rumblings that the Defense Department's Criminal Investigative Service (CIS) was looking into allegations of weapons trafficking and falsification of military IDs.

We had no sooner sat down than Koscielski was telling me he had given information to CIS about a former Crescent ops manager named Nate Seabrook. Seabrook, thirty-eight, was a light-skinned black guy who once served in the 82nd Airborne. He had grown up in Minneapolis with Paul Reuben and his twin brother, Patrick, and had gotten Paul his first job in Iraq before hiring him at Crescent. Seabrook and Patrick Reuben were still close friends. But Seabrook had made plenty of enemies while he was in Kuwait. Benjamin Borrowman, the mechanic they called "Red," told me, "My opinion of that man was that if he went north of the border he was gonna get whacked, and not by some unfriendly. It was gonna be by one of our own people. I'm not gonna say I was not above doing it myself."

Koscielski and Seabrook had once been friends, but now Koscielski had turned on Seabrook, too. He told CIS investigators that Seabrook, while visiting his gun store, had admitted to various "adventures" in Iraq. Those adventures, according to Koscielski, included providing false information to obtain U.S. military IDs, which Seabrook allegedly used to obtain weapons. An affidavit for a search warrant on Seabrook's apartment, filed in Minneapolis federal court, stated that "a person who previously worked with Seabrook provided Koscielski records that purportedly were obtained from Seabrook's computer when Seabrook was in Kuwait."

Seabrook denied the allegations. I often wondered about the motivations of Koscielski, a gun shop owner who had deputized himself in a kidnapping investigation and was now diming out an ex-friend to the same federal authorities he professed to despise. Patrick Reuben, a Minneapolis cop, refused to be in the same room with Koscielski, whom he believed was on a self-aggrandizing crusade involving his missing brother. As we sat in the booth, Koscielski said his only goal was to find Paul and the other hostages. "I'm a layman," he told me. "I just want my fucking friend back. I'm not the kind of guy who wants to cozy up to you and talk to you about current events and shit like that. I just want to get it done. And if you get in my way I will fuck you over good."

Despite his recent cooperation with the federal government, Koscielski said he was convinced that the FBI, among other things, had been stealing his trash, prompting him to buy a shredder. He said suspicious numbers kept popping up on his cell phone, but when he tried to call back no one was ever there.

"Me, too," said McCullough.

Koscielski said he wasn't paranoid. "I don't believe in black choppers over my head, or the CIA beaming beams into your brain. But . . . *hello*?"

I had heard enough and walked outside. Young's mother was smoking on the porch in the cold. We started talking about the case, and she said she was still optimistic. She said the government had recently told the families that "the boys are still alive."

An older woman with a raspy voice walked up and asked Sharon if she had heard from her kidnapped son. Sharon, unfazed by the absurdity of the question, said no, unfortunately she hadn't.

"You know over there they cut the heads off," the woman told her earnestly. "That's what they do, they cut off the heads."

"I don't think they do that anymore. I think Bin Laden told them that it was hurting their cause," said Sharon. "You don't think that I think about that all the time: how they're treating those boys, whether they're getting enough to eat?"

Sharon introduced me to Young's nineteen-year-old son, John Robert. He was wiry and blond like his dad, and slightly taller, about five foot nine. Even on this solemn occasion, he projected a kind of optimism and can-do spirit. He told me he was attending college while running a full-time lawn-care business. Every few minutes, his pretty girlfriend, Ashley, would sneak up on the porch and give him a kiss.

Young had gotten divorced when John Robert was a toddler. For a few years, Young tried to raise his son alone, but when John Robert was in second grade, Young sent the boy to live with his grandparents, Sharon and her second husband, Dennis DeBrabander, a database analyst. Sharon and Dennis ended up raising John Robert while Young struggled to keep his life together.

John Robert didn't seem to harbor the slightest resentment

about his father's choices, then or now. He called Young "a hero" and "my best friend."

"The last time he was here, we talked about everything, and I said, 'You are going to end up dying over there if you keep doing this.' I tried to talk him out of going back. And he said, 'Never live your life in fear. You have to live life to the fullest.'"

"I just think he was bored," John Robert said.

It was nearing midnight, freezing, winter fast approaching.

"Yeah, I think he was bored. He wanted some action."

John Robert paused.

"Well, he got his action," he said softly.

Inside the VFW hall, a band was playing "Riding the Storm Out" to a few stragglers. The door opened, and one of Young's friends, Gordon Love, staggered out on the porch, drunk, singing along with the band. "Riiiidin' the storm out," he sang. "Riiiidin' the storm out . . ." Love walked up and shook my hand. He began to tell stories about Young, about how he had fought with him and drank with him and hunted ducks with him in the woods outside Kansas City.

Then he turned to me and became sober. His face was just a few inches from mine. He said the last memory he had was sitting in Young's van the day before Young was scheduled to return to Iraq.

"I *told* him, man," Love said. "I don't know how I knew it, but [I] *told* him. We were just sitting there in the driveway and I told him, 'I got a feeling, man: don't go. Just don't go.'"

When I looked up from my notes, he was crying.

Picco invited me to Kuwait to get "the full story" behind the kidnapping.

As tempting as it was, the invitation gave me pause. It was hard to know what to expect from a company that would lock its own employee in a shipping container at gunpoint, or shoot policemen and leave them bleeding by the side of the road, or drive through a small Iraqi town, guns blazing. And those were the true stories. There were others out there—stories of beatings and mock executions, even murder—but you didn't know whether they were real or false or something in between. "Steve, whatever you do, do not meet them *anywhere* except in public," one former Crescent operator warned me. I laughed and told him he was being melodramatic, but it stayed with me.

When I told Francis and Nancy I was going back to Kuwait, they asked me to deliver a letter to Picco. It read:

Mr. Picco:

Several months ago we were awakened in the middle of the night by a telephone call from you telling us you were "very close" to getting Jonathon and the other four hostages back. You told us that you were confident that they would be released or captured soon. Although we tried NOT to appear anxious, with a phone call like that it was hard not to be. You told us that some of your sources had seen the men and that they were alive, BUT, **we have not heard from you since!**

We have **PATIENTLY** waited for word and have only heard discouraging news.

We are quite helpless in doing anything to secure their release other than waiting for word from YOU as to what you are doing or have done to secure their release.

What are you planning on doing?

PLEASE think about not only your employees but of the MANY family members and friends back home who trust that you will assist in their safe return to the United States.

We await word from you.

Francis and Nancy Coté

I arrived in Kuwait City with my luggage missing, seven hours late after being rerouted through Amsterdam. It was around 10:00 P.M. when I checked into the Kuwait City Marriott. I called Picco and told him I could take a cab to meet him the next day. He said he would send a car around to pick me up.

Late the next morning, a striking young Indian woman named Reema pulled up in front of the hotel in a white Suburban. The weather was typical for Kuwait—like being on the sun—and the air conditioning was broken in the SUV. It didn't strike me as a major problem, because I remembered that the Crescent villa was near downtown. But then I noticed that we were driving out of the city.

"Where are we going?" I asked.

Reema told me that Crescent had moved into a new villa, in Abu Hassaniyah, about forty-five minutes south of Kuwait City. Soon we were carving our way through the desert on the Fahaheel Expressway. I was drenched and apprehensive. Closing the window turned the truck into an oven. Opening it was like putting a hair dryer two inches from your face. I alternated until we finally arrived at a neighborhood of sandstone houses, just off the highway.

We parked in a dirt lot filled with two dozen Chevy Avalanches coated with dust—the entire Crescent fleet, grounded. One of the trucks was riddled with bullet holes. It turned out it was the Avalanche that Andy Foord had driven during the ambush. I walked inside the villa, jolted back to life by the cool air, and was led down to the basement, where Picco was sitting behind a desk in jeans and a white short-sleeve shirt, accompanied by his deputy, Paul Chapman. Someone brought me a Coke, which I chugged. I then handed Picco the letter from the Cotés, which was sealed inside an envelope. He set it aside without opening it.

Remarkably, Picco then launched into the same spiel he had given the Cotés months earlier, the spiel that led to the anguished letter now sitting on his desk.

"We know the guys are alive," he told me. "We've traced them down to a lot of locations over the past four months, okay? And we know the guys are alive and well—a bit unshaven, but alive and well. Basically we've got somebody working on the inside for us, which is costing us a lot of money, which we don't mind about. We've got some pretty high up people involved in the Iraqi echelons, okay? All I can say is we are extremely close. As long as all the ships sail in the right direction, then we'll get the guys back."

I had to hand it to Picco: with his accent and his smooth certitude, he was mesmerizing. He was a creature of this war, in which words—whether spoken at the U.N Security Council, or the Oval

Office, or the Republican Palace, or some basement in the middle of the Kuwait desert—rarely seemed to match reality. It was as if the people who ran the war believed that if you threw enough words at it, the WMD would materialize, the lights would go on in Baghdad, and Jon Coté would come walking through the door, talking about whipping up his famous jambalaya.

"My main concern is the families," Picco told me.

I started to get angry. If that was so, I asked, how could he have sent out seven of their sons to protect an indefensible convoy? Why did that convoy go north without the Iraqis? Why wasn't the convoy registered? Why was Crescent giving fake military IDs to Iraqis who clearly had a grudge against the company and probably the coalition? Why did Crescent have a domestic violence offender whose employment was prohibited by the U.S. military as its director of security? Why was Picco calling families in the middle of the night and raising their hopes, only to leave them twisting in the wind?

Picco deflected the questions almost cheerfully, like one long wink. At one point, Chapman got up and walked behind me. I tried to discreetly crane my neck, but I couldn't see him. And for that brief moment, I really wondered. I thought about the warning to meet Picco only in public. I thought about what I knew about the company. I thought about how I was sitting in the middle of the Kuwait desert, and no one else knew where I was. Then Chapman suddenly reappeared next to me, and I felt only embarrassed.

Picco said there was still time to get the hostages back. "Nothing will stop me on that. Not if it takes me fucking six months or two years, whatever. Unfortunately, to get them out is not as easy as everybody thinks it is. It's going to take force."

Picco said he was hamstrung, though, because the U.S. military was no longer allowing Crescent to operate freely. He said he believed the company had been unfairly targeted, that Crescent had run into problems with commanders up at Tallil who had wrongly accused the company of possessing illegal weapons.

"We think we're getting fucked because of the kidnapping," Picco said.

And then, the weirdest thing: while Picco was preoccupied by his computer, another Crescent employee slipped me a CD. It happened so fast and so unexpectedly that I wasn't initially sure what to do. I looked up at Picco, who was still gazing at his computer, and stuffed the CD into the computer bag at my feet.

When the interview ended, Picco had a driver take me back to my hotel. I loaded the CD into my laptop as soon as I walked in the door. It opened to reveal dozens of scanned U.S. military documents. In voluminous detail, the documents outlined the military's case against Crescent Security Group. One showed that an initial search of Crescent's living quarters on the base turned up a variety of offensive weapons, including fragmentation grenades, a Bushmaster rifle with its serial number scratched out, and four LAW rockets designed to counter tanks. The contraband also included 143 cans of beer—illegal on a dry U.S. military base—and dozens of samples of the anabolic steroid Dianabol. The military moved on to Crescent's storage containers and found still more banned weapons, including four .50-caliber machine guns, nine more LAWs, and thousands of rounds of ammunition. The military was also curious as to why a small private security company was in possession of M-113 armored personnel carriers.

Crescent tried to argue that the weapons were legal and that the company had been the target of a "vendetta." But the documents included a letter signed by Picco stating: "I accept full responsibility for my company's non-compliance."

Crescent was thus barred not only from Tallil Air Base but from every American base in the country "due to a blatant disregard" for U.S. military regulations, the documents showed.

And that's when it hit me: Crescent was dead.

Without the authority to operate on U.S. bases, the company couldn't work for the coalition. Picco had other businesses. I was told that he trying to move port-a-potties into Lebanon. But he was done in Iraq. His eventful and largely unknown contribution to America's war was over.

10

BLACKRWATEY FOR SPECIAL SECURITY

The "barment" of Crescent Security Group was not a vendetta, as Picco believed. It was part of a U.S. military strategy under the new American commander, General David H. Petraeus, to gain some measure of control over the private army. Petraeus took command of the coalition in early 2007 to implement the surge of American troops and the counterinsurgency doctrine outlined in *U.S. Army Field Manual No. 3-24*, which he coauthored. The manual dedicated just one section to the role of "private contractors from firms providing military-related services." But the implications of their actions ran through the entire 282-page document, which stressed "unity of effort" between the military and civilians and "ethical imperatives" that were critical to win over the local population, the ultimate goal.

Within a month of taking command, Petraeus began issuing "fragos"—fragmentary orders—to rein in the mercs. The first suspended all weapons permits issued to security companies not licensed by the Iraqi Ministry of Interior. Since few companies had bothered to apply for an operating license, they were immediately subject to having their weapons confiscated. The U.S. Army's Joint Area Support Group fanned out across the Green Zone in raids that netted hundreds of unauthorized weapons. It wasn't just the licenses: mercs were prohibited from carrying "offensive weapons" designed specifically for combat, but it was common for the companies to stockpile everything from .50-caliber machine guns and fragmentation grenades to rocket launchers and even the occasional TOW missile. Those were seized, too.

The response of the security companies was to resist, rather than obey, a direct order from the highest military authority in Iraq. They were led by Lawrence Peter, the director of the merc trade group, the Private Security Company Association of Iraq (PSCAI). Peter screamed that Petraeus had overreached. The Interior Ministry was weak and corrupt, he said, its licensing and weapons-registration procedures broken. "We received phone calls from all kind of offices, people who were either contractually involved or their clients, asking us why we were doing what we were doing," a commander involved in the weapons sweeps told me. "There were different levels of complaints to me, my immediate commander and then up the chain of command." In a letter to a U.S. Army lieutenant colonel, Peter suggested that he and the security companies would determine the fitness of the new Iraqi government:

> The Ministry of Interior . . . has yet to prove via standards of performance that it can be a completely trusted partner. . . . Now the MOI wants, as part of its new weapons card process, to obtain biometric data for every weapons card holder. That just is not going to happen for the ex-pats. The Association's position is that giving

such data to the MOI is wrong/WRONG, and puts its membership at risk. So, there are, to put it mildly, ISSUES.

Peter was quick to point out his unique dual role. Although he was PSCAI director, he wrote: "I also wear a Government hat, as a 'Special Category Employee' of the Pentagon."

Peter's complaints about the Interior Ministry were true enough. But that was Iraq. Petraeus soon issued another sharp frago. It began:

Iraq is a sovereign nation, and a major aspect of its sovereignty is the control of weapons and the administration of businesses that operate within its borders, specifically the Private Security Companies. The Iraqis have begun to express serious concerns at the way these companies are operating and many in the government have indicated a desire to ensure that private security companies operate within the law.

Petraeus gave the mercs until the end of 2007 to get their house in order. The frago, for the first time, defined legitimate security companies as "private businesses, properly registered with the Ministry of Interior and Ministry of Trade, that seek to gain commercial benefit and financial profit by providing security services." The requirements became standard language in Defense Department contracts, which meant that no company could be hired without a license and appropriate weapons permits issued by the Iraqi government. It was the strictest regulatory framework imposed on the security industry since the war began.

Except that none of it applied to Blackwater.

With its AH-6 "Little Bird" helicopters flitting around Baghdad, their door gunners training machine guns on the populace, and an array of offensive weapons, Blackwater was already a force unto itself. But its marriage to the State Department shielded it from the kind of regulation that Petraeus wanted to impose. It was exactly as Jack Holly had warned: the devil was in the contracts. Whoever held the contract ruled. In many ways, it was ironic: After four years of a failed war strategy, President Bush had installed a commander who seemed to understand the complexity of Iraq, the need for finesse as well as force. And yet Petraeus was seemingly powerless over a private company that could single-handedly undermine everything he was trying to accomplish. "There is no oversight or coordination of Blackwater by the U.S. military," Holly lamented one day. He felt that Blackwater's actions were contrary to the U.S. mission: "Their aggressive attitude is not what you would say is trying to mitigate disagreements between two societies."

So much for unity of effort. With the State Department's approval, Blackwater had been operating outside Iraqi law since 2005, the last time the company applied for an operating license. During that time, Blackwater's reputation only grew. Some of it was legend; after a while, anytime a merc popped off a round from an SUV, Blackwater would get the blame. But much of it had been documented in U.S. embassy archives, the incidents steadily piling up.

In June 2005, a Blackwater team shot an Iraqi in the chest in Hilla, killing him. The victim's brothers described the man, a father of six, as "an innocent person standing on the side of the road." A State Department email said Blackwater personnel "failed to report the shooting, covered it up, and subsequently were removed from Al-Hilla."

In October 2005, a Blackwater convoy traveling through Mosul encountered a vehicle that turned toward the motorcade. Following a warning, a Blackwater shooter opened fire. A bystander standing in the median was struck in the head by a stray bullet. Blackwater later reported a "probable killing" but never stopped.

In November 2005, a Blackwater convoy traveling to the Ministry of Oil in Baghdad collided with eighteen different vehicles (six on the way, twelve coming back). One merc reported that the Blackwater team leader "admitted giving clear direction to the primary driver to conduct these acts of random negligence for no apparent reason."

Reports of mayhem—the killing of the three civilians that sparked the protests in Kirkuk, another Hilla accident in which a red Opel burst into flames and Blackwater drove on—continued through 2006 until, on Christmas Eve that year, a merc named Andrew J. Moonen staggered drunk from a party inside the Green Zone.

It was close to midnight. Moonen, a former U.S. Army paratrooper from Seattle, wandered through a gate near the Iraqi prime minister's compound in a sector called Little Venice. He was confronted by a guard, Raheem Khalif, a thirty-two-year-old employee of Iraqi vice president Adel Abdul Mahdi. Moonen allegedly shot Khalif three times. Then he fled.

Panicked and reeking of alcohol, Moonen ran to a checkpoint manned by Triple Canopy, according to State Department documents later obtained by the House Committee on Oversight and Government Reform. He told the guards that he had gotten into a firefight with Iraqis who were chasing him and shooting at him. Moonen fumbled with his loaded Glock and one of the guards briefly seized it. Moonen denied that he had been drinking. The Triple Canopy guards handed Moonen back his pistol and escorted him from the checkpoint. Within minutes, a group of armed Iraqis showed up, searching for the Blackwater guard.

The Joint Area Support Group—the Green Zone police force—arrested Moonen at his trailer early Christmas morning. The soldiers took his pistol and gave him a Breathalyzer test. They concluded that he was too intoxicated to be questioned. When Moonen finally sobered up, he told U.S. Army investigators that an Iraqi guard had shot at him and he fired back in self-defense.

Later Christmas day, U.S. ambassador Zalmay Khalilzad received a furious call from Mahdi, the Iraqi vice president. He told Khalilzad that a drunk American wandering in the Green Zone had killed one of his guards. Khalilzad rushed to Mahdi's home, where Khalif's grieving family had gathered. Mahdi demanded that Khalilzad hand over the suspect to Iraqi authorities.

Instead, the next morning, Blackwater and the U.S. embassy shipped Moonen out of Iraq.

His travel arrangements were authorized by the State Department's senior regional security officer, Blackwater's U.S. government supervisor in Iraq. A Blackwater convoy ferried Moonen to Baghdad International Airport, where the security company was able to blow through checkpoints because of its U.S. government affiliation. Moonen flew on to Amman, then, apparently, home.

Once Moonen was gone, State Department officials scrambled to contain the shooting. A criminal investigation did not appear to be on the table. U.S. officials tried to calibrate apologies and pay-offs.

"Will you be following in up [*sic*] Blackwater to do all possible to assure that a sizeable compensation is forthcoming?" the embassy's chargé d'affaires wrote Randall Bennett, the senior regional security officer, in an email. "If we are to avoid this whole thing becoming even worse, I think a prompt pledge and apology—even if they want to claim it was accidental—would be the best way to assure the Iraqis don't take steps, such as telling Blackwater that they are no longer able to work in Iraq."

The chargé d'affaires first proposed a $250,000 payment to the victim's family, then $100,000. A diplomatic security official objected to such "crazy sums." The official was concerned it might encourage Iraqis to commit suicide by merc.

"This could result in incidents with people trying to get killed by our guys to financially guarantee their family's future," the official wrote.

> In the past we have paid out $2,500 for a disabled car, and in one instance $5,000 for a guy in a car and a wound to the leg. We don't want to get into too much here at post but we feel that a sum nearer to $15k–$25k or so would be more appropriate. Randall would like for BW management back there to work with you guys and perhaps DS legal to determine an appropriate figure keeping in mind the precedent it might set and the legal implications. BW is already working on a letter of condolences to go along with the compensation package.

The State Department eventually settled on the low end of the scale. Blackwater paid the dead guard's family $15,000. Moonen, it turned out, was fined almost exactly the same amount by the company: $14,697.00.

The fine came in the form of forfeited compensation. If the whole thing hadn't been so tragic, the breakdown of what Moonen lost could have been drawn up for a *Saturday Night Live* sketch:

Return airfare: $1,630
Completion bonus: $7,067
Fourth of July bonus: $3,000
Christmas bonus: $3,000.

Moonen had lost his Christmas bonus for allegedly shooting someone on Christmas Eve.

An Iraqi television network erroneously reported that a drunken American soldier, not a Blackwater mercenary, had gunned down Mahdi's guard. Blackwater apparently saw this as a ray of hope.

"Thought you might want to see this," a Blackwater employee wrote, forwarding the report to a supervisor. "At least the ID of the shooter will take the heat off us."

Two months later, Moonen got a job in Kuwait with Combat Support Associates, which operated under a Defense Department contract. The company, which provides security on U.S. military bases, later said it was unaware of Moonen's checkered performance history.

THE SAME MONTH AS THE GREEN ZONE SHOOTING, A U.S. Army veteran and counterterrorism specialist named Matthew Degn arrived in Baghdad as a senior policy adviser to the Interior Ministry. Degn, the program director for intelligence studies at American Military University, also worked as a consultant with companies such as SYColeman and MPRI, both of which had U.S. government contracts.

Degn, thirty-eight, lived in the Seattle area with his wife and five children. He was slender, with close-cropped red hair and a pleasant, clear-eyed demeanor, almost as if a street-savvy Ron

Howard had been dropped into the middle of Iraq. MPRI installed Degn on the seventh floor of the Interior Ministry, along with a team of U.S. military advisers. It was the ultimate consulting challenge. The Ministry of Interior, the hub for Iraq's new security forces, was like a fortress: checkpoints ran from the street all the way to the front door of many offices. Everyone, including the ministers, was armed. The building was riven by Shiite militias, including the Mahdi Army, which had fought the Americans off and on since 2004. "Every time we walked into the building we were in battle formation, armed to the teeth; a few soldiers even had grenades on their chests, as if we were going to war," said Degn. "But you were going in as a friend. We'd say, 'Hi, how you doin'?' to everyone we saw, but we never had our hands far from our weapons."

Degn advised the new intelligence directorate, headed by Major General Hussein Kamal, a tough, silver-haired Kurd. The two soon developed a close working relationship. The directorate's responsibilities included regulation of the exploding private security industry. As research for his new assignment, Degn read over the existing laws, including CPA Order 17. He came to section 4, paragraph 3: "Contractors shall be immune from Iraqi legal process with respect to acts performed by them pursuant to the terms and conditions of a Contract or any sub-contract thereto."

"You have no power," Degn told Kamal bluntly.

But the futility went well beyond permissive laws. The Intelligence Directorate, at best, was a nascent government agency with limited resources trying to regulate a billion-dollar industry. The private security office was a glorified cubicle. Licensed companies were listed on a smudged dry-erase board. The office was headed by a slight, intense young man known only as Colonel Ahmed to protect his identity for security reasons. In a corner of the room, beneath a clouded window, was a single bed where Colonel Ahmed often slept when it was too dangerous for him to leave the building.

The entire operation was suffused with a feeling of seething frustration, much of it directed at Blackwater. It wasn't only that the company, like many, operated recklessly and outside the law. It was Blackwater's smirking defiance, the total impunity the company appeared to enjoy. "The Iraqis despised them, because they were un-touchable," said Degn. "They were above the law." Sometimes, Blackwater's Little Bird helicopters buzzed the Interior Ministry roof, "almost like they were saying, 'Look, we can fly anywhere we want,'" said Degn.

Kamal told me he had four open cases (not including Moonen) in which Blackwater allegedly shot Iraqi civilians. When I asked him if he could describe the cases more specifically, he shrugged. "It's killing," he said. "No matter how you slice it, it's killing." But Kamal said he had neither the resources nor the authority to inves-tigate. "These cases will remain open until we find some kind of le-gal remedy," he said. "I imagine they have their own justifications for what happened, but the law should be applied. Order 17 has given them complete immunity."

One of the incidents occurred on February 7, 2007, just six weeks after Moonen allegedly shot the vice president's guard. A convoy of four SUVs filled with twenty Blackwater guards had escorted a U.S. diplomat to the Iraqi Justice Ministry, about a quarter mile from the Green Zone.

While the diplomat was meeting with Iraqi officials, Blackwater snipers took up positions on the Justice Ministry roof. Across the street was another government building: the Iraqi Media Network, one of the most prominent symbols of the new Iraq. Launched with the help of the U.S. government, the Iraqi Media Network operated newspapers, radio stations, and a flagship TV station called al-Iraqiya. The network had replaced the state-run media group that once dispensed propaganda for Saddam Hussein.

Two guard towers, one flying the Iraqi flag, overlooked the Iraqi Media Network's rear gate, which faced the Justice Ministry. Be-hind the towers, farther back inside the compound, was an aban-doned building where two security guards stood on a third-floor balcony. The balcony overlooked a traffic circle called King Faisal Square that separated the network from the eleven-story Justice Ministry. In the middle of the circle was a statue of the former Iraqi king on horseback.

That morning, twenty-three-year-old Nabras Mohammed Hadi

was sitting in a chair on a corner of the balcony. He wore dark green camouflage and held an AK-47. About twenty feet to his left, another security guard manned a belt-fed machine gun. Both were visible to the Blackwater snipers, about 450 feet away on the Justice Ministry roof.

Hadi had recently moved into the media network compound because insurgents threatened to kill him unless he gave up his government job. "He was the oldest son, and he supported his family," said Mohammed Adel Ali, one of Hadi's friends and a fellow guard. "He told me, 'If I quit, my family will be finished.'" Hadi sneaked home once a month to deliver his paycheck. It came to $231, less than half of what the Blackwater guards earned in a day.

Just before noon, a commotion broke out in the traffic circle between the two government buildings. "The problem started because some people wanted to park their car there," said Adel Saadi, another guard for the media network, who was standing near the gate. "Our guards didn't allow them, because we were worried about car bombs. But they kept insisting." Hadi stood up with his rifle. "I saw Nabras and he was yelling for people to move away," Saadi said. "He was holding his rifle. And then I saw smoke come from his body, and he fell."

"Nabras is hit! Nabras is hit!" yelled Ali, who also heard the shot. He and Saadi ran up the stairs with several other guards. When the guards reached the third floor, they, too, came under attack. At least three bullets lodged into the wall behind them. The guards crawled toward Hadi, shielded by a three-foot wall. They found him bleeding from his head next to his rusty chair and hundreds of cigarette butts piled up in the corner.

Azhar Abdullah al-Maliki, a thirty-one-year-old guard, raised his head above the wall as he tried to move Hadi. Another shot rang out and Maliki fell next to his friend. "People were yelling, 'Azhar, what's wrong? What's wrong?'" said Hussein Abdul Hassan, the head of the guard team. "When they went to move him, they saw the blood spurting from his neck." The guards quickly withdrew. They were replaced by an Iraqi army company that controlled the neighborhood of Salihiya. When the soldiers reached the balcony, Hadi was dead. Maliki was evacuated to a nearby hospital and pronounced dead of a gunshot wound to the neck at 2:00 P.M.

It was pandemonium inside the Iraqi Media Network. Journalists hid beneath their desks or ran for their lives. No one could figure out where the shots were coming from. People assumed that it was insurgents firing from the rooftops of Salihiya or even from inside the compound.

The Iraqi army commander, Captain Ahmed Thamir Abood, received a frantic call from the Justice Ministry. He was told that an American security team was firing from the roof. Abood rushed over in a Humvee with one of his lieutenants. The Blackwater team was gathered in the traffic circle, preparing to leave. Most of the men wore goatees and flak jackets and had tiny communication devices in their ears.

Abood, a short, stocky man who spoke halting English, advanced toward a Westerner wearing a blue blazer and khakis, presumably the diplomat in charge. A Blackwater operator stepped in front of him and refused to let the Iraqi captain pass.

"I want to speak with the guy who is in charge of this unit," Abood demanded.

The mercs began toying with him.

"He's in charge," said one, pointing at one of his colleagues.

"No, *he's* in charge," said another.

"They didn't care what I was saying," Abood told me.

The mercs climbed in their SUVs along with the diplomat, dropped smoke grenades in the traffic circle, and sped off toward the Green Zone in a green and orange cloud.

Minutes later, the Iraqi Media Network guards reassembled and noticed that a third guard was missing: Sabah Salman, a forty-year-old diabetic who took care of the weapons. Salman was also known as Abu Sajad. He cared for seventeen children: eight of his own, nine from a brother who was killed during the Iran-Iraq War.

The guards returned to the balcony and found Abu Sajad dead from a gunshot wound to the side. They said it appeared that he had gone up to the balcony to retrieve the weapons, only to be shot himself.

"He went up there without a gun," said Thair Salaam, one of the Iraqi Media Network's guards. "I don't know why they shot him."

That night, details of the bloody incident were broadcast on al-Iraqiya, which reached more than twenty-three million Iraqis. The network reported that Blackwater had killed three of its employees without any apparent provocation—in cold blood, essentially.

Over the next few weeks, the network conducted an internal investigation, which concluded: "On February 7, members of Blackwater opened fire from the roof of the Ministry of Justice building, intentionally and without provocation, shooting three members of our security team which led to their deaths while they were on duty inside the network complex."

A Salihiya police investigator, misspelling Blackwater, wrote in a report:

By collecting information and questioning the Ministry of Justice guards, it became clear that the armed personnel who came to the Ministry of Justice, who were using special security vehicles and caused the incident and killed guards of the Iraqi Media Network, they are working with the company of BlackRwatey for special security.

The police report described the shootings as "an act of terrorism."

I interviewed eight people who responded to the shootings that day, five others who were in the compound and at least a dozen more who were familiar with the case. Not one said the slain guards had fired on Blackwater.

The State Department did not interview a single witness except members of the Blackwater team. Neither U.S. embassy officials nor Blackwater representatives returned to the Iraqi Media Network to investigate, despite its long-standing relationship with the U.S. government and the fact that the media network compound was a quarter mile from the Green Zone.

The U.S. embassy Regional Security Office nevertheless concluded that Blackwater's actions "fell within approved rules governing the use of force," a diplomatic security official told me.

No U.S. official would speak for the record. A Blackwater spokeswoman, Anne E. Tyrrell, told me the team came under "precision small-arms fire" and fired back with "well-aimed shots." She refused to provide more information. "This was absolutely a provoked incident," Tyrrell said.

The Iraqi Media Network gave each family one million Iraqi dinars, or $812, to help with the burials. The network's legal adviser, Faisal Rahdi, told me the network tried to sue Blackwater to get more money for the relatives of the victims.

An Iraqi judge rejected the case, he said, citing the company's legal immunity under CPA Order 17.

"America doesn't need more enemies in Iraq," Rahdi said. "When someone loses one of his relatives or one of his friends gets killed by an American and that American is protected—untouchable—because of a law that was set by an American, this definitely will create new enemies for the United States."

THREE MONTHS AFTER THE AL-IRAQIYA SHOOTING, IN May, I got an email in California from a U.S. military adviser who worked inside the Interior Ministry. He wrote that Blackwater had been involved in two more shootings. He wanted me to know because the Iraqis he worked with were upset.

I contacted Matt Degn in Baghdad. It was much worse than that, he told me. After the second shooting, the U.S. military had to evacuate him from the Interior Ministry, fearing retaliation against Americans. The Interior Ministry had become "a powder keg" because of Blackwater, said Degn. He added angrily, "The American force here is being undermined by cowboys."

In the first incident, a Blackwater team had been ambushed in downtown Baghdad. A furious gun battle involving Blackwater, insurgents, U.S. and Iraqi troops, and Apache attack helicopters erupted near the Amanat, the city's municipal headquarters. Several people were killed. Interior Ministry officials heard the gunfire and the explosions and rushed up to the roof, where they had a perfect view of the city center going up in flames. Although it was Blackwater that had been attacked, the Iraqis, quick to believe the worst, blamed the company for the latest desecration of the storied capital.

The very next day, a Blackwater team was passing in front of the Interior Ministry when a man driving an unmarked sedan pulled out of a nearby gas station. One of the Blackwater shooters opened fire, killing the driver. Some witnesses told Iraqi officials that the shooting was unprovoked. There was one rumor that the driver had fallen out of the car, wounded, and that Blackwater had executed him in the street with two shots to the back of the head. There was no evidence to substantiate the rumor, but by then it was like a gathering bonfire in which fact and fiction all went up in flames.

Shortly after the shooting, the Blackwater team tried to return to the Green Zone. Dozens of Interior Ministry commandos descended on the convoy. The commandos leaped out of their trucks and trained their AK-47s on the surrounded Blackwater mercs, who responded in kind. "It was a Mexican standoff" in the middle of Baghdad, an American military official told me. "Everyone was just pointing their weapons and waiting for someone to fire."

The implications if someone had pulled the trigger—the fallout of such a bloodbath—were incalculable. But just then, a U.S. military convoy happened upon the scene. An American army colonel leaped out of his Humvee and persuaded everyone to lower their weapons. Soon a State Department official arrived and escorted Blackwater back to the Green Zone. The mercs refused to divulge their names or any details about the shooting to the Iraqis. By the time I contacted the U.S. embassy the following day, an official told me that a preliminary report had already determined that Blackwater responded appropriately. "When the progression of signals didn't slow the driver down, they opened fire at the sedan's grille, and when it continued, they fired into the windshield," the official said.

It was the stock explanation for every shooting: warning signals, escalation of force, targeted rounds. That explanation was applied to negligent women, distracted old men, wayward children, anyone who got in the line of fire. Every merc, it seemed, followed the rules for the use of force exactly as they were drawn up by Lawrence T. Peter, each and every time. When I asked the U.S. official, who of course refused to be identified, how the embassy determined in just one day that Blackwater had shot and killed a man justifiably, he grew testy.

"I'm not going to go into the detail," he said.

Why not? I asked.

"Because I don't feel it's necessary to do so."

As for the Americans who worked every day inside the Iraqi Interior Ministry, they found that Blackwater had changed their lives dramatically. "After that day, people looked at us a little different; you were always wondering, 'Is that guy thinking about *killing* me?'" said Degn. "There was a palpable feeling on the seventh floor that something monumental had happened, that we were in deep water. No one left the office alone or unarmed. And we felt like we weren't getting anything done. We were going up and coming down, but they weren't listening to a thing we were saying."

Kamal and Colonel Ahmed were ballistic that Blackwater could shoot an Iraqi right under their noses and they were powerless to do anything. "It had happened right on the Interior Ministry grounds. That's what made it so explosive," said Degn.

Kamal, as head of the intelligence directorate, attended weekly meetings of the National Intelligence Committee. The meetings were headed by Mowaffak al-Rubaie, Iraq's national security adviser, and attended by senior U.S. and Iraqi officials, including Brigadier General David B. Lacquement, the army's deputy chief of staff for intelligence. At the June 6, 2007, meeting, less than two weeks after the Interior Ministry shooting, Kamal told U.S. officials that they needed to crack down on Blackwater, according to minutes of the meeting. U.S. military officials responded that the company operated under State Department authority and was outside of their control. When I tried to contact Lacquement, his spokesman told me that for "reasons of classification and security" he could not comment on whether Blackwater was discussed at that meeting or any other.

It was now months into the troop surge. Petraeus had inserted American units directly into Baghdad neighborhoods, where they could operate more effectively. The military was co-opting former Sunni insurgents with cash and other resources. For the first time, violence seemed to be ebbing in a sustained way. The plan was straight out of Petraeus' own playbook. His goal was to get the violence down and create enough space to achieve a political solution in Iraq. The enemy was not only insurgents and militias but also allies who were out of step with the coalition. "When their actions are allowed to adversely affect each other, the populace suffers and insurgents identify grievances to exploit," Petraeus had written in *U.S. Army Field Manual No. 3-24.*

And yet Blackwater remained a wild card.

Matt Degn's own frustration was growing. Every day, he went to the Interior Ministry, one of the most dangerous assignments in all of Baghdad, only to see his work undermined by a company that had nothing to do with him. In some ways he felt conflicted. Degn respected Blackwater's ruthless efficiency; the company kept its clients safe, come hell or high water. Degn also understood the company's reluctance to deal with the Interior Ministry and thus the militias. He understood the ambiguities and complexity of the country in which they operated. But he feared that Blackwater did not.

"It's like one step forward, eight steps backward," Degn lamented.

He and Kamal sent memos to the U.S. embassy and the military chain of command, trying to get the Americans' attention that Blackwater was out of control. "I thought it was a huge issue and one which could likely lead to a disaster," said Degn. But he and Kamal never got a response.

"I mean, how many of these incidents does it take before you're finally aware?" said Degn.

On September 16, three months after Kamal's plea to the National Intelligence Committee, Ahmed Hathem al-Rubaie, a medical student, was driving his mother, Mahasin, in the family's white Opel sedan. They were running errands in western Baghdad. They dropped off Ahmed's father, Jawad, a pathologist, near the hospital where he worked. They picked up a college application for his sister Miriam. They were driving through Mansour, a once-affluent neighborhood of cafés and retail stores, long worn down by the war.

It was just after noon. About a mile away, Blackwater Chief of Mission (COM) Team 4 had escorted a U.S. Agency for International Development (USAID) official named Kerry Pelzman to a planning meeting for Izdihar, a joint U.S.-Iraqi infrastructure project. The meeting was at a secure compound about two miles from the Green Zone. While Pelzman was inside, a car bomb exploded about two hundred yards from the entrance to the building. Pelzman wasn't injured, but the Blackwater team requested backup, fearing a larger attack. Tactical Support Team 22 was dispatched from the Green Zone. The two teams evacuated Pelzman while a third Blackwater unit, Tactical Support Team 23, was sent out to provide support.

The third Blackwater convoy, consisting of four armored vehicles and approximately twenty shooters, arrived at a Mansour traffic circle called Nisoor Square. Iraqi policemen scrambled to halt traffic as the convoy approached. It was always dicey; the mercs often drove "counterflow" and people couldn't get out of the way. Ahmed, driving the white Opel with his mother in the passenger seat, approached the circle just as the Blackwater convoy arrived. He had not yet entered Nisoor Square when, suddenly, a Blackwater gunner opened fire with a belt-fed machine gun. The shots were aimed directly at Ahmed.

"The bullet went through the windshield and split his head open," said Sarhan Thiab, a traffic cop who was in the square that day.

Another officer, Ali Khalaf Salman, ran toward the Opel. When he reached the driver's-side window, he saw Mahasin, hysterical and soaked in Ahmed's blood, cradling her dead son.

"My son! My son! Help me! Help me!" she screamed.

Mahasin was a forty-six-year-old allergist. Hers was a family of medical practitioners in a country where doctors had fled in droves. Mahasin's brother-in-law Raad was a dialysis specialist. Her son Ahmed had spent three years studying to be a surgeon. But medicine couldn't help them now.

The Opel kept rolling toward the square, probably because

Ahmed's foot stayed on the accelerator after he was shot. Khalaf, the traffic cop, raised his left arm in an attempt to stop Blackwater from shooting. Thiab did the same. "I tried to use hand signals to make the Blackwater people understand that the car was moving on its own and we were trying to stop it," he said. "We were trying to get the woman out but we had to run for cover."

The Blackwater guards unleashed another barrage of gunfire, including, reportedly, a rocket-propelled grenade. "I saw parts of the woman's head flying in front of me, blow up," said Thiab. The Opel burst into flames.

Nisoor Square erupted in gunfire, the Blackwater team firing in all directions. At least three witnesses reported that Blackwater's Little Bird helicopters also fired down into the square. Some Iraqi civilians were shot as they tried to flee; two cars were found with their rear windshields shot out but the front windshields intact. "They were shooting from four cars," said Ahmed Ali Jassim, a nineteen-year-old maintenance worker. "People were fleeing, but where could they go?" Hussam Abdul Rahman, a twenty-five-year-old traffic cop, said, "Whoever stepped out of his car was shot at immediately."

Mohammed Hafiz, the thirty-seven-year-old owner of an auto parts business, was driving behind Ahmed and Mahasin. "We were six persons in the car: me, my son, my sister and her three sons. The four children were in the backseat."

Hafiz said about thirty bullets struck his car. One struck his ten-year-old son, Ali. "When the shooting started, I told everybody to get their heads down. I could hear the children screaming in fear. When the shooting stopped, I raised my head and heard my nephew shouting at me, 'Ali is dead, Ali is dead.' When I held him, his head was badly wounded, but his heart was still beating. I thought there was a chance and I rushed him to the hospital. The doctor told me that he was clinically dead and the chance of his survival was very slim. One hour later, Ali died."

Three weeks after the massacre, Hafiz, weeping as he described the ordeal to the Associated Press, said neighborhood kids, unaware his son had died, still came around to see if Ali could come out and play.

At some point, at least one of the Blackwater guards drew a weapon on his own colleagues, shouting, "Stop shooting!" and "No! No!" an American familiar with the investigation later told me. But still it went on, the shooting continuing even as Blackwater was exiting the traffic circle, witnesses said.

In all, seventeen Iraqis were killed. Many were poor or middle class. Their belongings piled up at Yarmouk Hospital: cheap watches, scuffed shoes, slim billfolds, a bag of vegetables. Mahasin's husband, Jawad, identified his wife by her dental bridge, his son by a piece of one of his shoes. Their charred bodies had been stuffed into black plastic bags. "My wife was a distinguished woman, a talented doctor," Jawad said. "My son was a gentle and cooperative person. He was on his way to becoming a doctor. They died while they were fasting in the holy month of Ramadan. They died as innocent people. I ask God's mercy on them."

Later that afternoon, the U.S. embassy put together a "spot report," an initial accounting of the incident. The report was stamped SENSITIVE BUT UNCLASSIFIED and was printed on Bureau of Diplomatic Security stationery beneath the State Department and Diplomatic Security Service seals. The report made it clear that Blackwater had come under fire and was not at fault: "Estimated 8–10 persons fired from multiple nearby locations, with some aggressors dressed in civilian apparel and others in Iraqi Police uniforms. The team returned defensive fire. . . ."

The spot report was drafted by Darren Hanner, identified as the Regional Security Office watch officer. It was approved by Ricardo Colon, identified as the embassy's deputy regional security officer.

It turned out that Darren Hanner was a Blackwater employee. The initial investigation into the shooting was thus conducted by Blackwater and written up as a State Department report. It contained not a single word about casualties, except to say: "There were no injuries to COM [chief of mission] personnel."

The episode almost certainly would have been buried but for the sheer number of people whom Blackwater killed and the volcanic anger that had built up inside the Iraqi government.

Within minutes of the shooting, soldiers from the U.S. Army's

First Cavalry Division arrived at Nisoor Square. The soldiers found the traffic circle flooded with Iraqi security personnel, including top generals. The Iraqi police were evacuating victims. The bodies of Ahmed and Mahasin were still in the charred white Opel.

Despite Blackwater's claim that it had been attacked by people dressed in civilian clothes and Iraqi police uniforms, the Americans could not find shell casings from AK-47 rifles commonly used by insurgents and police. The street, however, was littered with brass from American-made weapons: 5.56mm shell casings from M4 assault rifles, M240 Bravo machine-gun casings, M203 grenade launcher casings, and dunnage from stun grenades. There were more than forty bullet holes in Ahmed and Mahasin's car.

The First Cavalry put together a report based on observations from Nisoor Square, eyewitness accounts, and interviews with Iraqi police. Sudarsan Raghavan, the Baghdad bureau chief for the *Washington Post*, was permitted to view a storyboard that was forwarded to senior U.S. commanders. The U.S. military report was unequivocal and damning. It concluded that there was "no enemy activity involved" and described the shootings as an unprovoked "criminal event."

"I did not see anything that indicated they were fired upon," Lieutenant Colonel Mike Tarsa, the battalion commander whose soldiers gathered the information, told Raghavan.

The Iraqi government responded forcefully.

"We will not allow Iraqis to be killed in cold blood," said Prime Minister Nouri al-Maliki.

An Interior Ministry spokesman announced that the Iraqi government had revoked Blackwater's operating license. The company was summarily banned from Iraq, he said, and the government intended to prosecute all participants in the massacre.

It made for stunning headlines: US CONTRACTOR BANNED BY IRAQ OVER SHOOTINGS, read the front page of the *New York Times*.

IRAQ BANS SECURITY CONTRACTOR; BLACKWATER FAULTED IN BAGHDAD KILLINGS, read the front page of the *Washington Post*.

And, for awhile, people believed it.

In Washington, there were hearings. The House Committee on

Oversight and Government Reform blew up the wisdom of Jack Holly as a prop:

THERE IS NO OVERSIGHT OR COORDINATION
OF BLACKWATER BY THE U.S. MILITARY.

Jack Holly
Director of Logistics
U.S. Army Corps of Engineers

"Blackwater will be held accountable today!" the committee chairman, Henry A. Waxman, said as the hearing began.

Erik Prince, the company's thirty-eight-year-old founder, raised his right hand and swore to tell the truth. He wore his blond hair in a fresh military cut and tapped his pen during the questioning. When Prince was asked to concede that Blackwater had killed innocent civilians, he responded, "No, sir, I disagree with that. . . . There could be ricochets, there are traffic accidents. Yes. This is war." He told the committee, "I believe we acted appropriately at all times." He was so chastened by the experience he pocketed his MR. PRINCE nameplate as a souvenir before heading out the door.

The FBI sent a team of investigators to Baghdad, although no one knew what law, if any, might be applied. A joint U.S.-Iraqi commission on private security was established, and the State Department and the U.S. military began work on an agreement to cooperate more effectively.

But within three days of the Iraqi government's "ban," Blackwater's freshly painted trucks rolled out of the Green Zone.

The reality was that Blackwater didn't have an operating license for the Iraqi government to revoke. And the company couldn't be prosecuted in Iraq because of CPA Order 17.

The only authority that could keep Blackwater from working was its employer, the U.S. Department of State.

And without Blackwater, the State Department itself would have been cancelled in Iraq.

FAITH THAT LOOKS THROUGH DEATH

Seventeen people in fifteen minutes. "You gotta work hard to kill that many people, *really* hard," a friend wrote me later. He was disgusted. A former marine, he had come to Iraq in 2004 to make money and support the war. "I knew I was risking my ass but like others I was wanting to reconnect with that period in my life when men were honorable and we had esprit de corps," he wrote. "Undeniably the pay was a closer, but I wouldn't have done it without the other elements." Now they were all paid killers; Blackwater had pretty much taken care of that. "It fucking infuriates me," wrote my friend, who worked for another company, "especially knowing the level of ass-clownery that goes on with them and how they get away with it." For all the promises that were never realized—Blackwater's banishment from Iraq, the prosecution of the shooters in

Baghdad—the words "Nisoor Square" had entered the war's lexicon and acquired their own dark meaning, like Abu Ghraib. The massacre came to symbolize the impunity and violence of a largely invisible war that had somehow embedded itself in the Iraq conflict.

People tried to get their heads around it, but by then it was too big. Two weeks after the shootings, Waxman's office released a memo reporting that Blackwater had been involved in at least 195 "escalation of force" incidents since 2005. "This is an average of 1.4 shooting incidents a week," the memo reported. Prince, during his testimony, tried to put the numbers in perspective. "Since 2005, we have conducted in excess of 16,000 missions in Iraq and had 195 incidences of weapons discharge." That was less than 1 percent of all missions, he noted to the *Military Times*. "So the idea that the guys are trigger happy and shooting up the place is just grossly inaccurate."

What Waxman and Prince failed to mention, and perhaps failed to realize, was that it didn't matter how you spun the statistics, because in the end they were meaningless. No one had any idea how much shooting was really going on. The State Department and the military technically required companies to report each time they discharged a weapon, but whether they did so was up to them. Two security company officials estimated that just 15 percent of all shooting incidents were actually reported. One former Blackwater operator told me that his team averaged four or five shootings a week, nearly four times the rate Prince quoted for the entire company. More important, no one knew how many Iraqis got in the way. "We shot to kill and didn't stop to check a pulse," another former Blackwater operator noted.

Even the U.S. officials who compiled the data knew that it was a charade. "In my civilian life, if I were doing a process analysis on this thing, I would say, 'You know what, these numbers are suspect in terms of which companies are having the most incidents and what type of incidents they are,'" Major Kent Lightner, an army reservist who oversaw the monitoring system for the U.S. Army Corps of Engineers, told me. It was a statement of fact, not a frank admission. Most of the nearly three dozen companies on Defense

Department contracts didn't report *any* shooting incidents. Lightner's predecessor, Colonel Timothy Clapp, had arrived at the same conclusion: "In their contracts, it says they are supposed to report, but whether they do or not is up to them."

Every private security contract was like a rock: once you lifted it up, you never knew what you'd find.

Late one afternoon, just three weeks after Nisoor Square, an obscure Australian company called Unity Resources Group fired two dozen rounds into a white Oldsmobile on Karrada Street, a six-lane boulevard in Baghdad. Inside the vehicle were two Iraqi women, both Christians, on their way home from work.

"You won't find a head," a policeman told a reporter after the shooting. "The brain is scattered on the ground."

A Unity official in Dubai said the company regretted killing the two women. He quickly added the now-familiar merc mantra: the car had "failed to stop despite escalation of warnings."

Unity was under contract to protect employees who worked for a big North Carolina research firm called RTI International. RTI, in turn, held a $480-million contract with USAID to promote democracy in Iraq. USAID was affiliated with the State Department, but when I called a U.S. government spokeswoman, I was sent back to RTI. "USAID does not direct the security arrangements of its contractors," she informed me.

Internally, Unity had recorded thirty-eight shooting incidents over the previous two years while protecting RTI employees, I learned. On each occasion, Unity investigated itself, with predictable results: all thirty-eight shootings were deemed justified. One had occurred just three and a half months before Unity killed the two women, on almost the exact same spot, about 250 yards up Karrada Street. Witnesses said Unity gunners raked a white van with automatic weapons fire at 7:00 A.M. in front of a kindergarten. The driver emerged with his left hand attached only by skin.

Unity refused to answer questions about the incident, and when I contacted RTI, a spokesman first denied that it occurred. Later, when presented with witnesses, RTI discovered that, in fact, it had

internal records describing the shooting. Those records, a spokesman admitted, revealed that Unity had expunged all references to
casualties.

Karrada Street was like Upper Broadway in Manhattan. The
wide boulevard was crammed with restaurants and appliance stores,
social clubs and ice cream parlors, video emporiums and mosques. I
walked around the neighborhood, listening to local merchants describe how it had been turned into a shooting gallery for men in
SUVs. "Whoever gets near them, they will shoot them," said Sirry
Abdul Latif, a fifty-year-old furniture shop employee. Seven people
described yet another recent shooting in which armed civilians had
killed the driver of a Toyota sedan. No one was able to identify the
company, which sped away, but it happened on the same 250-yard
stretch of Karrada Street where the Unity shootings occurred.

Who exactly controlled Unity Resources Group?

I could never figure it out.

It wasn't the State Department or USAID. It wasn't the Iraqi
government or the Australian government. When I asked Kent
Lightner if the company reported to the U.S. military, he started to
say, "The real issue is that [Unity] is a company that is not a DoD
contractor, so whether they reported incidents or not is . . ."

Lightner didn't finish the sentence.

"I don't know, I'm walking the line on that one," he said finally.

To me, the bottom line was always the same, though. Just nine
days after the two women were killed, mercs employed by Erinys,
the British company, blasted an orange and white taxi near Kirkuk,
wounding the driver and two passengers.

At first everyone blamed Blackwater, which by then was routine.
Then Erinys took responsibility, adding quickly, of course, that the
taxi had failed to heed warning signals.

But it never mattered to the people who got shot.

"The Americans are responsible for this act by this security company," said a twenty-four-year-old woman who was hit in the
shoulder while in the backseat of the cab. She called the shooters
"wild monsters, criminals, and killers."

It was the Americans who were to blame, the woman said, "Because they are supporting them."

IN OCTOBER 2007, THE DEA AGENT WHO BECAME known as Joe from Basra touched down in southern Iraq's largest city to begin his search for the Crescent hostages.

The case and the men were fading into memory. The three videos, the last of which surfaced just after New Year's, had been followed by months of unbroken silence. The U.S. government and the families could only speculate as to why. After receiving the second video, Ahmad Chalabi had refused to contact the Americans, much less serve as an intermediary, cutting off one potential line of communication. The FBI, meanwhile, continued to investigate the case from a distance. The agency was still rotating agents in and out of Iraq every ninety days, making it almost impossible to gain traction. The case was still being run out of Baghdad, with oversight from the Washington, DC, field office.

Joe from Basra was in his midforties, five foot ten and athletic, with a square jaw, rugged good looks, and slightly receding charcoal gray hair that he combed from left to right with gel. In civilian life, he was formal: he wore ties that seemed to strangle him and rarely removed his sports coat. But his specialty was undercover work. He would disappear for months, transforming himself to blend into the underworld of narcotics trafficking. Joe's wife was also a DEA agent. They lived in Southern California and didn't have kids. In many ways, that made him perfect for the assignment: he had nothing to stop him from planting himself in Basra until he located the Crescent hostages, dead or alive.

Joe had never worked a kidnapping case, so his strategy was to pursue the hostages as he would six kilos of cocaine. Someone, he believed, would want to sell, negotiate, or at least discuss their possible acquisition. He started from that premise.

"If you're gonna be in the game, you gotta be near the field," he said as he headed south. It was a philosophy that the FBI had failed to embrace for eleven months. He embedded himself at the Basra airport, surrounded by the British military and protected by a U.S. Special Forces team. He spent the next four months working the case continuously, developing contacts through the Iraqi government, the Brits, the FBI, anyone who might have information.

Tips began to pile up. But in the echo chamber of Iraq, it was hard to know who or what to believe. There were layers of contacts: one guy who knew another guy, who knew another guy, and so on. One afternoon, a contact informed Joe that the Crescent hostages had been located. Joe had heard such claims before. He had told his contacts that he needed proof: articles of clothing, photographs, ID cards, evidence that he could confirm. The contact told him he would acquire the proof and report back. Weeks went by. In early February, Joe traveled up to Baghdad to update the FBI and other U.S. government officials on the case. While he was there, he received a call on his cell phone. The contact told him that a man was on his way to the Basra airfield to deliver the proof Joe had requested.

It was February 11, 2008—Jon Coté's twenty-fifth birthday. Joe called down to Basra to inform his Special Forces team that the contact was on his way.

The man arrived at the airport gate carrying a small plastic bag. He was escorted into the highly fortified compound, where the bag was then presented to the Special Forces team leader. The team leader, wearing plastic gloves, opened the bag carefully and felt a chill run through him.

Inside the plastic bag were five severed fingers. The man told him that they belonged to the missing Crescent hostages. The fingers had been separated, each in its own Ziploc bag. They were caked with dirt and badly decomposed. The fingers were only partially intact, more fingertips than fingers.

The team leader called Joe.

"I wish you were down here right now," he told him. "Here's what we think we have."

As macabre as the development was, it was the biggest break in the case yet. The fingers would have to be analyzed to confirm that they belonged to the missing men. The State Department dispatched a helicopter to Basra to retrieve the grisly package. Joe met the flight at LZ Washington, the Green Zone helipad, with an FBI forensics team. To avoid compromising the evidence, he put on gloves and took possession of the fingers without opening the bag. The fingers were sent to the Combat Support Hospital in the Green Zone with orders to stabilize the package for the flight to the United States, where the fingers were to be examined by forensics experts at Quantico.

Because of their deteriorated condition, only three of the five fingers elicited fingerprints. The analysis at Quantico showed that the fingers belonged to Jon Coté, Paul Reuben, and Ron Withrow, the American contractor whose name had appeared on the list of hostages discovered by the Brits the previous March. DNA analysis determined that the other two fingers belonged to Josh Munns and Bert Nussbaumer, the Austrian. The bag did not include a finger belonging to John Young, the missing Crescent team leader.

The FBI grappled with how to break the news to the families. To investigators, the decomposed fingers were almost certainly proof that the hostages had been killed: it was effectively proof of death. But the informant had been vague, and they still didn't have the bodies. Quantico said it was unable to determine whether the fingers had been removed from corpses or while the men were alive. The FBI decided to inform the families only that U.S. authorities were in possession of fingerprint and DNA evidence that had come from five of the hostages, excluding Young.

The government's decision to withhold information was motivated by "compassion for people who had already been through so much agony," according to an FBI official. But the decision backfired. At first, the families didn't know what to believe. They speculated about what the evidence was and what it meant; many thought the FBI had found items—cigarettes or drinking glasses, for example—with fingerprints on them. Three weeks later, news of the severed fingers was leaked to an Austrian news magazine. The story spread globally via the newswires and the Internet, quickly reaching the families in the United States.

Patrick Reuben, Paul's twin brother, called me in California, frantic. He said he had gotten a call from his seventeen-year-old niece, asking if it was true that her father was dead. Patrick asked if I knew anything. "I can't get any information out of the government," he complained. In Ridgefield, Washington, Jackie Stewart, Munns' mother, called her local FBI liaison. "We have no confirmed reports that any of this is true," the FBI told her. The agent cast doubt on the report, telling Stewart, "I just don't think it would be anything that macabre."

The FBI finally confirmed the macabre story in the late afternoon from Washington, DC. But the agency offered no guidance on whether the hostages were alive. "There's no way to accurately depict at this point whether it was prior to or after; scientifically I don't think they've been able to determine that," a source familiar with the investigation said. "It's possible they were removed while they were still alive and possible they were removed after they were dead."

"I'm just going crazy," Sharon DeBrabander, Young's mother, told me. "I mean, my kid's finger isn't even there. What does it *mean*?

"This is inhuman," she said. "I would like to think that this is a good sign, but I don't know. I think a mother knows these things, and I just don't feel good about this. How could it be a good sign that you have five decomposed fingers and my son isn't among them? I just don't understand why the FBI can't be truthful to the parents. I wonder if they've got the bodies and they're not going to tell us. Not knowing is killing us, and every day it's killing us more. It's so cruel."

Francis and Nancy Coté interpreted the gruesome discovery as proof of life. Nancy, of course, was the senior DEA agent in Buffalo, and her status had helped get Joe from Basra involved in the case in the first place. But in many ways she was left grasping like everyone else. "If it was a corpse, wouldn't you just take the whole finger?" she told me. "I really do think it came off a live body."

Francis shared the news with Chris. He told him he thought it was proof that his brother was alive. But Chris didn't want to hear it: he didn't share his father's unwavering faith, his eternal optimism. For months, Chris had become increasingly convinced that his brother and best friend was dead. This was only further proof—perverse, unimaginable proof—of what he already believed. Francis and Chris had never been further apart. They lived under the same roof, and yet it was as if they resided in different countries. Francis had Nancy and his God. Chris felt alone. The one person he would turn to in a crisis was the person who was missing, and now, it appeared, mutilated. And where was God?

That night, before they went to bed, Francis went to gather Chris in a consoling embrace. Chris slipped through it and disappeared into the darkness of the basement, alone.

ELEVEN DAYS LATER, SHARON NOTICED A CAR PARKED in front of her house in north Kansas City.

It was 8:00 P.M. on Easter Sunday. Sharon had offered a lift home to a friend who lived in the neighborhood. As she was backing out of the driveway, she noticed the car parked in the shadows next to the curb and the silhouettes of two people sitting inside. A man and a woman, well dressed, got out and walked toward the house.

Sharon recognized them as her local FBI contacts. At first she couldn't imagine what they were doing at her house on a quiet holiday evening. She stopped the car and stared, trying to figure it out. And then suddenly it hit her.

"Oh, Nancy, I know why they're here," Sharon cried to her friend.

She asked the agents to wait inside. When she returned a few minutes later, they were sitting in her living room, talking in soft voices with her husband, Dennis.

Sharon sat down and the female agent broke the news: "We are sorry to inform you that a body has been recovered in Iraq, and they have identified the remains of your loved one, John R. Young."

After sixteen months, Sharon found that she was all but cried out. More than tears, she had questions, many, many questions. She asked the agents to tell her how John had died. She asked them when he had died and where he had died.

But the agents didn't have any answers.

Sharon grew angry. Throughout the ordeal, from the kidnapping to the videos to the grim and mysterious discovery of five severed fingers that hadn't even included her son's, she had felt like she was groping her way through darkness. It made it harder to take: the endless not knowing. And now, even in his death, she still didn't know what had happened to him.

"I'm not asking; I'm demanding. Give me answers!" she told the agents. "I don't care what your bosses say. I'm demanding this. I'm his mother. I carried him nine months. You all didn't."

The agents were sympathetic; they promised they would ask. But what they couldn't tell her, and therefore convey, was how little they actually knew. That was the real distance between north Kansas City and Basra, Iraq. It was a long assembly line of death, and the two well-dressed representatives of the U.S. government who sat in her living room were merely at the end of the line. They had one task: to inform a mother that her forty-four-year-old son— a U.S. Army veteran, a father of two, "a gypsy with a soldier's heart," as Young's sister Joella described him—was gone.

The assembly line began with the killers themselves. And all that was known about them and what they had done was contained in a black plastic bag that had been dropped off at the Basra Air Base a few days earlier. The bag weighed roughly sixty pounds, the autopsy would later reveal, and contained what was left of John Young. His tattoos—a panther, a leering skull wearing a hat, and a feathered knife—were largely intact. But his amazing blue eyes and his lips were gone. His chest and his ribs had been crushed, and he had bled internally. Young's throat had been slashed so severely that his head was attached only by the spinal cord.

Young had been dead for months, although how many was never certain. He had been exhumed from a grave of dirt and sand before he was delivered anonymously to U.S. authorities.

His remains had been dropped off at the Basra airport with the body of Ron Withrow, the computer technician from Roaring Springs, Texas, who had been held with the Crescent hostages. Withrow's body was also in a plastic bag. The military placed the remains of the two men in silver caskets and shipped them to the United States in a cargo plane.

This was the beginning of the excruciating end for the families of the Crescent hostages. In the ensuing days, just answering the phone became a form of Russian roulette.

Who was next?

As Sharon was receiving the news about John in Kansas City, the phone rang at Keri Johnson-Reuben's house outside Minneapolis. She was afraid to answer it. When the agent told her that the bodies of Young and Withrow—and not her husband Paul—had been identified, Keri breathed a guilty sigh of relief. But it was only for a moment. "The next sentence out of their mouth, which made me physically sick, was that they've recovered three additional bodies and one that they were still attempting to recover," Keri said.

For the next three days, Keri barely ate or slept. And then, on March 26, a Wednesday, around 8:00 P.M., the agents pulled up in front of her house.

"They have identified the remains of your loved one, Paul Johnson-Reuben, and the remains of Joshua Munns," one of the agents informed her.

Keri fell to the floor and vomited. She became so sick that a friend had to drive her to the hospital. She spent the next two hours in the emergency room, catatonic, hooked up to an IV.

And still it wasn't over. Young, Reuben, Munns, and Ron Withrow had been pronounced dead. Almost certainly, the other body that had been turned in belonged to Coté or Nussbaumer. But that body still hadn't been identified.

And there was still a sixth body out there, somewhere in Iraq.

MONTHS EARLIER, IN A BIZARRE COINCIDENCE, THE families of the five Crescent hostages had agreed to assemble in Minneapolis at the end of March.

The gathering had been planned as an opportunity for the families to meet for the first time and compare notes on their common tragedy. But as they checked in to the Comfort Inn near the Minneapolis airport, the gathering had become something else entirely, almost a collective wake.

I flew in Thursday afternoon, one day after the bodies of Reuben and Munns had been identified. I met up at the baggage claim with Jackie Stewart, Munns' mother, who had flown in from Ridgefield, Washington. She wore jeans and a bulky white sweater, and her frizzy blond hair fell over her shoulders. She seemed remarkably composed. After grabbing our luggage, we drove to a sports bar and had a couple beers. Jackie told me she was at peace. "I know that Josh didn't feel anything," she said. "When you're about to die, your spirit leaves your body, so you don't feel any pain."

That night, the families met for dinner at an Outback Steakhouse connected to the Comfort Inn, down the street from the immense Mall of America. Jackie and I walked into the crowded restaurant and ran into Josh's father, Mark Munns. He was tall, about six foot four, like his son, only bulkier, with straight brown hair. You could feel the tension between him and Jackie; the two had never married and had been estranged for years. I knew that Munns sometimes blamed Jackie for helping Josh land the job with Crescent.

Now, without looking at her, he snapped, "She sold him to the Devil."

There was an awkward silence. Jackie was standing just a few feet away, her eyes wet, but she didn't look at Munns or say anything.

A hostess led us to the table, and the crowd grew. Sharon and Dennis had driven up from Kansas City. Lori Silveri, Coté's mother, had flown in from Ft. Lauderdale. Maria and Franz Nussbaumer, Bert's mother and brother, had come all the way from Gmunden, Austria. Munns had brought his wife, Crista, who had helped raise Josh. Several of Paul Reuben's relatives were there, including his wife, Keri, his mother, Johnnie, and his sister, Susie.

Reuben's twin brother, Patrick, had refused to attend. It was because of Koscielski, the gun shop owner, who was planning to brief the families on new information he claimed to have about the case. In late February, Koscielski had issued a press release, touting the event as an "International Summit on Kidnapping in Iraq." Francis and Nancy Coté had also backed out because of Koscielski, whom they considered unhinged.

To anyone in the restaurant, it would have seemed like a boisterous family reunion. There was laughter and loud talking, drinks piling up on the table. Every few minutes we needed more chairs. I was sitting next to Lori, and she marveled, "It's all so strange, all these different people from all these different places, who never even knew each other, coming together as families, and under such sad circumstances."

Lori said she didn't know how to feel. Three times in the past week, she had been visited by the FBI, moments of pure terror, only to learn that someone else's child was dead. As Lori looked across the table, she began to cry. "These people are all so brave," she sobbed. "They all have closure. But where's Jonathon?"

Suddenly, the table grew quiet and I noticed that everyone was staring behind me. I turned to see two identical beautiful women removing their coats. The women—girls, really—looked exactly alike: tall and angular, with pale brown skin and dark brown hair pulled into tight ponytails. One was hauling a baby carrier containing a wriggling infant covered in a pink and white blanket.

They were Reuben's twin seventeen-year-old daughters, Casey and Bree. The five-month-old baby was Bree's; her name was Ka'Leah, and she had been conceived and born while her grandfather was in captivity. I introduced myself and explained to Casey and Bree that I had interviewed their father before he disappeared. I made faces at Ka'Leah, who was giggling.

"Do you like the man?" Bree cooed to her daughter. "Do you like him? He saw grandpa before he got kidnapped."

Bree and Casey talked over one another and finished each other's sentences. I tried to memorize which was which, but then one of them would move, and I'd get confused. They were funny and spacey and charming, like their dad, and it was heartbreaking just to be around them. They said they still had to get dresses for their prom, which was two weeks away.

Bree and Casey said the last time they talked to their father, he was petrified by the bombing that had killed the two Iraqis.

"He was *soooo* scared. It was like there was this car bombing and in this car bombing he had gotten stuff all over him and he was like, 'Girls, I know that could have been me. I just want to f——ing get out of here.'"

I could tell it was Bree talking because the baby had started crying and she picked her up.

Then Casey said, "And he was like, 'It's really, really dangerous here right now. This is gonna be my last mission.'"

"And I begged him," said Bree. "I said, '*Please*, Dad, just drop everything now; just come home *right now*. And he said, 'No, I can't. I have to do just one more mission.'"

"And that one more mission cost him his life," Casey said.

People would ask you all the time: Is it worth it? Is it worth a job, worth a story, worth a paycheck? After a while you'd tell them anything, because the answer was implicit in the question, wasn't it?

I often thought about an exchange I had with Reuben the week before he was kidnapped. We were sitting in my room at the Kuwait City villa. He had told me about the same bombing he described to his daughters. Except that it hadn't been just one more mission; there had been many more missions, and still Reuben stayed. Finally I asked him why.

"I kind of like doing it," he said. "I've been in the Marine Corps. I've been in the Army National Guard. I've always liked this kind of work. And I'm getting caught up on some bills and stuff like that."

He paused and smiled.

"And I heard they're coming out with that new Dodge Challenger in 2008. I want that."

He was joking, sort of. In the end, that couldn't be the risk/reward: the most beautiful daughters in the world vs. a new car.

The morning after the family dinner, Koscielski held his international summit in the Brisbane Room of the Comfort Inn. An off-duty Bloomington cop wearing a bulletproof vest beneath a tan polo shirt guarded the door with a Taser. There was a kid's birthday party in the room next door. The still-grieving families filed in and, for the next three hours, heard Koscielski describe his "intelligence," a stew of rumors and wild speculation. When the international summit concluded, I drove out to Patrick Reuben's house for a barbecue. Bree and Casey were coming over with their mom, Paul's first wife, Kathy, and Jackie Stewart, who was staying with Patrick and his wife, Jennifer.

Patrick commuted to his job as a Minneapolis cop from New Richmond, Wisconsin, about an hour east of the city. It was jarring to see him come to the door. Like his twin nieces, he was an exact replica of his brother: about six foot four, 280 pounds, with a warm and mischievous smile. He had less hair than Paul, but the same laugh, the same voice (maybe an octave lower), the same surprising agility for a large man, and the same slightly warped sense of humor. After Paul was kidnapped, Kathy sometimes found it haunting to be around Patrick, and he would quip, "You hate me, don't you?"

Patrick led me down to the basement. We sat surrounded by toys and kid videos; every few minutes his four-year-old son, Mac, or five-year-old daughter, Marilynn, would come bursting into the room.

"He just wanted to have a fun time," Patrick said of his brother. "He would make rude noises. He was open about his life. I think he was a fibber, too. I think he was ashamed of some of the stuff he did."

Patrick said he and Paul started getting into their mother's liquor when they were "very young, maybe six or seven." The habit stayed with Paul his entire life. Everyone loved him, though, and wanted to help. It was only after he signed a "last chance agreement" and got pulled over again that he was forced to resign from the St. Louis Park Police Department after nine and a half years. That job had been perfect for Paul, combining his love for people and excitement. "Everything went downhill from there," said Patrick. "That is when he started drinking heavily. We went to a Van Halen concert in 2005 and he was mixing drinks in the car." By then, Paul had filed for bankruptcy, his marriage to Kathy was over, and he was scraping by on dry-walling jobs that a friend occasionally threw at him.

It was an exciting opportunity—private security in Iraq—that ultimately saved him. Paul applied for a job over the Internet. No one seemed concerned about his drinking. He worked for three different companies: DEH Global, Securiforce, and, finally, Crescent. And then the job that saved him killed him.

I followed Patrick upstairs. After dinner, we all sat around talking and laughing, Patrick, Kathy, and the girls trading stories about Paul. Kathy was a sunny, down-to-earth white girl from Indiana; she worked as a secretary for a Minneapolis engineering firm. She and Paul had met in Hawaii when he was in the marines. He had followed her down the street, "this tall guy with the biggest smile I ever saw. Paul was like that: from the moment you met him, he was all smiles and good feeling." Kathy had kicked Paul out of the house twice, the last time for good, but you could tell the warm feeling had never left her. She remembered him coming home after working the overnight shift as a cop, too tired to move. "He was asleep on the floor, and his feet were so ticklish," she said. "I would tickle his feet and he couldn't move to defend himself. We just laughed and laughed."

Bree and Casey said they had been saving things to show their dad when he got home: newspaper clippings, photos of Ka'Leah, a chronology of everything that happened while he was away.

"I always thought about the day he was coming home," said Bree.

"I did the same thing; I was going to never let him out of my sight," said Casey.

"All that hoping," said Bree, "what do I do now?"

Soon it was time to go; the girls had school in the morning. I drove back to my hotel and turned on the computer. There was a press release from the FBI: Bert Nussbaumer's body had been identified.

There was only one left.

CHRIS COTÉ WAS BOMBING HIS NISSAN DOWN BUF-falo's Audubon Highway around 3:30 A.M. Just ahead, he could see the light changing from yellow to red. He knew he wouldn't make it, but he blew through it anyway.

Chris was working eighty hours a week at the Yamaha dealership. It was a routine that kept him moving and breathing and numb. Early each morning, he would surface from the basement and head off to work. He returned late at night, avoiding his family, especially his father.

That night, friends had coaxed him out to dinner. Someone had bought him a beer. Normally Chris was the first to quit. But he no longer cared: the floor had dropped out of his life. Chris had another beer, then another, then some shots. He followed his friends to another bar and gulped down several Red Bull and vodkas. He lost count of how many. Then he got in the car.

A second light turned red and Chris blew through it.

A cop appeared behind him and pulled him over. The officer asked if he'd been drinking. Chris described his evening in detail: two bars, beers, shots, Red Bull and vodkas. It was as if he wanted to get punished. The officer gave him a Breathalyzer test. He was twice the legal limit.

Buffalo, of course, has the Bills and Niagara Falls, but it's still a small town.

Another officer walked up.

"Are you the one whose brother is in Iraq?" he asked.

"Yes, sir," said Chris.

The officer asked about his stepmother, the number-one DEA agent in town.

"What would Nancy think about this situation?" he said.

"She wouldn't be happy at all," said Chris.

The officers left the Nissan in a parking lot and drove him home. They made Chris wake up Nancy and hand her his keys, which he did.

The next morning, Nancy, not his dad, drove Chris back to his car.

"Listen, Chris, I don't know what to tell you, but you and Jon are like my own sons," Nancy told him. "We love you very much and we want you to know that. I'm worried about you. I'm worried about what happened last night."

"I guess you should be worried," said Chris.

He felt ashamed the rest of the day.

Francis wanted desperately to speak with his son. For all his faith and optimism, with five bodies now accounted for, Francis clung to hope but knew in his heart that Jon probably wasn't coming home. And now his other son was on an emotional precipice. One night, the family heard screaming coming from the basement. It was Chris, raging at the world.

Francis had lost his father to a drunk-driving accident. His son Jonathon had fled to Iraq after being arrested for drunk driving. And now this: his responsible son, Chris, hammered, barreling through stoplights as if he didn't care. Francis wanted somehow to reach out. But he didn't know how. His youngest son was missing, almost certainly dead, and his only other child was cut off from him. Chris felt only alone. His religious faith, the faith that his father felt so strongly, had long ago been undermined by his parents' divorce—and now it was decimated. He and Francis shared the same grief but spoke different languages. It was like there was a locked door between them.

In late March 2008, Iraqi prime minister Nouri al-Maliki launched an offensive to root out the militias and criminal gangs that ruled Basra. Thousands of Iraqi troops fought running gun battles with Mahdi Army fighters in the narrow streets. American F-18 warplanes fired cannon rounds against the militias, the air strikes booming through the city and lighting up the night. Basra, a sweltering port city of three million people, was under siege: electricity and water cut off, civilians cowering in their homes. The fighting spread to other Mahdi Army strongholds throughout Iraq, including Sadr City, the sprawling Baghdad slum.

And somewhere in the middle of it was Jon Coté.

As the fighting engulfed Basra, the recovery of what the U.S. government referred to as the "sixth body" had stalled.

On April 4, John Young's funeral was held in Lee's Summit, Missouri. The pastor described him as "a regular American, but a hero." Young's former Crescent colleagues, Benjamin "Red" Borrowman, Shannon McCullough, Gary Bjorlin, and Kevin Baker, served as pallbearers. The men posed for a picture inside the Langsford Funeral Home, their clenched fists displaying custom-made rings inscribed with the words *Proeliator Aeternus*, Latin for "eternal warrior," and bearing a winged sword, a mercenary symbol. Young received a military burial, after which the American flag was lifted from his casket, folded by an honor guard, and placed on Sharon's lap.

On April 12, one thousand people attended the funeral of Josh Munns in Anderson, California, near Redding. Munns was buried at the Northern California Veterans Cemetery with military honors, amid a sea of American flags, following a rifle salute and taps.

I talked to Francis the day after Munns' funeral. He told me that sometimes he caught himself speaking of Jon in the past tense. Then he would correct himself. "I know you could say, 'Well, there were six of them and five of them are dead, so what are the odds of Jon making it home alive?'" he said. "But I still do not want to think that way and I'm not going to allow myself to think that way."

Francis had begun to hear the stories from the other families about the condition of the bodies when they came home, the torture some of the men had apparently endured. Sometimes he'd find himself going to the refrigerator, opening it up, and forgetting what he was looking for.

Basra was in flames, engulfing the search for his missing son. And yet he never seemed to break. I asked him how he got through it.

"It's all about making sure that you reconcile with God every morning and every evening and that you're living the life he wants you to live, and that you stay in touch with him and listen to what he wants you to be in this world," he told me. "You know, life is what it is. We even pray for the individuals that captured these guys, that they turn their hearts to God and they understand what they did was wrong and they repent. That's our faith."

I asked him if he ever felt a need for vengeance.

"I mean, there was a time once, where I'd have picked up my shit, and I'd get a sniper rifle and I'd be picking them off one at a time at different times of day and night in Basra. I'd use the same tactics that they use. But you know what? There's no good that can come of it, there's really no good."

The following day, April 14, Iraqi troops stormed a house in central Basra and liberated a British cameraman named Richard Butler. He had been kidnapped two months earlier while on assignment for *60 Minutes*. The Iraqis overpowered his captors and found him with his hands bound, wearing a hood that he said had covered his head during most of his ordeal.

Within days, the Iraqi forces had taken control of Basra.

On April 19, a Saturday, two FBI agents came to the house and informed the Cotés that the sixth body had been found. It was being flown to Dover Air Force Base for identification.

On April 24, a Wednesday, Chris went into work early; he was certain that would be the day, and he wanted to be prepared. He told his boss he planned to take some time off. Shortly after lunch, the receptionist, her eyes red, grabbed Chris and pulled him into the ladies' room. She told him that his father had called and the FBI was on its way to his house.

As Chris reached the outskirts of Radcliffe Estates, he noticed four cars snaking through the streets. He followed the procession as it slowed and then turned toward his house. "And that's when I knew I was right behind the FBI and everybody who was coming to tell me that my brother was dead."

It was spring, sunny; Buffalo had thawed. Chris walked up to the porch. The front door was open, but the screen door was locked. Through it, he could hear Christian music drifting from the kitchen. Nancy, shaken and in tears, couldn't unlock the door. She went off to get Francis. As Chris waited on the porch, four FBI agents—two men and two women—joined him.

"We're so sorry," one of them said.

Chris had played out the moment when he would get the devastating news, turning it over and over in his head until it had become almost familiar. But this wasn't it: standing on his porch, locked out of his house, a whispered condolence in the air. He had an urge to say, "For what?"

The group moved through the house to the deck outside the kitchen and sat down at the patio table beneath an umbrella: Chris, Francis, Nancy, and the four agents, all dressed in dark suits. A female agent with long red hair looked directly at Francis. She told him that the tests had been completed and it had been determined that the sixth body was "your son, Jonathon Coté."

The air filled with the silence beyond words and all that we expect from the world. Slowly, it gave way to the perfunctory detail that orders our lives, even in death, and then more silence, until Chris and Nancy finally walked the FBI agents to the door, leaving Francis at the table on the deck.

After the agents were gone, Nancy turned to Chris.

"I wish there was something I could do," she said.

"Nancy, there's just nothing you can do," Chris replied.

Fathers and sons—they are us, and we are them. That evening, as the house filled with friends and relatives, and plates of food piled up on the counter, Chris led his father into the family room so they could be alone. Francis had been drinking since the afternoon, and he sank heavily into the couch. Chris sat before him on the footrest, his chin on his fist, staring at the man he had avoided for months and now understood completely.

Francis, his strength depleted, began to wail.

He shouted at God and sobbed, "Why did you take your son from me?"

Chris could see the pain coursing through him. He stood up and draped himself over his father, like a blanket.

"It's okay," Chris told him. "It's okay."

"No, it's *not* okay," Francis raged.

"Yes, it is. It's okay," Chris said softly.

"Christopher, don't ever leave me, if you ever leave me—"

Chris cut him off.

"Dad, I'm never leaving you," he said.

Nancy appeared at the front of the room. Chris walked downstairs into the basement. Two of his and Jon's oldest friends, Micaela Lumsden and D.J. Szymanski, came over to sit with him. Soon they were all trading stories in the basement. Micaela, a Buffalo social worker, was thin, with straight dark hair. She was to be married in the fall, and she had hoped that Jon would be home for her wedding. Years earlier, out of the blue, Jon had confessed that he loved her. It was impulsive, typical Jon, but now Micaela started to cry, wondering if she had dated him whether everything might have turned out different. D.J. was six two, about 270 pounds, with a pale shaved head and tattoos. Jon used to pick up a rubber exercise ball, hold it against his stomach, and ask D.J., a former Canisius College lineman, to get down in a football stance and blast him. In the winter, D.J., Chris, and Jon would tether a sled to the back of Chris' Nissan and take turns pulling each other through Radcliffe Estates.

It was after midnight when Micaela and D.J. left. Chris was alone. Jon's clothes—sweaters, his ski jacket, his army uniform—were still in the closet, and they smelled like him. Chris put on a video of his favorite movie, *A River Runs Through It*, the adaptation of Norman Maclean's classic book about fly-fishing and his murdered younger brother. Chris had watched it a half dozen times, for Maclean's story, in many ways, was his own. He turned on the movie and there on the screen was his wild younger brother, trailing him through a field, and slaying the girls, and defying the strictures of their stern and loving father, and courting death.

In the movie, long after his son is killed, the father, a Presbyterian minister, tells his congregation, "Each one of us here today will at one time in our lives look upon a loved one who is in need and ask the same question: We are willing to help, Lord, but what, if anything, is needed? For it is true we can seldom help those closest to us. Either we don't know what part of ourselves to give or, more often than not, the part we have to give is not wanted. And so it is those we live with and should know who elude us. But we can still love them—we can love completely without complete understanding."

Chris knew that was true. Our loved ones, they elude us. They smoke too many cigarettes and they drink before they drive and they escape our world to places where death, in many respects, is the cost of doing business.

And sometimes they don't come back.

EPILOGUE

THE BOOK OF WISDOM

As US Airways Flight 1860 eased into gate four at Buffalo Niagara International Airport, the pilot came over the intercom to announce, "Can I please have your attention. We are carrying with us tonight the remains of a fallen American in Iraq. Please remain seated for the movement of the remains and for the American escorts to deplane."

The cabin fell silent. No one moved as the two men seated in the first row rose to gather their belongings. They were the master sergeant who had accompanied Jon Coté's body from Dover Air Force Base and the drug enforcement agent known as Joe from Basra.

The two men were led down to the tarmac, and the master sergeant climbed up into the belly of the plane. He draped an American flag over the silver casket and made sure that the body was placed feetfirst onto the conveyer belt.

There was a light drizzle, the temperature forty degrees. A bitter wind blew off Lake Erie, snapping a half dozen flags held by members of the Patriot Guard Riders of New York, a biker group that supports the families of fallen troops. Police flashers and a Buffalo TV crew threw light and shadows over the massive plane. From the ground you could see the passengers, still in their seats in the lighted cabin, gazing out over the spectacle, and the baggage handlers, waiting off to the side in orange vests and knitted caps.

I stood with Francis, Nancy, Chris, and Lori underneath the wing to the right of the plane, buffeted by the freezing wind. Joe from Basra, immaculately dressed in a dark suit, a pressed white shirt, and an overcoat, walked across the tarmac and embraced Francis and Nancy, who thanked him. The casket then began its descent.

Five men and one woman from New York's 107th Air National Guard met the casket at the bottom of the belt. Led by the master sergeant, they marched it to a hearse parked about twenty-five yards from the plane. I could hear Lori and Nancy sobbing. Francis saluted his son. As the door to the hearse closed and we started to walk away, he reached over and squeezed my hand. I started to lose my composure. I found myself thinking about all the people I knew in Iraq who had died: Iraqis and Americans, soldiers and reporters, marines and mercs. And wondering exactly why.

The thunder of fourteen Patriot Guard Harleys led the long procession from the airport to the Dengler & Roberts Funeral Home in East Amherst. It was a redbrick two-story building with white columns. Dozens of tiny American flags had been planted on the lawn next to the carport. The casket was removed from the hearse and set down on the grass. Edward Kornowski, a fifty-seven-year-old Vietnam vet and Patriot Guard Rider wearing a motorcycle jacket, recited the Serenity Prayer:

> *God grant me the serenity*
> *to accept the things I cannot change;*
> *courage to change the things I can;*
> *and the wisdom to know the difference.*

Then he said, "Jonathon, thank you for your service to the United States of America. Welcome back to American soil."

The casket was lifted from the ground and moved inside the building, light glowing from every window. Jon's family and friends lingered in the shadows of the carport, exchanging hugs as the formally dressed funeral home staff passed around peppermints.

After a few minutes, the cars began to peel away. I was riding with Chris, and before we left, he told me he had to take care of something. He ran inside the building and returned a few minutes later. He said he had a question for the funeral director. He wanted to know when he could view his brother's remains.

THE COTÉ FAMILY HAD BEGUN TO GATHER IN BUFFALO: aunts and uncles and waves of cousins. They arrived from Florida and California, Michigan and New Jersey, the French-speaking relatives, from Montreal. The brick house in Getzville was constantly filled, the kitchen counter replenished every day with cold cuts and lasagna and buffalo wings, chips and dip and myriad desserts. Francis was once again a rock. "I've got it under control now," he said when someone commented on his composure. He occupied himself with formidable tasks in which all were invited to participate. One afternoon, he rigged up a pair of straps that enabled us to move a five-hundred-pound hot tub into the backyard.

Another afternoon I showed up and some guy was turning the garage into a gas station. After the New Year, Francis had bought a green Honda Civic that ran on natural gas. It cost about a dollar a gallon to fill the tank, which was built into the trunk. Now, on the week of his son's funeral, Francis was having a natural gas pump installed in his garage so he could fill up the Honda himself.

"So, Francis, what's the reason you're doing all this?" his brother, Serge, asked as we observed the installation. Serge was taller than Francis, bearded and sardonic. He was an inspector for the FAA outside Detroit.

"Is it because of the environment? Is it because of the cost?"

"It's because of Iraq," said Francis.

I asked him what he meant.

Francis held up his middle finger.

"Fuck your oil, fuck your war," he said, smiling. "Fuck Iraq."

After a while we walked back inside the house. Nancy was in the kitchen and she was talking about how the funeral director had told her that under no circumstances would he allow Chris to view the body. "I don't care what anyone says: I'm not opening that box," the funeral director had said, according to Nancy.

Francis was relieved. He was proud of Chris, whose strength seemed to have emerged from some hidden wellspring. The day after Jon's body was identified, the Cotés had held a press conference at a local hotel. Chris had brought some of the reporters to tears. At the end, he was asked, "If you could ask your brother one last question, what would it be?"

Chris took a breath.

"Do you forgive those who did this to you?" he replied, his voice cracking. "If he can, then I know I can."

But Francis didn't want Chris to view his brother's desecrated remains. He thought it might permanently scar him; he wanted the family to remember Jon as he was. Chris felt he needed to see his brother to make it real.

"You can't tell him what to do; he's an adult," Maude Coté, one of Chris' closest cousins, told Francis.

Maude was a young immigration lawyer from Montreal, bespectacled and sweet natured. Upon hearing of Jon's death, she had rushed down to Buffalo, where she spent her days dispensing hugs and washing dishes.

"Chris can make his own decisions," Maude said.

"It's my son who's in that box," Francis told her. "It's not Christopher's son."

FRANCIS, LORI, CHRIS, AND THE COUSINS FILLED UP a room of the funeral home with reminders of Jon. In one corner they placed his red snowboard, two hockey jerseys, snowboard boots, and a hockey stick. There was an easel with Jon's certificates of achievement from the military and school. His army dress uniform hung on the back wall. Throughout the building, video monitors looped hundreds of photos of Jon and his family to music that Chris had selected.

Jon lay inside a dark wooden casket at the front of the rectangular room, which had a low ceiling and green carpeting. Behind it was a blown-up photo of him wearing a gray sweater over a white T-shirt and smiling wanly. On top of the casket rested a Bible open to the book of Wisdom, chapter 3: "But the souls of the just are in the hand of God, and the torment of death shall not touch them. . . ."

More than a thousand people filed through during the two-day wake; the receiving line stretched out the door into the parking lot out back. Many were strangers who had merely followed the story on the news or had seen the emotional press conference. The Buffalo chief of police, FBI agents, and Nancy's DEA colleagues came by. A dozen former members of Jon's platoon in the 82nd Airborne greeted the Cotés together—some in uniform, others who had gotten out and resumed their lives as civilians.

The Patriot Guard Riders stood vigil outside, circling the building with American flags. They included Mike and Sandy Kraig, who had lost their son Travis, a private first class in the 25th Infantry Division, in Iraq.

By the end of the wake, the receiving line was still so long that Francis and Nancy walked back through to make sure everyone had been greeted. When the crowd finally thinned out, I ran into Jenny Goldin, one of Jon's closest friends. She was bright and petite, an elementary school teacher who had known his many sides. In one of her favorite memories, Jon strolled into a bar with her and Chris one night wearing snowboard boots and a pink T-shirt that said "Stroke My Ego."

Jon noticed a girl staring at him and, of course, thought instantly she was interested.

Jenny cracked up.

"Jon, she's staring at you 'cause you're wearing those stupid moon boots and a pink shirt that says 'Stroke My Ego.'"

Jenny witnessed Jon's emotional descent after he got out of the army; once she dragged him to a VA clinic in downtown Buffalo to see a counselor. But he stared at the floor and said little, and he only went once. Later, Jon stood in the backyard of Jenny's parents' house and announced that he was going to the University of Florida to be an accountant, at which point Jenny and her entire family burst out laughing.

Jon the accountant: the ultimate oxymoron.

I asked her how she was doing. "I don't know," she said somberly. "You spend so much time with someone, and then you'd give anything to have just a single moment. It all has to be for a reason, even if it's for a *bad* reason. There has to be a reason. Otherwise it's just meaningless."

I was driving Chris around in my rented Ford Fusion, and before we left he asked me to give him some time with his brother. I wandered around a mall for about forty-five minutes until he sent me a text message that he was ready to go home.

When I returned, the funeral home was virtually empty. I was met by a man who asked if I would make sure that Chris was okay. The staff had become concerned, he said: someone had peeked into the room and saw Chris on top of his brother's casket, sobbing, nearly hysterical.

When I walked in, Chris was kneeling before the casket and the photo of his brother. He turned around, red-eyed, and I drove him home.

On the way, he told me he had given up trying to view Jon's remains. Later, he would say he was glad it didn't happen. For when the autopsies came back—one from Dover, one from Buffalo General Hospital—they revealed the extent to which Jon had been violated.

His right thumb was missing, as well as part of his right pinkie, which showed "clear evidence of a tool mark for which resulted in the removal," according to the military's report. The mummified pinkie had been wrapped in gauze and placed in a plastic container. Jon's body was also missing its head, which was never found. The Buffalo pathologist told Francis that the head appeared to have been severed, although it was unclear how.

When he died, Jon was wearing "hospital scrub like pants," a sleeveless cotton undershirt, and a cotton short-sleeved shirt with a dark collar. His remains were covered in mud and weighed seventy-four pounds. The date and time of his death were "undetermined due to advanced decomposition."

"DEAR GOD, PLEASE HELP US GET THROUGH THIS. Please give Francis strength to give a eulogy that honors You and honors Jonathon."

Nancy grasped Francis' hand. They were sitting in the natural-gas-powered Honda, waiting for the funeral procession to start.

The sky was slate gray. The morning was warm, threatening rain. Francis followed the vehicles—the Patriot Guard Riders, Buffalo police cruisers, New York state troopers—onto Transit Road as the procession slowly made its way through the brick suburbs and marshlands of northeast Buffalo.

The Nativity of the Blessed Virgin Mary Church was in Williamsville, about three miles down the road. Parked out front was Harris Hill Fire Engine No. 6, its ladder dangling a huge American flag over Main Street. Patriot Guard Riders lined the walkway, each holding a flag.

The church was crammed with some eight hundred people; TV crews filled the balcony. The pallbearers, led by Chris, walked the flag-draped casket down the aisle, trailed by the family, which settled into the first two rows. Lori was wearing a black suit and, on her left index finger, the purple butterfly ring that Jon had fussed over while he was having it made for her in Kuwait City.

The organ fell silent. The flag was removed from the casket and replaced with a white shroud.

"November 16, 2006, and the months that followed, bear witness to the reality of sin and evil in this world," Randy Rozelle, the Coté family pastor, told the mourners.

The answer, he said, was God's own son, who like Jon was taken hostage. "Our lord Jesus was spit on and mocked and beaten with rocks," Rozelle said. "And scorched and stripped of his clothing and crowned with thorns and nailed to a cross to be killed. I don't know the pain and hurt that you are suffering right now, but your heavenly father in heaven does."

Francis rose, pressed his left hand to Jon's casket, and walked heavily to the podium. He thanked everyone for coming in English and French. For the next thirty minutes, he then recounted an American life that began at 7:52 A.M. on February 11, 1983, at Long Beach Naval Hospital in Southern California and ended somewhere in Iraq, the time and date unknown.

Francis thought of himself as patriotic but not very political. He was generally skeptical of politicians, now more than ever. But in the middle of his eulogy, his voice echoing through the church, he took a moment to describe the strange and unfamiliar world in which his son had been killed, and the circumstances that led to its creation. Private contractors, he told the mourners, had become a reality of modern warfare, their numbers ten times greater than "in the First Gulf War in which I served."

"They shoot, they get shot, and sometimes they get killed," Francis said. "The United States is putting hired help behind the front lines to ease the burden of its understaffed and overworked armed forces. That's the price we pay for having an all volunteer military. By paying civilians to handle tasks previously handled by the military, the administration is freeing up U.S. troops to do the actual fighting. But the use of contractors also hides the true costs of war. Their dead aren't added to official body counts. Their duties—and profits—are hidden by closed-mouthed executives who won't give details to Congress as their coffers and roles swell.

"Although Jon was not in the armed forces at the time he was killed, he was *again* serving our country in this war," said Francis.

Chris then rose and walked toward the podium. He and Francis were just about to pass one another when Chris reached out, grabbed his father, and embraced him.

Chris's eulogy was brief, and it left everyone in tears.

"Jonathon was an artist to me, a beautiful person with his own rhythm," he said. "His life was his artwork and he wished to share it with anyone whom he met."

He recited the passage from *A River Runs Through It*, the affirmation of our ability to "love completely without completely understanding."

"I loved Jonathon completely," said Chris, "and I know that love for Jonathon is shared by everyone here today."

ALONG THE ROUTE TO THE CEMETERY OUTSIDE OF Buffalo, people stood and watched the long procession go past. I saw a woman in a white sweater standing in her front yard with her hand over her heart. There were little kids saluting and young men gathered on their porches, staring and wondering.

Undoubtedly, some of them thought they were watching the funeral procession for an American serviceman who had been killed in Iraq. That was technically true. Jonathon Coté fought in the U.S. Army and was killed in Iraq. But of course it was far more complicated than that.

The official American death toll on April 24, 2008, the day Jon's body was identified, was 4,047. That did not change. Five years into the war, the mercs still weren't counted, alive or dead, even though hundreds and perhaps thousands had perished. The laws that governed their actions remained, at best, vague. In May, the State Department, rather than expelling Blackwater, extended the company's contract for another year, even as a Washington, DC, grand jury was investigating the killings at Nisoor Square. Meanwhile, Jack Holly, who for months had warned of Blackwater's abuses under State, was no longer welcome in Iraq. That summer, a U.S. military sweep turned up disputed weapons, including some belonging to a private security firm, in an armory on his compound inside the Green Zone. After nearly five years in Iraq, Holly tendered his resignation as head of logistics for the U.S. Army Corps of Engineers' Gulf Region Division. As this book was going to press, the circumstances of Holly's departure were in many ways as murky as the industry on which he had been wholly dependent. But it appeared that his alliance with private security, in the end, was as tenuous as the one that had been forged by the U.S. government from the very beginning.

Throughout Iraq, violence under Petraeus' command had dissipated to the point where the Iraqi government was now planning to open up the oil fields to foreigners. That was perceived as good news for the mercs, who believed that the oil companies, in turn, would hire them to provide security, allowing them to expand into a lucrative new market. "It's just gonna get better and better," Lawrie Smith, deputy director of the Private Security Company Association of Iraq, told me.

It creates a lot of ambiguity when you hire people to fight your war. For all the grief and emotion that Jon's kidnapping provoked, there was always an undercurrent of tension over his motives for going. Once, while he was still missing, the *Buffalo News* ran a small article about a fund-raiser his family had held to raise money for a possible ransom. The article elicited dozens of comments on the newspaper's Web site—some supportive, some critical to the point of cruelty:

One person wrote: A drunken, poor student decided to go for the big bucks, hired on with a sorry company and went to Iraq. He didn't like the constraints the U.S. military had on him when he was an actual soldier, and he thought he could have more fun as a mercenary. . . . Whitewash it any way you want to, but this guy is paying the price for his greed and his family is willing to support terrorism to bail him out.

One of Jon's friends responded: WOW EVERYONE, DON'T HOLD BACK YOUR CONDESCENDING JUDGEMENTS, PLEASE. Can we try a little sympathy for a young man who may have made a dangerous decision, who felt scared for his safety at the end there and was all set to come home and be done with it within 2 weeks of his capture? He's a good kid and we miss him terribly.

Another person wrote sympathetically: You're a young man [and] we all know how tough it is these days. You decide that when your military tour is up that you still want to help your country. You go over there, escort MILITARY convoys for other countries etc. to help out the "cause" and you're captured. The company says little to nothing, the gov't says little to nothing, no one has heard anything.

I never really resolved the ambiguity. I liked Jon Coté the moment I met him and I fell in love with his family. But it was an ugly business he had gotten himself into, perhaps the ugliest business there was. The U.S. government had fostered it as a manifestation of our failures in Iraq, a method for shifting responsibility and hiding the human toll, the stain of original sin. Private Security Contracting—what a name for it—but it fit the times. For Iraq wasn't Vietnam. It was and is a war fought on the margins of our consciousness, in that faraway place where people starve and tsunamis engulf entire cities and life goes on, unaltered. Unless you were there, of course. As Iraq came apart, not soon to be pieced back together, the private security contractors helped confine it to that faraway place, tens of thousands of shadow soldiers, their roles and identities as vague as the war itself. You didn't have to draft them, or count them, or run them through Congress. You didn't even have to know they were there.

Of course there were consequences; there had to be. The Bush administration had turned over responsibility for deciding who can kill and die for our country to the likes of Franco Picco and Erik Prince. Because the mercs weren't soldiers anymore; many of them never were. They never got stop-lossed or returned to duty after getting wounded or had to pull a fifteen-month tour, or *three* tours. They could walk away at any time and often did, contract-hopping their way through a war and another people's nation with a gun. The money, it was always there and that was the ultimate goal: not peace, not victory, not a better Iraq.

The money changed everything.

"You can get away with taking life if your country sends you; you can eventually forgive yourself," said Patrick McCormack, who joined the military after 9/11 and served with Jon Coté in the 82nd Airborne. "But when you do it because you want to buy a house, that's when you really begin to have existential questions."

THE PROCESSION FILED INTO RIDGE LAWN CEMETERY in Cheektowaga. Hundreds of people stood on the vast green lawn beneath the clouds. Jon's casket was placed next to a World War II vintage howitzer. His family sat beneath a tent as an honor guard fired off three shots. The mournful sound of taps drifted in the wind and a helicopter flew overhead. The American flag was then lifted from the casket, folded, and presented to Lori, while another folded flag was presented to Francis.

"This flag is presented on behalf of a grateful nation," the white-gloved master sergeant told them.

Jon had given his life while working for Crescent Security Group, but not a single representative of the company was present.

The crowd filed past the casket, hundreds upon hundreds of people. Some bent down to kiss it. Others whispered, "I love you, Jon." Others ran their fingers lightly over the wood, from one end to another, or pressed down with both hands, bowing their heads while roses and red and white carnations piled up on top.

After everyone had cleared out, a dozen young men approached from a low clearing. They were sobbing, most of them, and as they filed past the casket they left not only flowers but pieces of their past. From their pockets and the lapels of their jackets they produced combat infantryman badges (CIB)—the U.S. Army's prestigious award, handed out to infantrymen who engage in close combat—and Airborne wings. One of the men walked stiffly, from two thirteen-inch rods that had been inserted into his back. He wore his Class A uniform, his dress greens, decorated with overseas service stripes, a Ranger tab, a combat patch, a good conduct medal, and a CIB, among other awards.

Staff Sergeant Nicholas Ford had last seen Coté in Kuwait. Ford, then twenty-one, was preparing to enter Iraq with the 82nd Airborne. Jon had a day off from Crescent and had come to visit his old unit. He wore Abercrombie & Fitch blue jeans, flip-flops, and a sleeveless T-shirt. They spent the day together, shooting the shit in the barracks, and then Jon returned to his job. Ford went on to Samarra, where one afternoon the road exploded beneath him, barrel-rolling his Humvee fifteen feet in the air. He woke up a month later, his vertebrae shattered, his jaw shattered, both hips broken, his left lung collapsed, third-degree burns the size of a human hand covering his left thigh. Three of Ford's fellow paratroopers were dead.

Ford spent months at Walter Reed Army Medical Center, hooked up to a catheter, teaching himself to walk again. Some mornings he didn't want to open his eyes. To get through the next minute, he would think about Coté, by then six months into captivity, "probably living in some shit-hole, getting the shit kicked out of him every day, alone while I had my wife and my family. That's what kept me going, thinking about what he was going through."

Ford removed the Purple Heart the U.S. Army had given him for his wounds from the lapel of his coat. He placed it on top of the casket, to leave the earth with the brother who had fought and died in the same war but no longer qualified for medals.

The men of the 2nd Platoon, Alpha Company, 2nd Battalion, 505th Parachute Infantry Regiment of the 82nd Airborne Division then walked away, their arms thrown over each other's shoulders, their bodies hunched together against the wind and their grief.

As they walked away in terrible silence, one of them said finally, "Let's go drink some beer." And together they all laughed.

SOURCE NOTES

This book began as a reporting project for the *Washington Post* on the private armies of Iraq. Most of the material was gathered during four trips to Iraq between the fall of 2006 and the fall of 2007, and also in interviews—in person, by phone, and occasionally via email—with people connected to the private security industry in the United States, Europe, Latin America, and Asia. I have also drawn upon my earlier experiences covering U.S. troops. In total, I made eleven trips to Iraq from the fall of 2004 through 2007.

Despite its enormous expansion, the private security industry, as indicated by its name, remains a largely closed world. Some contracts explicitly prohibit employees from speaking publicly; violations can result in dismissal and/or large fines. Although most of the people quoted in this book are named, a small percentage requested anonymity because of concerns for their safety or their employment status. In nearly all cases, U.S. government officials, in particular those representing the State Department, demanded anonymity as a condition for describing how private security companies in Iraq were regulated and how shooting incidents were investigated. These officials invariably cited U.S. government policy or security concerns.

From the moment I arrived in Iraq, I benefited from the generosity and expertise of my colleagues at the *Washington Post*. In particular, I was able to draw on the reporting of Jonathan Finer, Joshua Partlow, and Sudarsan Raghavan, the *Post*'s Baghdad Bureau chief throughout 2007, as well as the research, translation, and incomparable reporting of Naseer Nouri, Saad al-Izzi, and Khaled Alsaffar.

A wealth of information, including articles and videos, on the Crescent kidnapping and its aftermath can be found at www.freecote.com, a Web site administered by the family of Jon Coté.

Unless cited below, the information contained in this book came from interviews or public sources.

PROLOGUE. ON THE BORDER

xiii *"The U.S. military, which catalogued troop fatalities by more than thirty potential causes"*: Fatalities from Operation Iraqi Freedom are cataloged in a *Washington Post* database.

xv *"Soon it's a $100 billion industry"*: P. W. Singer, a senior fellow at the Brookings Institution and author of *Corporate Warriors: The Rise of the Privatized Military Industry* (Cornell University Press, 2003), estimates that private security has grown into a $100 billion industry with several hundred companies operating in more than a hundred countries. The figure has been widely cited. See, for example, Joseph Neff, "A Business Gets a Start," *News & Observer*, July 29, 2004.

CHAPTER 1. SOCIAL STUDIES, INC.

4 *"UF was the third-largest school in the country"*: Figures from the Integrated Postsecondary Education Data System. See http://www.ir.ufl.edu/nat_rankings/students/enrlmt_old.pdf.

14 *"I know it all came up fast"*: Email from Mike Skora to Jon Coté, July 10, 2006.

14 *"That same afternoon, he filed his application to withdraw"*: Coté's application to withdraw from all courses was submitted on July 10, 2006, and signed by the University of Florida dean of students two days later.

CHAPTER 2. I WANT TO KILL SOMEBODY TODAY

18 *"The company had been founded at the start of the war"*: For an account of Triple Canopy's origins, see Daniel Bergner, "The Other Army," *New York Times Magazine*, August 14, 2005.

18 *"The CEO, Lee Van Arsdale, was a former Delta Sabre Squadron commander"*: From the Triple Canopy Web site: www.triplecanopy.com.

18 *"By 2006, Triple Canopy had nearly $250 million in contracts"*: This number was generated in mid-2007 from the database of FedSpending. org, a nonpartisan Web site that monitors federal government expenditures.

19 *"None of the prevailing laws"*: In theory, security contractors were subject to the Military Extraterritorial Jurisdiction Act of 2000, a civilian law that allows the Department of Justice to prosecute contractors employed by the Pentagon on foreign soil. But the law had not been tested in Iraq.

22 *"The Pentagon estimate was 25,000"*: As late as August 2008, five and a half years into the war, a Congressional Budget Office report noted the variance of data on the number of armed security contractors operating in Iraq. The report cited a 2005 Pentagon estimate of 25,000. In February 2008, according to the report, the Private Security Company Association of Iraq estimated 30,000. See Report from the Congressional Budget Office, "Contractors' Support of U.S. Operations in Iraq," p. 14–15, August 2008.

22 *"The GAO estimate was more than twice that: 48,000"*: Report from the Government Accountability Office, "Rebuilding Iraq: Actions Still Needed to Improve the Use of Private Security Providers," July 2005. The Private Security Company Association of Iraq also publicly stated that the number of security contractors in Iraq was 48,000, then lowered that estimate to 30,000 for the Congressional Budget Office report without explanation.

22 *"It had started small"*: There are numerous detailed accounts of the Bush administration's and the U.S. military's failure to prepare for and address the challenges of Iraq. See especially Rajiv Chandrasekaran, *Imperial Life in the Emerald City* (Knopf, 2006); Larry Diamond, *Squandered Victory* (Times Books, 2005); Michael Gordon and Bernard E. Trainor, *Cobra II* (Pantheon, 2006); George Packer, *The Assassins' Gate* (Farrar, Straus and

Giroux, 2005); Thomas E. Ricks, *Fiasco* (Penguin Press, 2006); and Bob Woodward, *State of Denial* (Simon & Schuster, 2006).

22 *"The International Republican Institute, chaired by John McCain"*: The IRI was protected by Blackwater Worldwide, the National Democratic Institute was protected by Unity Resources Group.

22 *"the market so hot it became known as the 'Iraq Bubble'"*: Alec Klein, "For Security in Iraq, a Turn to British Know-How," *Washington Post*, August 24, 2007.

24 *"By 2008, there were an estimated 190,000"*: Report from the Congressional Budget Office, "Contractors' Support of U.S. Operations in Iraq," August 2008.

24 *"But there were never any statistics"*: Partial casualty figures for contractors were kept by the Department of Labor under the Defense Base Act.

24 *"The U.S. Army Corps of Engineers employed at least a half dozen companies"*: In 2007, those companies included Aegis Defence Services, ArmorGroup International, Erinys Iraq, Falcon Group, and Threat Management Group.

25 *"I cannot say if the shots were aimed at us"*: Robert Bateman, "Blackwater and Me: A Love Story It Ain't," *Chicago Tribune*, October 12, 2007.

25 *"I'm a first-year student here at SAIS"*: A transcript of the exchange as well as Rumsfeld's remarks to the Johns Hopkins, Paul H. Nitze School of Advanced International Studies, December 5, 2005, can be found at http://www.defenselink.mil/transcripts/2005/tr20051205-secdef4421.html.

25 *"Two months later, the commander in chief, George W. Bush"*: Video of the exchange as well as his remarks on the "global war on terror" to the Johns Hopkins, Paul H. Nitze School of Advanced International Studies, April 10, 2006, can be found at: http://www.sais-jhu.edu/mediastream/videoOndemand/gwbush04102006.html.

28 *"Later, the four men would produce three distinct accounts"*: I have tried to present these accounts, drawn from interviews, after-action reports, company documents, and court records, to highlight their differences and similarities. Readers are left to draw their own conclusions about what occurred.

28 *"But he seemed confused"*: An incident report dated July 11, 2006, three days after the shootings, by Triple Canopy project manager Mark Alexander stated that Naucukidi initially told him that Washbourne had opened fire on the bongo truck. Naucukidi altered his statement to say that it was Schmidt, not Washbourne, who fired on the truck. In a written statement, an interview, and a sworn deposition, Naucukidi identified Schmidt as the shooter.

31 *"That night, the mercs held a going-away party"*: Shane Schmidt, incident report to Triple Canopy, July 10, 2006.

31 *"Schmidt later wrote that he briefly attended"*: Ibid.

31 *"By the time Schmidt and Sheppard came forward"*: Ibid.

32 *"The Milwaukee project manager, Mark Alexander, filed a seven-page report"*: Alexander incident report, July 11, 2006.

32 *"Alexander recommended firing J-Dub"*: Ibid.

32 *"Schmidt and Sheppard responded by filing a lawsuit"*: The suit was filed in Fairfax County Circuit Court on July 31, 2006. On August 1, 2007, a jury ruled that Triple Canopy did not wrongly fire Schmidt and Sheppard but criticized the company for what a jury note described as: "poor conduct, lack of standard reporting procedures, bad investigation methods and unfair double standards amongst employees." The case was under appeal as of this writing. See Tom Jackman, "Security Contractor Cleared in Two Firings," *Washington Post*, August 2, 2007.

35 *"Triple Canopy sent a two-page report"*: Incident report from Kelvin Kai, Triple Canopy's Iraq country manager, dated July 12, 2006.

35 *"It concluded that the three shooting incidents 'did in fact occur'"*: Ibid.

CHAPTER 4. WE PROTECT THE MILITARY

48 *"His book, **A Bloody Business**"*: Colonel Gerald Schumacher (retired), *A Bloody Business* (Zenith Press, 2006).

48 *"The entry for Crescent Security Group"*: Schumacher, *A Bloody Business*, p. 275.

50 *"Weiss was later immortalized"*: Tish Durkin, "Heavy Metal Mercenary," *Rolling Stone*, September 9, 2004.

50 *"Then, one night in 2004"*: Schumacher, *A Bloody Business,* p. 180–185.

62 *"Schneider, I later learned, had pleaded guilty"*: The allegations against Schneider and his accounts of the incidents are outlined in reports on file with the Lenawee County (Michigan) Sheriff's Office, Case No. 1994-0012888 and Case No. 1995-00000373.

62 *As a domestic violence offender, Schneider was prohibited"*: See U.S. Code 18 U.S.C. §922(g)(8): It shall be unlawful for any person who has been convicted in any court of a misdemeanor crime of domestic violence, to ship or transport in interstate or foreign commerce, or possess in or affecting commerce, any firearm or ammunition; or to receive any firearm or ammunition which has been shipped or transported in interstate or foreign commerce.

CHAPTER 5. THE STORIES YOU TELL

68 *"The company held a certificate of membership"*: Crescent was listed as a member company on the Private Security Company Association of Iraq Web site until articles about the company's lawlessness appeared in the *Washington Post* in July 2007.

68 *"Coté visited the Crescent Web site"*: The site has since been disabled.

69 *"One of the first measures"*: Coalition Provisional Authority Order Number 17 (Revised): Status of the Coalition Provisional Authority, MNF-Iraq, Certain Missions and Personnel in Iraq, June 27, 2004.

69 *"You are ready now for sovereignty"*: Rajiv Chandrasekaran, "U.S. Hands Authority to Iraq Two Days Early; Fear of Attacks Hastens Move; Interim Leaders Assume Power," *Washington Post,* June 29, 2004.

69 *"It granted mercenaries and other contractors immunity"*: CPA Order 17, June 27, 2004.

69 *"Never in the history of American warfare"*: Defense Federal Acquisition Regulation Supplement 252.225–7040, paragraph (b), "prohibited contractor personnel from using force or otherwise directly participating in acts likely to cause actual harm to enemy armed forces."

69 *"On October 3, 2005"*: "Contractor Personnel Authorized to Accom-

pany U.S. Armed Forces," Department of Defense Instruction, No. 3020.41, October 3, 2005.

70 *"Private security contractor personnel are . . . authorized"*: Defense Federal Acquisition Regulation Supplement, "Contractor Personnel Authorized to Accompany U.S. Armed Forces (DFARS Case 2005-D013)," *Federal Register*, Vol. 71, No. 116, p. 34826, June 16, 2006. The provision became a final rule on March 31, 2008. See *Federal Register*, Vol. 73, No. 62, p. 16764, March 31, 2008. The final rule stated that private security contractors are not mercenaries but that they merit special designation to "reflect the broader authority of private security contractors with regard to use of deadly force."

70 *"They included Brian X. Scott"*: On one occasion, Scott, citing the Anti-Pinkerton Act, single-handedly held up (temporarily) the awarding of the largest private security contract in Iraq. See Alec Klein and Steve Fainaru, "Judge Halts Award of Iraq Contract," *Washington Post*, June 2, 2007.

70 *"And the American Bar Association"*: The chairman of the ABA's Section of Public Contract Law, Michael A. Hordell, filed a seventeen-page objection, dated September 18, 2006. The letter stated: "The changes made by the Interim Rule may enhance the ability of DoD to employ PSCs to provide security for military facilities in hostile areas. Nevertheless, the changes also significantly blur the LOAC (Law of Armed Conflict) protections for all contractor personnel and fail to adequately address how contracting officers, contractors and military officers are to ensure LOAC violations do not occur."

70 *"The most pointed objection"*: Fenster's blistering critique, dated August 9, 2006, questioned the Pentagon's assumption that contractors would be limited to defensive functions: "The utter impossibility of such an assumption is well-demonstrated by the experience of nearly all the battlefield contractors who have been deployed in the current engagements. The defense of themselves and their property (including the property of the government) has clearly necessitated combat operations that can only be described as 'offensive' (whether or not they literally include 'preemptive attacks')."

71 *"While serving as a Bremer adviser"*: Peter said he played no role in the

formulation of CPA Order 17, which granted contractors immunity from Iraqi law.

71 *"The first sentence, in capital letters"*: Coalition Provisional Authority Memorandum Number 17, "Registration Requirements for Private Security Companies (PSC)," Annex A: Use of Force, June 26, 2004.

CHAPTER 6. NOW YOU ARE GOING TO DIE

All information on the events of the November 16, 2006, attack and subsequent kidnapping comes from Andy Foord and Jaime Salgado, the two surviving Crescent operators. Foord and Salgado provided written statements to British military investigators and later agreed to extensive interviews, including follow-up questions via email. Foord and Salgado were interviewed separately. Although their general recollection of events was the same, they differed on some key points. Foord said Jon Coté initially believed the convoy was being searched as part of a routine Iraqi police checkpoint. Salgado said Coté and the Crescent team leader, John Young, were both confused.

CHAPTER 7. YOUR BLOOD

111 *"The scope of this hijacking"*: Edward Wong, "Allies Wage Raid in Iraq, Seeking Abducted Guards," *New York Times*, November 18, 2006.

111 *"Basra's provincial governor said"*: Thomas Wagner, "Gang Suspected in Iraqi Kidnappings," Associated Press, November 18, 2006.

111 *"The chief of operations for the Basra police force"*: Ibid.

111 *"The police invited the media"*: "Coalition in Iraq Search for Hostages," Associated Press, November 20, 2006.

111 *"That evening, a man wearing a white headscarf"*: Hannah Allam, "After Three Weeks, No Word on Abducted Contractors," McClatchy Newspapers, December 7, 2006.

119 *"On the screen was a video"*: The video was never made public. The description of it comes from Hannah Allam, "Abducted Contractors Appear in Videotape," McClatchy Newspapers, December 27, 2006.

CHAPTER 8. SCOPE OF AUTHORITY: GOD

122 *"Eight days later, a video"*: Christopher Torchia, "New video shows 5 contractors who were kidnapped in southern Iraq," Associated Press, January 4, 2007. The video can still be seen on www.freecote.com.

123 *"After the kidnapping, I wrote"*: The article was published as a two-part series on July 29–30, 2007, in the *Washington Post*.

125 *"From 2004 to 2007, the U.S. military paid $548 million"*: Steve Fainaru, "U.S. Pays Millions in Cost Overruns for Security in Iraq," *Washington Post*, August 12, 2007.

125 *"Aegis gained notoriety"*: Jonathan Finer, "Contractors Killed in Videotaped Attacks; Army Fails to Find 'Probable Cause' in Machine-Gunning of Cars in Iraq," *Washington Post*, June, 11, 2006.

125 *"By then, the military had privatized"*: Steve Fainaru, "Iraq Contractors Face Growing Parallel War," *Washington Post*, June 16, 2007.

126 *"It was founded by a swashbuckling"*: For a comprehensive history of Tim Spicer and the Sandline Affair, see Robert Young Pelton, *Licensed to Kill* (Crown, 2006); P. W. Singer, *Corporate Warriors* (Cornell University Press, 2003); and Lieutenant Colonel Tim Spicer, *An Unorthodox Soldier* (Mainstream Press, 2000).

126 *"Tim Spicer is a mercenary"*: Steve Fainaru and Alec Klein, "In Iraq, a Private Realm of Intelligence Gathering," *Washington Post*, July 1, 2007.

127 *"By early 2006, his network"*: Figures from U.S. Army Corps of Engineers Gulf Region Division, Baghdad.

128 *"Of the twenty men on Convoy 1047"*: The attack is described in detail in an internal history of the U.S. Army Corps of Engineers Gulf Region Division. The description of the aftermath appears on pages 128–129. The company was purchased by G4S plc in May 2008.

129 *"In 2005, one out of every eighteen"*: Figures from U.S. Army Corps of Engineers Gulf Region Division, Baghdad.

130 *"ArmorGroup was a publicly traded company"*: From ArmorGroup media fact sheet, www.armorgroup.com. The company was purchased by G4S PLC in May 2008.

130 *"And yet half of its $273.5 million in revenue"*: From ArmorGroup media fact sheet, www.armorgroup.com.

131 *"In 2006, ArmorGroup ran 1,184 convoys"*: Figures provided by ArmorGroup sources.

131 *"The company had lost 30 employees"*: Figures provided by Armor-Group sources. The only official source of contractor casualty figures comes from the Department of Labor, which compiles workman's compensation claims under the Defense Base Act.

131 *"The PSCAI, the merc trade association"*: Later, after a spate of negative publicity about security contractors stemming largely from Blackwater shootings, the PSCAI listed only member companies.

136 *"Over time, the 'market for force'"*: Deborah D. Avant, *The Market for Force* (Cambridge University Press, 2005).

136 *"By 2007, the military had brought charges"*: From *Washington Post* database of military personnel charged with homicide or manslaughter since the start of Operation Iraqi Freedom.

137 *"The company employed more"*: Erik Prince testimony, Hearing of the House Committee on Oversight and Government Reform, October 2, 2007.

137 *"Blackwater had surveillance blimps"*: See www.blackwaterusa.com.

137 *"If the Iraq war had an official sponsor"*: For a detailed and highly critical account of Blackwater's rise, see Jeremy Scahill, *Blackwater* (Nation Books, 2007).

137 *"the company had made a billion dollars off the war"*: Contract figures provided at Hearing of the House Committee on Oversight and Government Reform, October 2, 2007.

137 *"when four of its operators were ambushed"*: Scahill's *Blackwater* contains a detailed account of the Fallujah attack.

138 *"Except that Blackwater"*: Steve Fainaru, "Where Military Rules Don't Apply," *Washington Post*, September 20, 2007. Blackwater was exempted from a variety of military regulations, including restrictions on the use of offensive weapons and procedures for reporting shooting incidents.

CHAPTER 9. HOSTAGE AFFAIRS

146 *"the 'grim perversities of smut and death,'"*: Chris Hedges, *War Is a Force That Gives Us Meaning* (PublicAffairs, 2002).

147 *"His first three days were 'a total waste'"*: From Koscielski trip report.

148 *"a U.S. Army patrol came under attack"*: Joshua Partlow, "Insurgent Video Claims Captured U.S. Soldiers Are Dead," *Washington Post*, June 5, 2007.

148 *"The army sent four thousand Americans"*: Ibid.

149 *"I ain't stopping till they kill me"*: Ibid.

149 *"As the families began to speak out"*: Wes Smith, "Hope for UF Student Captured in Iraq Fades," *Orlando Sentinel*, July 8, 2007.

149 *"Shortly after, Schumacher got an email"*: Email exchange between G. Alexander Crowther, Ph.D., and Colonel Gerald Schumacher (retired).

151 *"A career drug enforcement officer"*: Dan Herbeck, "Another Passage for Stepmother of Coté; Nightmare Followed by DEA Retirement," *Buffalo News*, July 8, 2008.

154 *"An affidavit for a search warrant"*: The affidavit was submitted in U.S. District Court, State and District of Minnesota, and was signed by Kevin Gjertson, special agent with the Criminal Investigative Service.

CHAPTER 10. BLACKRWATEY FOR SPECIAL SECURITY

161 *"The manual dedicated just one section"*: U.S. Army Lieutenant General David H. Petraeus and U.S. Marine Corps Lieutenant General James F. Amos, *Counterinsurgency FM 3-24*, Department of the Army, 2006.

162 *"The first suspended all weapons permits"*: Modification 6 to Multi-National Forces Iraq Frago 05-134: "Clarification of Iraq Weapons Policy and Extension of Expiration Date for Temporary Weapons Cards," March 9, 2007.

162 *"In a letter to a U.S. Army colonel"*: Letter from Peter to Lieutenant Colonel John Burk, dated February 21, 2007.

163 *"Petraeus soon issued another sharp frago"*: Modification 7 to Multi-National Forces Iraq Frago 05-134: "Clarification of Iraq Weapons Policy and Extension of Expiration Date for Temporary Weapons Cards Pending New Card Issue," April 27, 2007.

164 *"In June 2005, a Blackwater team shot an Iraqi"*: Memorandum from House Committee on Oversight and Government Reform: "Additional Information about Blackwater USA," October 1, 2007. The committee, which was investigating Blackwater, said it had compiled 437 "internal Blackwater incident reports" and thousands of pages of documents, including emails, relating to Blackwater and fourteen other security companies.

164 *"In October 2005, a Blackwater convoy traveling"*: House Committee on Oversight and Government Reform memorandum, October 1, 2007.

164 *"In November 2005, a Blackwater convoy traveling"*: Ibid.

164 *"another Hilla accident"*: Ibid.

165 *"a merc named Andrew J. Moonen staggered drunk"*: House Committee on Oversight and Government Reform documents, October 1, 2007, and John M. Broder, "Ex-paratrooper Is Suspect in Drunken Killing of Iraqi," *New York Times*, October 4, 2007.

165 *"He was confronted by a guard, Raheem Khalif"*: House Committee on Oversight and Government Reform memorandum, October 1, 2007.

165 *"Panicked and reeking of alcohol"*: The committee memorandum cited the statement of a Triple Canopy guard.

165 *"The Joint Area Support Group—the Green Zone police force"*: Committee on Oversight and Government Reform memorandum.

165 *"Later Christmas day, U.S. ambassador Zalmay Khalilzad"*: Karen DeYoung, "State Department Struggles to Oversee Private Army," *Washington Post*, October 21, 2007.

165 *"the U.S. embassy shipped Moonen out of Iraq"*: The committee memorandum stated that Blackwater, after firing Moonen for violating its policy against possessing a weapon while intoxicated, arranged to have him flown out of Iraq. The State Department was informed of the arrangements and received a copy of his itinerary, according to the memorandum.

166 *"Once Moonen was gone, State Department officials scrambled"*: The committee compiled an email record of the response.

166 *"Will you be following in up [sic] Blackwater"*: Email from U.S. Embassy chargé d'affaires to U.S. embassy regional security officer, December 25, 2006.

166 *"The chargé d'affaires first proposed a $250,000 payment"*: U.S. embassy email, December 26, 2006.

166 *"This could result in incidents"*: Diplomatic Security Service email, December 26, 2006.

166 *"In the past we have paid out $2,500"*: Ibid.

167 *"was fined almost exactly the same amount"*: Email from Blackwater to Diplomatic Security Service, January 8, 2007.

167 *"An Iraqi television network erroneously"*: Blackwater internal email, December 27, 2006.

167 *"Thought you might want to see this"*: Ibid.

167 *"Two months later, Moonen got a job"*: Richard Lardner, "Congressman Says Fired Blackwater Guard Found Work with Defense Contractor, Associated Press, October, 6, 2007.

168 *"He came to section 4, paragraph 3"*: CPA Order 17.

176 *"When their actions are allowed"*: U.S. Army Lieutenant General David H. Petraeus and U.S. Marine Corps Lieutenant General James F. Amos, *Counterinsurgency FM 3-24*, Department of the Army, 2006.

177 *"a mile away, Blackwater Chief of Mission (COM) Team 4*: From U.S. embassy spot report, September 16, 2007.

177 *"While Pelzman was inside, a car bomb exploded"*: Steven R. Hurst and Qassim Abdul-Zahra, "Pieces Emerge in Blackwater Shooting," Associated Press, October 8, 2007.

177 *"Tactical Support Team 22 was dispatched"*: Embassy spot report.

177 *The third Blackwater convoy, consisting*: Steven R. Hurst and Qassim Abdul-Zahra, "Pieces Emerge in Blackwater Shooting," Associated Press, October 8, 2007.

177 *"The bullet went through the windshield"*: Sudarsan Raghavan and Josh White, "Blackwater Guards Fired at Fleeing Cars, Soldiers Say; First U.S. Troops on Scene Found No Evidence of Shooting by Iraqis; Incident Called 'Criminal,'" *Washington Post*, October 12, 2007.

177 *"Another officer, Ali Khalaf Salman"*: Steven R. Hurst and Qassim Abdul-Zahra, "Pieces Emerge in Blackwater Shooting," Associated Press, October 8, 2007.

177 *"My son! My son!"*: Ibid.

177 *"Mahasin was a forty-six-year-old allergist"*: Ibid.

177 *"The Opel kept rolling toward the square"*: Joshua Partlow, "Embassy Restricts Diplomats' Iraq Travel; U.S. Order Follows Shooting by Guards," *Washington Post*, September 19, 2007.

178 *"Khalaf, the traffic cop, raised his left arm"*: Steven R. Hurst and Qassim Abdul-Zahra, "Pieces Emerge in Blackwater Shooting," Associated Press, October 8, 2007.

178 *"The Blackwater guards unleashed"*: Ibid.

178 *"Blackwater's Little Bird helicopters also fired down"*: Ibid.

178 *"Some Iraqi civilians were shot"*: Joshua Partlow, "Embassy Restricts Diplomats' Iraq Travel; U.S. Order Follows Shooting by Guards," *Washington Post*, September 19, 2007.

178 *"They were shooting from four cars"*: Sudarsan Raghavan, "Tracing the Paths of 5 Who Died in a Storm of Gunfire," *Washington Post*, October 4, 2007.

178 *"Hafiz said about thirty bullets struck his car"*: Steven R. Hurst and Qassim Abdul-Zahra, "Pieces Emerge in Blackwater Shooting," Associated Press, October 8, 2007.

179 *"But still it went on, the shooting continuing"*: Sudarsan Raghavan and Josh White, "Blackwater Guards Fired at Fleeing Cars, Soldiers Say; First U.S. Troops on Scene Found No Evidence of Shooting by Iraqis; Incident Called 'Criminal,'" *Washington Post*, October 12, 2007.

179 *"In all, seventeen Iraqis were killed"*: James Glanz and Alissa J. Rubin,

"From Errand to Fatal Shot to Hail of Fire to 17 Deaths," *New York Times*, October 3, 2007.

179 *"Many were poor or middle class"*: Sudarsan Raghavan, "Tracing the Paths of 5 Who Died in a Storm of Gunfire," *Washington Post*, October 4, 2007.

179 *"My wife was a distinguished woman"*: Steven R. Hurst and Qassim Abdul-Zahra, "Pieces Emerge in Blackwater Shooting," Associated Press, October 8, 2007.

179 *"the U.S. embassy put together a 'spot report,'"*: Steve Fainaru, "Blackwater Faced Bedlam, Embassy Finds; 'First Blush' Report Raises New Questions on Shooting," *Washington Post*, September 28, 2007.

179 *"Darren Hanner was a Blackwater employee"*: CNN.com: "Blackwater Contractor Wrote Government Incident Report," October 2, 2007.

179 *"not a single word about casualties"*: From U.S. embassy spot report.

179 *"soldiers from the U.S. Army's First Cavalry"*: Sudarsan Raghavan and Josh White, "Blackwater Guards Fired at Fleeing Cars, Soldiers Say; First U.S. Troops on Scene Found No Evidence of Shooting by Iraqis; Incident Called 'Criminal,'" *Washington Post*, October 12, 2007.

179 *"the Americans could not find shell casings"*: Ibid.

180 *"The First Cavalry put together a report"*: Ibid.

180 *"revoked Blackwater's operating license"*: Sabrina Tavernese, "U.S. Contractor Banned by Iraq over Shootings," *New York Times*, September 18, 2007.

181 *"Blackwater will be held accountable"*: Dana Milbank, "The Man from Blackwater, Shooting from the Lip," *Washington Post*, October 3, 2007.

181 *"He was so chastened"*: Ibid.

CHAPTER 11. FAITH THAT LOOKS THROUGH DEATH

183 *"Two weeks after the shootings"*: House Committee on Oversight and Government Reform memorandum, October 1, 2007.

183 *"Prince, during his testimony"* House Committee on Oversight and Government Reform Hearing, October 2, 2007.

183 *"That was less than 1 percent":* "We Can Take Those Lumps; Blackwater CEO talks about his firm's controversial place in military operations," *Military Times,* July 21, 2008.

183 *"just 15 percent of all shooting incidents":* Steve Fainaru, "Guards in Iraq Cite Frequent Shootings," *Washington Post,* October 3, 2007.

183 *"it was a charade":* Ibid.

184 *"You won't find a head":* Joshua Partlow and Sudarsan Raghavan, "Guards Kill Two Women in Iraq," *Washington Post,* October 10, 2007.

184 *"Unity was under contract":* Steve Fainaru, "Iraqis Detail Shooting by Guard Firm," *Washington Post,* November 26, 2007.

199 *"Iraqi prime minister Nouri al-Maliki launched an offensive":* Erica Goode, "U.S. Airstrikes Aid Iraqi Army in Basra Siege," *New York Times,* March 29, 2008.

SELECTED BIBLIOGRAPHY

Avant, Deborah D. *The Market for Force: The Consequences of Privatizing Security*. New York: Cambridge University Press, 2005.

Hedges, Chris. *War Is a Force That Gives Us Meaning*. New York: Public Affairs, 2002.

Miller, T. Christian. *Blood Money: Wasted Billions, Lost Lives, and Corporate Greed in Iraq*. New York: Little, Brown, 2006.

Pelton, Robert Young. *Licensed to Kill: Hired Guns in the War on Terror*. New York: Crown, 2006.

Petraeus, U.S. Army Lieutenant General David H., and U.S. Marine Corps Lieutenant General James F. Amos, *Counterinsurgency FM 3-24*. Washington, DC: Department of the Army, 2006.

Scahill, Jeremy. *Blackwater: The Rise of the World's Most Powerful Mercenary Army*. New York: NationBooks, 2007.

Schumacher, Colonel Gerald. *A Bloody Business: America's War Zone Contractors and the Occupation of Iraq*. St. Paul, MN: Zenith, 2006.

Singer, P. W. *Corporate Warriors: The Rise of the Privatized Military Industry*. Ithaca, New York: Cornell University Press, 2003.

ACKNOWLEDGMENTS

I AM, FIRST AND FOREMOST, GRATEFUL BEYOND MEASURE to the families of the Crescent hostages, for their bravery and compassion, for their unwavering commitment to expose the truth about what happened to their loved ones, and for bestowing me with their trust. My heartfelt thanks to Francis and Nancy Coté, Christopher Coté, Lori Silveri, Patrick and Jennifer Reuben, Kathy Reuben, Casey and Bree Reuben, Keri Johnson-Reuben, Sharon and Dennis DeBrabander, John Robert and Jasmyn Young, Mark and Crista Munns, Jackie Stewart, and Maria and Franz Nussbaumer.

I am forever indebted to the Cotés and Silveris, who embraced me as family while at the same time insisting that I write unflinchingly about Jon's life and death.

Phil Bennett, the managing editor of the *Washington Post*, and my editor, mentor, and friend for fifteen years, first approached me with the idea of writing about the private war in Iraq. This book, and the work that preceded it, is the result of that initial spark. Even in these difficult times, there is no other newspaper like the *Post*, which somehow continues to combine collegiality, humanity, and an unparalleled tenacity to seek out hard truths. The *Post*'s coverage of the Iraq war is a manifestation of those qualities. The newspaper's executives, chairman Don Graham (formerly of the First Cavalry Division), and Bo Jones, the publisher during my time in Iraq, have encouraged and supported dozens of journalists who have passed through Baghdad, impelling them to produce their best work. I am especially grateful to executive editor Len Downie, whose retirement after forty-four years at the *Post* caps a career that stands as monument to the most powerful journalism of our time, and to my editor and friend, David Hoffman, whose intelligence and passion for the work touches everything he does.

I am also indebted to my colleagues in Baghdad and Washington for their support and encouragement. I am especially grateful to Anthony Shadid, who has enhanced our understanding of Iraq more than any other American journalist; Tom Ricks, who took me under his wing to impart his uncommon wisdom and military expertise from the moment I set foot in Baghdad; and Karl Vick, the ideal colleague, correspondent, and friend. None of us would have been able to work without the support, assistance, and bravery of our Iraqi colleagues, whose contribution to the coverage of this war can now be measured in thousands of stories. I am especially thankful to Omar Fekeiki, Bassam Sebti, Naseer Nouri, Saad al-Izzi, and Naseer Mehdawi, and to the *Post*'s amazing Baghdad Bureau: Dhia Ahmed, Marwan al-Ani, Khalid Alsaffar, Omar Asaad, Dlovan Brwari, Naseer Fadhil, Sabah Fadhil, Falah Hassan, Muayad Jabbar, Mona Jawad, Wijdan Jawad, Mohammed Mahdi, Rifaat Mohammed, Mohammed Munim, Jawad Munshid, Fawziya Naji, Saif Naseer, Ghazwan Noel, and Muhanned Salem.

The price of information in Iraq was driven home again on Sunday, October 14, 2007, when our colleague, *Post* correspondent Salih Saif Aldin, thirty-two, was shot and killed while reporting in Baghdad. The sacrifice of Iraqi journalists in this war has been enormous: as of this writing, 110 Iraqi journalists have been killed since the March 2003 invasion. We remember Salih and miss him terribly. *Mushtaqeelak, Salih.*

Julie Tate's "research" skills include investigative reporting, copyediting, brainstorming, fact-checking, and general musing, all served up with warmth, intelligence, and melting sarcasm. Her work is in nearly every line of this book.

I am also grateful to my *Post* colleagues (some, sadly, now former colleagues) in Baghdad, Washington, and other environs: John Ward Anderson, Cameron Barr, Rajiv Chandrasekaran, Liz Clarke, Jon Finer, James Grimaldi, Bill Hamilton, Tiffany Harness, Scott Higham, Tom Jackman, Mary Jordan, Ellen Knickmeyer, Molly Moore, Andy Mosher, Amit Paley, Josh Partlow, Sudarsan Raghavan, Keith Richburg, Michael Robinson-Chavez, Dave Sheinin, Mary Beth Sheridan, Keith Sinzinger, Dita Smith, Jackie Spinner, Joe Stephens, Doug Struck, Kevin Sullivan, Liz Visser, Liz Ward, Scott Wilson, Chris White, and Josh White. Thanks also to Colin McMahon and Rick Jervis, traveling companions from Chilpancingo to Tal Afar.

Several people read the manuscript and made suggestions to improve it. They include Mark Fainaru-Wada, Karl Vick, Mike Arrighi and Julie Tate. A special thanks to Arrighi, the ultimate Baghdad host and war-zone chef, who took time to read and offer suggestions even as he moved between Iraq, Afghanistan, and the United States. Maureen Fan "heard" the entire book from China, offered sage advice on each chapter, and kept me sane (mostly). Special thanks to God for Maureen.

Robert Shepard, my agent, in many ways understood this project long before I did. His editing, guidance, and straightforward advice were indispensable at every turn. Bob Pigeon, my editor at Da Capo, is a true professional whose suggestions improved every chapter.

Thanks also to my friend Brad Mangin, as well as Ashley St. Thomas, Kate Kazeniac Burke, Alex Camlin, Christine Marra, John Radziewicz, and Fred Francis.

I am grateful to the men of 2nd Platoon, Alpha Company, 2nd Battalion, 505th Parachute Infantry Regiment of the 82nd Airborne

Division, for entrusting me with their memories of Jon Coté and their difficult tour in Iraq. Also the men of Sigma Phi Epsilon in Gainesville, Florida, in particular Joey Dal Santo and Matt Sloan.

Long before the mainstream media discovered the world of private security, several writers, journalists, and academics were tackling the subject from all sides of the political spectrum. Each was unfailingly generous and helpful. They include Peter W. Singer, Deborah D. Avant, Jeremy Scahill, Pratap Chatterjee, R. J. Hillhouse, and Robert Young Pelton.

Colonel Gerald Schumacher (retired), the author of *A Bloody Business*, was the first person I met when I began this project. Gerry, a writer-photographer-warrior, introduced me to Crescent, offered keen insights on the private war, plied me with amazing photos, and even provided weapons training in the Nevada desert. He is a colleague and a friend.

Thanks also to my friends Liz Clarke, Bonnie Cohen, Greg Fernbacher, John Gaines, Bud Geracie, Cynthia Gorney, Sean Horgan, Kevin "Moose" Huhn, Bruce Jenkins, Claudia Kalb, Jackie MacMullan, Leigh Montville, Scott Price, Ray Ratto, Glenn Schwarz, Dave Sheinin, Mary Beth Sheridan, Don Skwar, and Ian Thomsen.

And to Cal DeAlmeida, the mathematician-chef of the Bronx, and Caitie DeAlmeida, the talented young writer.

The it-takes-a-village theory of child-rearing also applies to this book. I could not have completed it without the wonderful Poinsett crew of El Cerrito, California. Special thanks to the Nealy's: Mike, DeLisa, Andrew, Weston, and Gia; and Rick Cobb, Patrice Paul-Cobb and Kenia Cobb.

The story of Jon Coté and Crescent Security for me became inextricably intertwined with the death of my father, Bob Fainaru, whose voice I can still hear, and whose humor and humanity will be with us always. At one point, my amazing mother, Ellen Gilbert, had one son on his way to prison and another in Iraq, and through it all gave us only unconditional support. My wonderful sister-in-law, Nicole Fainaru-Wada, is always there for laughter and a wise and understanding ear. Thanks to Max and Ella, my nephew and niece, who are excellent readers and savage wrestlers. And, of course, to Will, my beautiful boy, the Usain Bolt of Poinsett Park.

Somehow I was blessed with the greatest brother of all time, Mark Fainaru-Wada—revealer of truths, my best friend, everything.

INDEX

Page references in **bold** refer to text graphics.

Abood, Ahmed Thamir, 171
Abu Ghraib Warehouse, 132–135
Aegis Defence Services
    Correa and, 112
    shooting at civilians, 125–126
    Spicer and, 126
Agility, 132, 141–142
Ahmad, Shihab, 139
Ahmed, Colonel, 168, 175
Al Afem, 64
Al Alam news network, 111
Al-Iraqiya TV station, 169–173
Al-Maliki, Azhar Abdullah, 170, 171
Al-Maliki, Nouri, 180, 199, 200
Al-Rubaie, Ahmed Hathem
    background/killing of, 176–178,
        177, 179, 180

father, Jawad, 176, 179
    mother, Mahasin, 176–178, 179, 180
    sister, Miriam, 176
Al-Rubaie, Mowaffak, 175
Albany Times Union, 142
Albright, Madeleine, 22
Alexander, Mark, 32
Ali, Mohammed Adel, 170
Ali, Rizgar, 139
All the President's Men, 45
Allam, Hannah, 118–121
American Bar Association (ABA),
    70
American Military University, 167
Andrade, Fernanda, 5, 15
Aristide, Jean-Bertrand, 133
ArmorGroup, 59, 89, 129–131
Arrighi, Mike, 20, 21, 26, 138
Arsdale, Lee Van, 18
Avant, Deborah, 136

Bagram Air Base, Afghanistan, 100
Baker, Kevin, 200
Balad, xvii, 60, 113, 124
BALCO steroids scandal, 39–40, 41, 46
Barnes, Leroy ("Nicky"), 152
Basheer (Iraqi with Crescent), 78, 79, 81–82
Basra
    al-Maliki's offensive in, 199, 200
    description, xiii
    trip to, xiii–xiv, xvi, xvii
    See also Joe from Basra
Bateman, Bob/Kate, 25–26
"Belushi, John" (Wissam Hisham), 88, 91, **92–93**, 94–95
Bennett, Randall, 166
Berman, Chris, 129
Bernstein, Carl, 37
"Big Boy Rules" of mercenaries, 19, 26, 69, 136
Bjorlin, Gary, 200
Black Hawk Down affair, 18
Blackwater USA/Worldwide
    al-Iraqiya shootings, 169–173
    background, 136–138
    "ban" and, 180, 181
    equipment overview, 137
    Fallujah ambush, 137, 138
    as hated, 135, 136, 137–140, 163–164, 168–169, 172–183, 185
    impunity of, 25–26, 137–140, 163–167, 168–183, 213
    killings by, 139–140, 164–167, 169, 170–174, 176–181
    Kirkuk killings, 139–140, 164
    lawlessness of, 25, 137–140, 163–167, 168–183
    Nisoor Square killings, 177–180, 182–183, 213
    reporting on shootings, 183

Triple Canopy and, 18, 137
Washington hearings, 180–181
Bloody Business, A (Schumacher), 48–49, 149
Bonds, Barry, 39–41, 42, 46, 152
Borrowman, Benjamin ("Red"), 65–66, 154, 200
Botes, Jaco, 22
Boyle, Jason, 79, 99, 112
Bremer, L. Paul, 69, 71, 137
Bright Lights, Big City, 83
Buffalo News, 214
Bush, George W.
    Aristide, 133
    Iraq, 25–26, 118, 129, 164, 215
    Mark Fainaru-Wada, 40
Butler, Richard, 201

Caldwell IV, William B., 111
Camp Anaconda, **viii**, **ix**, 63
Camp NAVISTAR, **viii**, **ix**, 50
Castlegate, 88
Casualty counting, xiii, 24, 212, 213, 215
Chalabi, Ahmad
    background, 118
    Bush administration and, 118, 120, 186
    interview of, 118–121
    video of hostages, 119–121, 123, 186
Chapman, Paul, 112, 158, 159
Chong, Joseph, 132
Clapp, Timothy, 184
Clark, Geoff, 71, 142
Coalition Provisional Authority Memorandum Number 17. *See* CPA Memorandum 17
Coalition Provisional Authority Order Number 17. *See* CPA Order 17
Colon, Ricardo, 179

Combat Support Associates, 167
Corporate Warriors (Singer), 126
Correa, Raul
  background, 112–113
  as mercenary, 112–113, 114, 115–116
Coté, André, 151
Coté, Chris
  eulogy for brother, 212–213
  family gathering/brother's funeral,
    206, 207, 208, 210
  kidnapping and, 106, 189–190,
    198–199, 201–204
  parents/family life, 83, 106–107,
    108–109
  personality, 7, 8, 10, 107
  relationship with brother, 7, 10, 12,
    106–107, 108–109, 203, 208,
    212–213
  relationship with father, 189–190,
    198, 199, 202–203
  work/career, 7, 109, 198
Coté, Francis
  background, 107–108, 109, 212
  eulogy for son, 211, 212
  families meeting and, 194
  family gathering/son's funeral,
    206, 207–208, 209, 210, 216
  gas station of, 207–208
  kidnapping and, 109, 143–144, 145,
    156–157, 189, 200–203
  personality/description, 107–108
  relationship with Chris, 189–190,
    198, 199, 202–203
Coté, Jon
  burial, 216–217
  church service for, 211–213
  description, xii, 2, 4–5, 66–67,
    72–73, 81
  family gathering/funeral, 207–210
  gift for mother, 83, 211
  parents/family life, xvii, 66, 83,
    106–107, 108–109

  personality, xii, xvi, 2, 4–5, 7, 8,
    72–73, 81, 107
  relationship with brother, 7, 10, 12,
    106–107, 108–109, 203, 208,
    212–213
  remains, 205–207, 208, 210–211
  stepbrother Max, 109
  stepsister Samantha, 106, 109
Coté, Jon/kidnappings
  death confirmation, 201–202
  on hostage list, 144–145
  as missing, 98, 110
  November 2006 convoy attack, 86,
    89, 91, **92–93**, 94, 98, 100
  remains, 207, 208, 210–211
  videos, 119, 123
  See also Crescent Security Group
    kidnapping
Coté, Jon/mercenary
  Basheer's remains, 81–82
  beginnings, 11–12, 13–15
  danger of work, 74–75, 83–84
  death pact, xii, xvii
  Facebook, 73
  Fainaru's advice to, 83–84
  meeting Fainaru, 66–67
  money and, xvii, 11–12, 73–74
  November 2006 convoy attack, 86,
    89–90, 91, **92–93**, 98
  plans to return to school, xii, 67,
    84, 86
  pranks, 72, 85, 86
  reasons for becoming, 83, 85–86,
    124–125
  return, 68, 72, 73–75
  telling his story to Fainaru, 67, 72,
    73–75
  trip to Basra with Fainaru, xiii, xiv,
    xvi–xvii
Coté, Jon/military
  decorations/citation, 3
  firing on wedding celebration, 2–3

Coté, Jon/military (*continued*)
   ManPad Suppression mission, 1–2
   nightmares/post-traumatic stress,
       8, 11, 209–210
   overview, xii, 1–3, 4, 109
Coté, Jon/University of Florida
   friends, 4–9, 10, 11–12
   major/studies, xii, 4, 5, 10, 67, 210
   motorcycle, 9–10, 12–13
   partying/drinking, 4–6, 7, 8, 11,
       12–13, 15, 74
   Sigma Phi Epsilon, 4, 6, 10–11, 84
Coté, Lori (Lori Silveri)
   background, xvii, 83, 108–109, 109
   family gathering/funeral, 206, 216
   gift from son, 83, 211
   kidnapping, 110, 194
Coté, Maude, 208
Coté, Nancy
   background, 106, 109, 151–152, 198
   Chris and, 198–199
   family gathering/Jon's funeral,
       208, 209, 211
   kidnapping and, 106, 109, 143–144,
       145, 151–152, 156–157, 194, 201–203
Coté, Serge, 207
Coulrophobia, 18
"Counterflow" driving, 115–116, 177
CPA Memorandum 17
   Blackwater and, 172, 174–175
   use of force and, 71
CPA Order 17
   Blackwater and, 173, 181
   immunity and, 69, 136, 168
Crescent Security Group
   description, 48–49, 54, 55, 64, 65,
       68, 75
   end of, 153, 158, 159–160, 161
   "fake IDs," 63, 71, 154, 159
   investigations of, 153, 159–160
   Iraqis salary/work inequalities,
       55–56, 64–65, 87–88

Italian military and, 59, 63, 81, 99
lack of equipment/supplies, 51, 52,
    62, 71, 78–79
money and, 55–56
office politics/factions, 65, 87–88
reputation/lawlessness, 53, 62, 63,
    71, 99, 112–113, 138, 142, 153,
    156–157, 158–160
risks to employees, 53–54, 74–75,
    83, 84
stories, 77–82
Wolf's Den, 58, 65, 75, 87, 88, 100,
    115
See also specific individuals
Crescent Security Group kidnapping
   British military/intelligence and,
       110–111, 115
   demands of kidnappers, 112, 123
   diagram, **92–93**
   effects on company, 112, 114,
       115–116, 153–154, 159–160, 161
   families and, 116–117, 143–144,
       145–146, 147–148
   families going public, 147–148, 151
   families meeting, 193–196
   FBI and, 110, 121, 145–146, 147–148,
       149, 151, 152, 155, 186, 187, 188, 189,
       190, 194, 197, 201–202
   information bits/rumors, 111, 142,
       144, 145
   Iraqi security forces and, 88–89, 91,
       92–93, 94, 96, 97, 110, 111, 114, 115
   lack of information/investigation,
       111, 114–115, 117, 140–141, 142,
       145–152
   severed fingers, 187–190
   torture, 200, 210
   unequal treatment by U.S.
       government, 148–150, 151–152
   videos, 111–112, 119–121, 122–124,
       145, 186
See also specific individuals

Crescent Security Group November
2006 convoy
attack, **ix**, 90–91, **92–93**, 94–98
checkpoints, 89–90
gathering for, 86–87, 88–89
lack of Iraqi security, 88–89, 110
See also specific individuals
Criminal Investigative Service
(CIS), 153–154
Crowther, G. Alexander, 149
Custer Battles, 112

Dal Santo, Joey, 4, 5, 6–7
"Davis, Sammy," 110
DEA and kidnapping, 110, 151–152
See also Joe from Basra
DeBrabander, Dennis, 155, 190, 193
DeBrabander, Sharon
families meeting, 193
kidnapping and, 146, 152–153,
154–155, 189
son's death confirmation, 190–191
Degn, Matthew
Blackwater and, 173, 175, 176
description, 167–168
family, 167
MOI and, 167–168
role/position, 167, 168, 173
DEH Global, 51, 197
Delta Force, 18
DHL, 54
Dogs of War, The (Forsyth), 126
DynCorp, 18, 52, 137, 139, 150

82nd Airborne, 2, 5, 13, 63, 74, 100,
112, 154, 209, 215, 216, 217
Erinys Iraq, 59, 125, 185

Fainaru, Steve
Barry Bonds and, 40–41
divorce, 39, 41–42
father's cancer/death, 102–105

son, 39, 43, 47
trip with father/brother, 36–38, 42,
43–44, 45–46
Fainaru, Steve/Iraq
abstractions and, 117
Balad patrol/attack, 124
CD from Crescent employee, 160
post-Iraq malaise, 38, 41, 44,
46–47
reasons for going/staying, 38, 39,
41, 124–125
Sadr City bombing incident,
38–39
suicide bomber/bombings, 117–118
Fainaru, Steve/kidnapping
article on, 123–124, 150
learning of, 106, 110
return to Iraq after, 124–125
visit with Picco, 156–160
Fainaru, Bob
cancer and, 37, 38, 42–43, 102–104
death, 104–105, 117, 124, 152
trip with sons, 36–38, 42, 43–44,
45–46
Fainaru-Wada, Mark
father's cancer/death, 102, 103–105
legal case, 37, 39–40, 43, 152
as reporter/BALCO steroids
scandal, 39–40, 41
sentencing, 43, 44–45, 46
statement, 45
trip with father/brother, 36–38, 42,
43–44, 46
wife Nicole, 40, 44–45
Falcon Group, 70, 132–134
Fallujah, xii, 55, 56, 60, 119, 137
battle, 60–61, 137
Blackwater and, 137
Farsi language, 8
Federal Register (U.S.), 69
Fenster, Herbert L., 70
Foo, Jenny J., 145–146

Foord, Andy
    after attack, 94, 95, 98–99, 100–101,
        110–111, 113, 115
    background, 58, 86–87, 96, 113
    firings by, 87, 96
    November 2006 convoy attack, 86,
        88–91, **92–93**, 94, 95–99
Ford, Nicholas, 216–217
Forsyth, Frederick, 126
Fragmentary orders
    mercenaries deadly force use, 69,
        168
    regulating mercenaries, 162–163
    See also CPA Memorandum 17;
        CPA Order 17
Furkan Brigades, 122–123

Game of Shadows (Fainaru-Wada and
    Williams), 41
Gem bar, Triple Canopy, 17, 19–20, 31
Geneva Conventions, 19
Gilbert, Ellen, 44–45
Goldin, Jenny, 209–210
Granite Tactical Vehicles, 129

Hadi, Nabras Mohammed, 169–171
Hafezi, Shiva, 4, 5, 7–9, 13–15, 84
Hafiz, Mohammed/Ali, 178
Halliburton, 18–19
Hankins, David, 5–6, 10
Hanner, Darren, 179
Hartig, Michael J., 35
Hassan, Hussein Abdul, 170
Hassan (Iraqi with Crescent), 78,
    79–80
Hawija accident, 80–81
"Head bomb," 117
Hedges, Chris, 146
Hilla, Iraq, 17, 26, 34, 112, 164–165
Hisham, Wissam ("John Belushi"),
    88, 91, **92–93**, 94–95
Holly, Jack
    background, 126–127, 135

on Blackwater, 135, 136, 137–138,
    163–164, 180–181
Convoy 1047 attack, 128
description, 126–127
on mercenaries, 127–128, 135–136
role with Corps of Engineers, 126,
    180–181, 213
switch to armored vehicles, 129
Horner, David, 63, 64–65
House Committee on Oversight and
    Government Reform, 165,
    180–181
Howard, Ragen T., 13
Hussein, Saddam, 132, 150, 169
Hutchinson, Eric L., 13

I Don't Know But I've Been Told
    (Correa), 112
International Contractors
    Association, 22
International Peace Operations
    Association, 21
International Republican Institute,
    22
"Iraq Bubble," 22
Iraq-Kuwait border conflict, 88
Iraq maps, **viii–ix**
Iraq War
    as faraway, 215
    government reasons, xiv
Iraqi Media Network, 169, 171, 172
Iraqi Ministry of Interior
    ArmorGroup and, 131
    Blackwater and, 173–176
    Crescent and, 68
    licenses/weapons permits and,
        162–163
    security of, 168
    See also specific individuals
Iraqi Ministry of Trade, 68, 163

Jackson, Chris, 56–57, 112
Jamison, Sammy, 131

Jassim, Ahmed Ali, 178
Joe from Basra
after Coté's death confirmation,
205, 206
background, 152, 186
description, 186
hostage search, 186–188, 189
severed fingers and, 187–188
Johnson-Reuben, Keri, 144, 192,
193
Johnson-Reuben, Paul. *See* Reuben,
Paul
Joint Contracting Command for
Iraq and Afghanistan, 35
Junkyards in Iraq, 57

Kai, Kelvin, 32, 35
Kamal, Hussein, 168, 175, 176
Karate Kid, The, 23
Karrada Street killing, 185
KBR Inc., 18–19, 35
Khalif, Raheem, 165
Khalilzad, Zalmay, 165
Kidnappings
description, 114–115
Withrow, 145
See also Crescent Security Group
kidnapping; *specific individuals*
Kirkuk, 117, 133, 139, 164, 185
Knight-Ridder newspaper, 118
Kornowski, Edward, 206–207
Koscielski, Mark
families meeting and, 193–194, 195,
196
investigations by, 146–148
at Young's fund-raiser, 153–155
Kraig, Mike/Sandy/Travis, 209
Kurds
Falcon Group, 70, 133–134
Kirkuk, 133, 139
Kuwait City, xiii, 48, 49, 54, 55, 66, 72,
75, 79, 83, 106, 112, 114–115, 147,
157–158, 195, 211

Lacquement, David B., 175
Laguna Construction, 18–19, 35
Latif, Sirry Abdul, 185
Lewis, Robert, 108
Licensed to Kill (Pelton), 126
Lightner, Kent, 183–184, 185
Lloyd-Owen International (LOI), 87
Logistics and Movement
Coordination Center (LMCC),
99
Logistics Directorate, 24
Love, Gordon, 156
Lumsden, Micaela, 203

Maclean, Norman, 203
Magazin, Anja, 4, 5, 15
Mahdi, Adel Abdul, 165, 167
Mahdi Army, 168, 199
ManPad Suppression mission, 1–2
MapQuest use, xiv
Maps of Iraq, **viii–ix**
Masirewa, Jona, 31, 32
McCain, John, 22
McClatchy, 118
McCormack, Patrick, 215
McCullough, Shannon, 153, 155, 200
MedEvac, 79
MEJA (Military Extraterritorial
Jurisdiction Act), 136
Mercato del Golfo, 54
Mercenaries
1893 law prohibiting, 70
ambiguity/tension over, 215
beginnings/evolution, xi, xiv–xv,
22–24, 103, 127–128, 129–130,
135–136
coalition relationship, 59–60
convoy attack frequencies, 129
description overview, xi, xiv–xv,
22–24
hatred of Americans and, 137–140,
163–164, 168–169, 172–183, 185–186
on the job training, 63

Mercenaries (*continued*)
  law and, 19
  lobbyists, 21–22
  need for, xi, xiv, 22, 212
  non-financial reasons for
    becoming, xvi, xvii, 182
  numbers of, 21–22, 23–24
  oil company protection, 214
  payoffs for killings by, 166–167
  protests against using, 69–70
  quality disparity, 52, 62, 62–63
  regulating, 161–163, 168, 175, 176
  reporting/data on shootings,
    183–184
  responsibility question, 25–26
  sayings of, xv, 20
  shooting explanation, 174, 184, 185
  turnover, 60, 113
  unequal treatment by military/
    U.S. government, 79–80,
    148–149, 151
  unions, 21–22
  as unprecedented, 69–70
  uses overview, 22, 23–24
  weapons confiscation by military,
    162
  See also Military/mercenaries;
    Private security firms; *specific*
    individuals
Military
  bravery/selflessness, 60, 61
  lack of troops, xi, xiv, 22, 212
  pre-mission patrol briefing, 53–54
  rules/accountability, 33
  troop fatalities cataloging, xiii
  "winning the war," xvi–xvii
Military Extraterritorial Jurisdiction
  Act (MEJA), 136
Military/mercenaries
  blurring line between, 70, 129–130,
    132, 133, 212, 215
  bonding in, 60, 62

  counting casualties and, xiii, 24,
    212, 213, 215
  equipment/supplies disparities, 62,
    78–79
  unequal treatment by government,
    79–80, 148–149, 151
  "unity of effort," 161–162
Military Times, 183
"Miyagi," 23
Moonen, Andrew J.
  alleged killing by, 165–166
  job after killing, 167
Morita, Pat, 23
Mosul, 80, 164
MPRI, 167, 168
Muhammad, Khursheed, 139
Muhammad, Nidham Qadir, 139
Mujahedeen of Jerusalem Company,
    111–112, 121, 123, 140–141
Munns, Josh
  background, xii, xii–xiii, 60–62
  description/personality, xii, 52, 60,
    61–62, 81
  fiancé, xiii, 62, 144
  funeral/burial, 200
  as mercenary, xii, xiii, xiv, xvii
  PTSD, 61
Munns, Josh/kidnapping
  death confirmation/remains, 192
  as missing, 98, 110
  November 2006 convoy attack,
    86, 89, 91–92, **92–93**, 94, 95, 98,
    100
  videos, 119, 123
  See also Crescent Security Group
    kidnapping
Munns, Mark/Christa, 60, 61, 193
Muqtada al-Sadr, 118
Muslim Public Affairs Council of
  Western New York, 151
Mustafa (Iraqi with Crescent), 78,
    79–80

Nadir, Khalid Mahmood, 139
Nasiriyah, 50, 59
National Democratic Institute, 22
National Intelligence Committee,
    175, 176
National Islamic Resistance in Iraq:
    The Furkan Brigades, 122, 123,
    141
Naucukidi, Isireli ("Isi")
    background, 19, 34–35
    J-Dub alleged killing man and, 27,
        29, 31, 32, 34–35
    SUV accident/cover-up, 17, 21
New York Times, 180
Nisoor Square killings, 177–180,
    182–183, 213
Numaniyah trip/hit, 77–80
Nussbaumer, Bert
    background, 86
    kidnapping, 98, 110, 119, 123, 145,
        188, 197
    November 2006 convoy attack, 86,
        88, 90, 91, **92–93**, 94, 98, 100
    Qusay and, 87
    See also Crescent Security Group
        kidnapping
Nussbaumer, Franz, 193
Nussbaumer, Maria, 193

Office of American Citizens
    Services and Crisis
    Management, 145–146
Orlando Sentinel, 149

Papua New Guinea and mercenaries,
    126
Patriot Guard Riders of New York,
    206, 209, 211
Peck, Timothy L., 13
Pelton, Robert Young, 126
Pelzman, Kerry, 177
Permuy, Lauren, 5, 15

Peshmerga, 133
Peter, Lawrence T.
    on Blackwater, 138
    CPA Memorandum 17 and, 71,
        174
    Iraqi MOI and, 162–163
    PSCAI and, 70–71, 127, 162–163
Petraeus, David H.
    Blackwater and, 164
    regulation of security companies,
        161–163, 176
    surge and, 161, 175–176
Picco, Franco
    after Iraq, 160
    after kidnapping, 88, 112, 114
    background, 54, 55
    on Crescent, 63
    Fainaru's visit, 158–160
    hostage families and, 143, 144,
        156–157
    money and, 55–56
    See also Crescent Security Group
Prince, Erik, 138, 181, 183
Private Security Company
    Association of Iraq (PSCAI),
    22, 68, 70–71, 127, 131, 138,
    162–163, 214
Private security contractor. *See*
    Mercenaries
Private security firms
    "legitimacy" of, 68–69
    numbers, xiv, 22, 131–132
    ratio of operators to tractor-
        trailers, 89
    variety, xiv
    See also specific firms
PSCAI (Private Security Company
    Association of Iraq), 22, 68,
    70–71, 127, 131–132, 138, 162–163,
    214
Public Warehousing Co. (PWC) of
    Kuwait, 128–129, 132

Quantico, 188
Qusay ("Mongo"), 87, 96

Raghavan, Sudarsan, 180
Rahdi, Faisal, 173
Rahman, Hussam Abdul, 178
Raising a Modern-Day Knight
    (Lewis), 108
Ramadi, xiii, 41, 55
Reconstruction Operations Center
    (ROC), 137–138
Reema, 157–158
Regulating mercenaries, 161–163, 168,
    175, 176
Reuben, Patrick
    background, 154
    description/personality, 196
    families meeting and, 193, 196–197
    family of, 196
    kidnapping, 188–189
    Koscielski and, 154, 193
Reuben, Paul
    Coté/Skora joke on, 85, 86
    daughters Casey and Bree, 51, 144,
        194–195, 196, 197
    description/background, 51, 197
    drinking, 53, 196, 197
    first wife Kathy, 196, 197
    granddaughter Ka'Leah, 194, 197
    kidnapping, 98, 110, 119–120,
        123–124, 146–147, 153, 192
    military background, 51, 195
    November 2006 convoy attack, 86,
        89, **92–93**, 94, 98, 100
    Numaniyah trip/hit, 77–80
    reasons for staying in Iraq, 195
    role with Crescent, 51–52, 78, 79, 80
    See also Crescent Security Group
        kidnapping
River Runs Through It, A (Maclean),
    203, 213
ROC (Reconstruction Operations
    Center), 137–138

"Rock" vehicles, 129
Rolling Stone magazine, 50
Route Irish, 27
Route Irish (IED Alley/Death
    Street), 29
Route Tampa, **viii**, **ix**, xvi, 16, 20, 58,
    73, 81, 90, 97, 98, 100, 114, 115
Rozelle, Randy, 211–212
RTI International, 184–185
Rumsfeld, Donald H., 25
Ruth, Babe, 40, 42

Saadi, Adel, 170
Saddam Hussein, 133, 150, 169
Sadr City, 38–39, 199
Sadr City bombing incident, 38–39
Safwan, **ix**, 58, 87, 89, 111, 122, 145
Salaam, Thair, 172
Salgado, Jaime
    after attack, 97, 99, 100–101,
        110–111, 113, 115
    background, 87, 96
    November 2006 convoy attack, 86,
        88–89, 90–91, **92–93**, 94, 95–99
Salman, Ali Khalaf, 177, 178
Salman, Sabah (Abu Sajad), 171–172
San Francisco Chronicle, 39, 40, 44, 46
Sandline Affair, 126
Sandline International, 126
Schmidt, Shane ("Happy")
    background, 27
    drinking, 34, 62
    J-Dub alleged killing and, 27–30,
        31, 32, 33
    J-Dub on, 34
    lawsuit by, 32
Schneider, Scott
    after kidnapping, 112, 116, 144
    background, 50, 61, 62–63
    Borrowman and, 65
    description, 49
    on "fake IDs," 63
    mission to Nasiriyah, 57

role with Crescent, 49, 50, 55, 58, 65, 75, 87
shooting incident, 116
Schumacher, Gerald, 48–49, 58, 149–150
Scott, Brian X., 70
Scott, Darryl A., 126
Scott, George C., 127
Seabrook, Nate, 153–154
Securiforce International, 51, 59, 101, 113, 197
Sharon, Leon, 133–135
Sheppard, Chuck ("Shrek")
  J-Dub alleged killing and, 27–30, 32, 33
  law and, 19
  lawsuit by, 32
Shining Path, 23
Sierra Leone and mercenaries, 126
Silveri, Lori
  background, xvii, 83, 108–109, 109
  family gathering/funeral, 206, 216
  gift from son, 83, 211
  kidnapping, 110, 194
Simpson, Cameron, 89, 130
SINCGARS radios, 78
Singer, P. W., 126
60 Minutes, 201
Skora, Mike
  after attack, 101, 110, 114, 115, 116
  background, 100
  Crescent investigations and, 153
  recruiting Coté, 13–14, 74, 82, 85–86, 100
Sloan, Matt, 6, 11–12
Small, David W., 35
Smith, H. C. Lawrence ("Lawrie"), 71, 138, 214
Smith, Patricia, 32
SOC-SMG, 112
Social Studies, Inc., 10–11
Spicer, Tim, 126
Sports Illustrated, 41

St. Denis, Traci, 141–142
Starr, Ann Exline, 139
Steroids scandal, 39–40, 41, 46
Stewart, Jackie, xiii, 61, 189, 193, 196
Stryker collision with armored personnel carrier, 80
Sunni Triangle, 55, 72
Surge, 129, 148, 161, 175–176
SYColeman, 167
Szymanski, D.J., 203

Tallil Air Base, **viii**, 59, 66, 72, 73, 77, 81, 86, 87, 89, 96, 99, 114, 115, 153, 159, 160
Tarsa, Mike, 180
"TCNs" (third-country nationals), 31
Thiab, Sarhan, 177, 178
Thomason, Ryan ("Rhino"), 18, 21, 31
  J-Dub and, 31
Threat Management Group (TMG), 59, 131, 132–133, 141
Toohey, Jim/Jan, 44
Triangle of Death, xiii
Triple Canopy
  Blackwater and, 18, 136
  description, 17, 18–19
  Gem bar, 17, 19–20, 31
  killing/investigation, 19–20, 31–33, 34–35
  Milwaukee project, 18–19, 20, 27–31
  Moonen and, 165
  See also specific individuals
Tyrrell, Anne E., 173

Umm Qasr, 141, 142
Uniform Code of Military Justice, 19, 25, 136
Unity Resources Group, 184–185
University of Florida
  description, 4
  See also Coté, Jon/University of Florida

U.S. Army Corps of Engineers
    compound, 70, 125
    Iraq reconstruction, 125
    mercenaries hired by, 24, 125, 126
    PSCAI and, 70
    See also Holly, Jack
U.S. Army Field Manual No. 3-24
    (Petraeus as coauthor), 161–162,
    176
U.S. Army's Joint Area Support
    Group, 162, 165
U.S. Central Command, 35
USA Today, 112
USAID (U.S. Agency for
    International Development),
    177, 184, 185

Vic's Auto Home Trim Shop, 108
Vietnam veterans, 44, 63
Vietnam War, 23, 60, 215
Vincent, Fay, 37

Washbourne, Jake ("J-Dub")
    background, 17
    description, 16, 20
    drinking, 17–18, 34
    killing/investigations, 26–35
    SUV accident/cover-up, 16–17,
        20–21, 26
    work of, 16–18, 19
    wounding civilian/cover-up, 17,
        20–21, 26
Washington Post, 33, 40, 123–124, 150,
    180
Waxman, Henry A., 181, 183
Weber, Mike, 141
Weiss, Wolf, 50, 54, 58
Whiskey Room, 6, 11, 12
White, Jeffrey R., 43, 45, 46

White House Correspondents
    Dinner (2005), 40
Williams, Lance
    legal case, 39–40, 44–45, 46
    as reporter/BALCO steroids
        scandal, 39–40, 41
Withrow, Ronald J., 145, 188, 191–192
Wolf's Den, Crescent Security
    Group, **ix**, 58, 64–65, 75, 87, 88,
    100, 115
Worldwide Personal Protective
    Service contract, 18

Young, John
    background, xiii, 59, 76–77
    description/personality, xiii–xiv,
        76–77
    family fund-raiser, 152–156
    funeral/burial, 200
    kidnapping, 98, 110, 119, 122–123,
        144–145, 190–192
    marriages/children, 77
    November 2006 convoy attack,
        86–87, 88, 90, 91, **92–93**, 95, 98
    sister Joella, 191
    See also Crescent Security Group
        kidnapping
Young, John/mercenary
    Basra trip and, xiv
    on leave from, 76
    mission to Nasiriyah, 59
    non-financial reasons, xiii–xiv, 76
    November 2006 convoy attack, 86,
        88–89, 90, 91, **92–93**, 94, 95, 98,
        100
    Numaniyah trip/hit, 77–80
    role with Crescent, 58–59, 76, 77,
        87
Young, John Robert, 155–156